CHRONICLES

of the FRIGATE

MACEDONIAN

1809–1922

The Natural Superiority of Left-Handers

The Battle of Stonington

Meet Martin Luther King, Jr. (for young readers)

W.W. Norton & Company   New York • London

CHRONICLES

of the FRIGATE

MACEDONIAN

1809–1922

James Tertius de Kay

The text of this book is composed in Palatino with the display set in Diotima
Composition by Crane Typesetting Service, Inc.
Manufacturing by The Courier Companies, Inc.
Book design by Chris Welsh

Library of Congress Cataloging-in-Publication Data
De Kay, James Tertius.
Chronicles of the frigate Macedonian, 1809–1922 / James Tertius de Kay.
p. cm.
Includes index.
1. Macedonian (Ship) 2. United States—History, Naval—To 1900.
I. Title.
E182.D35   1995
973.5'25—dc20   95-1722

ISBN 0-393-03804-1

ISBN 0-393-32024-3 pbk.

W. W. Norton & Company, Inc.
500 Fifth Avenue, New York, N.Y. 10110
www.wwnorton.com

W. W. Norton & Company Ltd.
10 Coptic Street, London WC1A 1PU

1 2 3 4 5 6 7 8 9 0

For my beloved
BELINDA

CONTENTS

USS *Macedonian*, 36 guns (Rebuilt)

U.S. Sloop-of-War *Macedonian*, 20 guns (Razeed)

Photographs appear following page 144

PREFACE

The Frigate *Macedonian*

Hᴵˢ Mᴀᴊᴇsᴛʏ's Fʀɪɢᴀᴛᴇ *Mᴀᴄᴇᴅᴏɴɪᴀɴ* ᴡᴀs ʟᴀᴜɴᴄʜᴇᴅ ᴀᴛ Wᴏᴏʟᴡɪᴄʜ in 1810, at the height of the wars against Napoleon. In 1922, on the same day her last remains burned to the ground in the Bronx, a young Babe Ruth hit his fifth home run of the season. The story of the *Macedonian* is an informal history of that tumultuous span of years, writ small.

Ships are rarely very interesting in themselves. It is the people who sailed in them, and the things they did, that are worth paying attention to. For various reasons, the *Macedonian* had more than her share of larger-than-life skippers, from her very first captain, the aristocratic Lord William FitzRoy, who cooked her books with patrician arrogance, to the flamboyant and eccentric visionary Uriah Phillips Levy, America's first Jewish commodore. In between there was the right honorable William Waldegrave, who enjoyed watching pink young boys spread-eagled on the gratings and flogged; Stephen Decatur, who captured the *Macedonian* and never stopped lying about it; John Downes, who used the ship to build his own personal fortune; and Matthew Calbraith Perry, who used her twice—once to ensure the security of the African colony of Liberia, and later to force open the Empire of Japan.

She is barely remembered today, but in her time the *Macedonian* was recognized the world over as the most important prize of war ever taken by the American Navy—a distinction she holds to this day. Her capture from the British in the War of 1812 was seen as proof of American daring and skill, and the nation's leaders took every opportunity to show her off. It was largely thanks to her cachet as a trophy ship that she served so prominently for so many years, and participated in so many of the events that defined her times, including the liberation of Latin America, the war against the slave trade, the Great Irish Famine, and the Civil War.

In the cut and thrust of global politics during the nineteenth century it was the presence of warships—sometimes to fight, sometimes to protect, sometimes to intimidate, and sometimes simply to show the flag—that made the difference, and determined a nation's success or failure. It was called "gunboat diplomacy," and it worked.

Because the decision to send those warships into international waters was always sensitive and made at the highest levels of state, the *Macedonian* can be viewed not simply as a military artifact but quite literally as an instrument of national policy. As such, a close reading of her comings and goings over the years, and an understanding of the various ways she was employed, can tell us more about the political ambitions and moral ambiguities of the powers she served than an entire library of state papers.

HIS MAJESTY'S

~~~~~~~~~~~~~~~

FRIGATE

~~~~~~~~~~~~~~~

MACEDONIAN,

~~~~~~~~~~~~~~~

38 guns

WOOLWICH

~~~~~~~~~~~~~~~~~~

E ARLY ON A MORNING IN LATE MARCH 1809, EDWARD SISON,
Master Shipwright of Royal Woolwich Dock Yards, stood
hunched over a table in his office, meticulously examining a
fresh new set of ship's plans by the pale sunlight filtering in
through his office window.

The large sheets, which had recently arrived from the Navy
Board, a few miles upriver in London, were the drafts for a new
frigate—as yet unnamed—a ship of the fifth rate, with a nominal
armament of thirty-eight guns. The plans consisted of six separate pages, defining every detail of the proposed vessel, each
drawn with exquisite precision to a scale of 48:1, so that every
inch on paper represented four feet of actual ship. The signature
of Sir William Rule, Surveyor of the Navy, scrawled across the
top sheet, attested to the authenticity and correctness of the
plans.

Sison could see at once that there was nothing particularly
novel about the drawings in front of him. The ship he was
looking at was virtually identical to the *Lively*, which he had
built in 1804, and the *Undaunted*, which he launched in 1807,
and though he was thoroughly familiar with almost every detail,
he conned each page with a practiced eye to refresh his memory,
keeping alert for anomolies or possible errors in copying.

Having at last assured himself that Sir William's latest design
held no surprises, Mr. Sison shucked himself into his heavy
greatcoat, tucked the rolled-up plans under his arm, and addressing a few last-minute instructions to his chief clerk, plucked

his hat from its peg near the door and stepped out into the brisk morning air.

The cold wet winds of March coming off the Thames managed simultaneously to chill to the bone while whispering a promise of spring, that most glorious of English seasons. The first daffodils could be expected any day.

From his office doorway the Master Shipwright could take in the entire length of the yard, which stretched about a half mile along the riverbank, from the rigging house at the eastern end to the mast house in the west. Here, in one concentrated place, were gathered all the machines, raw materials, and talent necessary to create a wooden warship from scratch. Each morning nearly two thousand shipwrights, loftsmen, smiths, coopers, sawyers, and scavelmen came through the gate to build and repair the enormous fleets Britain required to maintain her command of the seas in this, the sixteenth year of the wars with France.

Woolwich was only one of a string of royal dockyards stretching around the coast of Great Britain and as far away as Nova Scotia and Bombay. Taken together, they comprised the largest military-industrial complex the world had ever seen, servicing and supporting a huge navy of over a thousand vessels that guarded the routes of Empire and held Continental Europe in blockade.

Turning eastward toward the feeble equinoctial sun, Mr. Sison made his way briskly between the sawpits and the noisy smithery, past the pitch house with its pungent smell of hot tar, and beyond the sheds of sided timber that crowded the pathways and occupied every unused foot of ground.

All along the river's edge, in stately array, great wooden warships stood high out of the water, looming over the graving docks and building slips, each with her own gangs of workmen clambering over her like teams of Lilliputians examining a group of sleeping Gullivers. Some were new ships abuilding, others were old ships under repair. Out in the Thames itself, a line of ships "in ordinary" stood moored stem to stern, waiting to be refitted and sent back to sea.

Moments later Sison arrived at his destination, an empty

building slip at the water's edge, where a group of workmen stood waiting for him, huddled out of the wind and chatting quietly, their breath hanging in the cold air. These were the men who would actually build the new frigate. They were craftsmen for the most part, shipwrights and other "artificers," who had spent years of apprenticeship learning their trade. For all their training, they were, as Sison well knew, only second-rate craftsmen at best. The most skilled shipbuilders in Britain worked at the private yards, where the pay was higher. Woolwich, as a government dockyard, could only offer the lower salaries mandated by Parliament, and in consequence Sison was forced to settle for the leftovers, including the drunks and malingerers turned down by the private yards.

Despite their inadequacies, the men gathered around the Master Shipwright were considered of such vital importance to the national interest that every one of them carried an official "protection" from the government, a piece of paper that specifically exempted him from the clutches of the dreaded press gangs that roamed the waterfronts of England, pouncing on any likely prospect, and forcing him without recourse into an ill-paid, dangerous, and degrading life on board one of His Majesty's warships.

Mr. Sison greeted the men cheerfully, and no doubt made some idle but obligatory chat about the weather before setting the crew to work on the first and most significant step in the construction of any wooden ship, the laying of her keel.

The keel of a wooden frigate was simplicity itself, little more than a long, straight beam, cut square, about 150 feet from end to end, that ran the entire length of the bottom of the ship. The job of fitting the pieces of the keel together and setting the finished beam atop the line of oaken blocks that ran down the center of the building slip was for the most part straightforward and uncomplicated; but because the keel was the largest and most important single timber in a ship—it literally held the vessel together—it was a matter of high seriousness that this first step be done right. A well-laid keel made for a sound ship. A poorly laid keel guaranteed trouble. It was as simple as that.

As was customary with English ships of the period, the keel was built of best-quality elm, a clear, close-grained wood that could stand up to prolonged immersion in salt water and was impervious to the deprivations of the *toredo*, or ship worm. It was to be constructed from six separate baulks of elm, each one a little over twenty-five feet long and hewn from the trunk of a single tree. Under Mr. Sison's supervision, the men heaved and chivvied these great clumsy elements into place with block and tackle, then sealed the butts with hot pitch and flannel, and locked the baulks end to end by means of complex Z-shaped fittings called scarphs. Finally, each scarph was drilled through with an auger, and thick copper rods were inserted into the holes, permanently bolting the baulks together. By late afternoon the job was done, and it only remained now to "fair" the keel, that is, to knock it precisely into line with mallets and secure it to the supporting blocks with oaken dowels called treenails.

Within a matter of days the new keel sprouted a curving bow at one end and a straight stern post at the other, and began to look, at least two-dimensionally, distinctly ship-shaped. Soon the vessel was "floored up" forward and aft, giving her a third dimension. Even to the untutored eye, she now resembled a Viking longboat.

The size of the work crews arriving at the building site each morning grew larger every week, and by early summer half a dozen different teams were busy shaping, fitting, and raising into place the massive arched framing timbers, which, like enormous ribs, defined her final shape.

Of all the wooden warships of the day, frigates were the public's favorites. They were swifter than the huge, clumsy battle ships-of-the-line, yet they packed sufficient destructive power in their gun batteries to inflict serious damage on the enemy. They were often sent off on solitary duty, and frigate captains who captured or sank enemy ships in single-ship combat—the Royal Navy had an impressive number of such Hornblower prototypes—were national heroes, lionized in the press and as often as not received at court.

Every maritime nation produced its own style of frigate. Dutch frigates were shallow-bottomed, to compensate for the shoals of the Friesian coast. The French, who used frigates sparingly, and almost always for reconnaissance and communication, favored sleek, hydrodynamically pure hulls, to maximize speed and maneuverability. The British, on the other hand, built their frigates primarily for blockade duty: strong enough to withstand Channel winters and capacious enough to hold months of provisions.

Of American frigate design, which was to play a decisive role in the history of the *Macedonian*, we will have more to say further on.

IN KEEPING WITH Admiralty directives, the frigate now taking form on the ways at Woolwich was no sleek, elongated clipper, but a plain, tough, seagoing gun platform. There was hardly a straight line in her, yet the new ship, with her blunt prow and chopped stern, had a decidedly squarish cut to her, and was built roughly to the dimensions of a shoebox.

By August she was as tall and massive as a large public building, divided now into five separate levels, each designed to fulfill a specific function. Her lowest level, the hold, was large enough to carry supplies for up to six months of blockade duty. The very bottom of the hold, directly over the keel, was reserved for ballast and the heaviest provisions, such as iron shot and water kegs, in order to keep the ship's center of gravity low. Above the hold was a sort of half deck that ran only part of the length of the ship, called the orlop. It too would be used primarily for storage. Directly over the orlop was the lower deck, where the entire ship's company, with the exception of the captain, would sleep. All three of these levels were below the waterline, and would receive no direct sunlight once construction was completed.

Above the lower deck was the business level of the frigate,

the main deck, sometimes called the gun deck because it carried the ship's principal battery of cannon, poking out through the square ports cut into the sides of the ship. Finally, open to the elements and forming a roof over the main deck, were the frigate's two top decks, both on the same level, one forward and one aft, separated by an open space called the waist. The forward deck, which covered the front third of the ship, was called the forecastle. The aft section, stretching from the main mast all the way to the taffrail at the stern, was the quarterdeck. This area, which housed the steering wheel, and which roofed over the captain's quarters, would become the nerve center of the ship, the place from which the vessel was governed. It was center stage, officers' territory, off limits to all except those who had a duty to be there.

With the return of cold weather, workmen planked over the upper deck beams with stout fir boards three inches thick, creating a strong, solid gun platform and providing shelter so that laborers and craftsmen could continue working throughout the winter, protected against the worst of the weather. Crews of shipwrights below decks began fitting a seemingly endless number of lodging knees, hanging knees, crutches, transoms, and sleepers throughout the inner reaches of the ship, timbers that would help maintain her rigidity and shape against the battering of storms, battles, and high seas.

There was, among shipwrights in the age of sail, a profound appreciation and understanding of the properties of different kinds of wood. Construction contracts defined the type, grade, and quality of wood for every part of the ship: elm for the keel and the garboard strakes; fir for the masts and spars; Prussian deal for the quarterdeck (except for the two outer planks, which were to be of English oak). No detail was too small to escape the specifiers' attention: boxwood for the compass gimbels, cherry for the railings, lignum vitae for the sheaves that turned inside the blocks.

But of all the woods used in the construction of a ship, the most important by far was oak. Oak accounted for 95 percent of all the wood that went into a warship, and over forty acres of oak forest would eventually find its way into the *Macedonian*. Properly cured oak was strong, long-lasting, and resistant to water. The oak of England, nurtured in a moderate climate and at high latitudes that ensured long summer days of growth, was deemed particularly strong and superior to all others. For hundreds of years the great forests of England—the forests of Sussex, Surrey, Hampshire, and Kent—provided the oak that built an Empire, and it was not until Britain marshaled its forces to repel Napoleon that it discovered it had plundered its forests one time too often, and there was now almost no oak left with which to wage war against the greatest threat since the Armada.

Frantic efforts to secure fresh supplies met with only partial success. In the emergency, shipbuilders began importing oak from the Baltic. They called it "Danzig Oak," and it was cut from forests as far away as Silesia and the Carpathians, in what are now Poland and Russia. Continental agents assured Royal Navy contractors that their oak was of the highest quality, comparable in every way to the best of England, but there is more to oak than a salesman's assurance. Oak had to be cut in winter, when the sap was low, and seasoned for at least two years in freshwater mud to leach out the acids before it was finally slow dried to reduce the moisture content below 15 percent. Only then was it fit to be shaped into ships of war.

Because foreign brokers could not be held to a strict adherence to proper seasoning practices, with each passing year more and more of the Danzig Oak that found its way into British ships was of inferior quality. The results were ships that leaked, sagged, and crumbled into dust with dry rot years before their time.

If there was one overriding anxiety in Mr. Sison's mind during the months in which the *Macedonian* slowly took shape, we can safely guess that it centered on the quality and quantity of the supplies of oak at Woolwich Dock Yard. The subsequent history of the *Macedonian* would in no small part be shaped by the crisis that British shipbuilding was undergoing at the time of her construction over the quality and availability of oak.

* * *

SIXTEEN MONTHS AFTER construction began, the anonymous frigate at last had a name: *Macedonian*. In recognition of this fact, a carved wooden figurehead of the noblest of the Macedonians, Alexander the Great, now graced her bow. The conqueror's heroically proportioned bust was clad in a crested helmet and full armor. He had the lordly nose of a Hogarth rakehell, and his gigantic eyes stared arrogantly forward, searching the horizon in a most fierce and determined manner. His thrusting chin seemed set to cleave the waves, and was clean shaven in keeping with the historical tradition that Alexander forbade his troops to grow beards lest the enemy use them as handholds.

The Royal Navy had a long tradition of employing classical names for its ships, and of applying the same name to new vessels when the old were lost or broken up. By 1810 there had already been six *Minervas*, four *Apollos*, and seven *Hectors*. But the growing need for vessels had now forced the Admiralty to come up with new names, including *Macedonian*. Subsequent events would dictate that it was a name that would never be used again, at least in the Royal Navy.

At this stage, the new ship was ready to be launched. She still had no masts, no yards, no sails, no rigging. Neither did she as yet have her guns, the very reason for her being. Such incidental elements were known as "furniture," and would be added once she was afloat.

THE LAUNCHING OF a wooden ship the size of the *Macedonian* was a nervous occasion for all concerned. As with a human birth, the potential for disaster was always present. She might get stuck on the ways, requiring drastic action to free such an unwieldy weight. She might topple sideways, or foul the slip, crushing onlookers and irreparably damaging her scantlings. To protect her against such calamities, in the last week of May a team of workmen began building the huge cradle which would carry the full weight of the *Macedonian* down the greased ways and into the Thames.

The day before the launch, workmen with axes moved slowly

along the line of supports that ran down the middle of the slip, methodically cutting away one by one the oaken blocks that had held the great weight since the laying of the keel. The entire ship now settled in all its massiveness into the waiting cradle.

On the appointed day—June 2, 1810—and at the appointed hour, which coincided with the fortnightly spring tide so that the *Macedonian* might have the minimum distance to travel before she reached the water, a crowd of workmen and officials, naval officers and their wives, and other interested parties assembled along the shore, and with flags flying and the dockyard bell tolling proudly, the last of the stanchions which had supported the *Macedonian* for over a year were knocked away. Without a tremor, as smoothly as one of Mr. Watt's pistons, the great vessel began to slide, slowly at first, but with ever-increasing velocity, into its natural element. The crowd, deeply moved by the magnificent sight, responded with a spontaneous cheer. A large wave, pushed up by the entrance of the new ship's stern into the river, rolled ponderously out toward the opposite bank of the Thames and disappeared in midchannel.

The newborn *Macedonian* wobbled unsurely and rode far too high in the water, but that was to be expected. Coppering and furniture, as well as permanent ballast and a large crew with full provisions, would increase her draft soon enough. As a gaggle of oared riverboats made their way to the new ship, signaling and calling out to the little figures on deck to send down lines so they might escort her to her new moorings, the witnesses on shore turned and drifted back to their everyday occupations.

Within a month, she would be ready to go to sea. It was time now to find her a crew.

FITTING OUT

~~~~~~~~~~~~~~

T HE SINGLE MOST IMPORTANT MEMBER OF THE *MACEDONIAN*'S crew—the twenty-nine-year-old aristocrat the Admiralty had selected to be her captain—had his mind on other things than sailing ships during the early summer of 1810. He was hunting for a rich wife.

His name was Lord William FitzRoy, third son of the Duke of Grafton, a member of the highest levels of the British aristocracy and a young man of enormous self-absorption. His absence from Woolwich did not betoken any sense of disinterest on his part. There is every reason to believe that Lord William very much desired a frigate command, and had exercised his considerable influence to snare such a plum. His absence simply reflected certain realities peculiar to the upper classes.

Thanks to the laws of primogeniture governing inheritance, third sons of dukes were likely to be left penniless on the death of their father, and it therefore behooved such men to seek alternative sources of revenue if they wished to continue to live in the style to which their birth had accustomed them. The simplest and least painful solution to the problem was a favorable marriage, and when Lord William's sister, the Duchess of Marlborough, invited him down to Blenheim, her magnificent palace in Oxfordshire, he jumped at the chance to mingle with the rich and fashionable set that attended her, in the not unreasonable hope that he might find there some well set up young lady willing to trade her dowry for a good name.

Spouse hunting can be a time-consuming enterprise, but not every moment at Blenheim was given over to lordly romance.

One morning, as a favor to Lady Marlborough, FitzRoy interviewed a thirteen-year-old boy—the son of one of his sister's servants—and agreed to take him into the crew of his new ship. The eager young man, whose name was Samuel Leech, would in time come to rue his decision to follow the sea. Many years later he would publish a detailed memoir of his experiences in the *Macedonian* that provides one of the few surviving accounts of the sometimes harrowing and degrading life in the Royal Navy as seen from below decks.

It was not until Lord William's amatory pursuits had met with failure that he finally made his way up to London and thence to Woolwich, where he found the *Macedonian* moored offshore and already in commission. He stood now at quayside, resplendent in his cocked hat and full-dress uniform displaying the twin epaulets of a post captain, admiring his new command from a distance while he waited for the ship's boat.

She had changed dramatically since the day of her launching. Her entire bottom was now coppered, and workmen had installed over seventy tons of pig iron ballast in her hold. The combined weight of these additions significantly increased her draft, which in turn lowered her profile and did much to correct her previous top-heavy look.

Above decks, she now sprouted a small forest of spars. Three stubby lower masts had been stepped fore, aft, and amidships, and carpenters and riggers had already fitted equally tall topmasts to each, securing them with miles of standing rigging drawn tightly to the fighting tops and chain plates on either side of the ship. These weblike shrouds served to hold each mast square and true, and horizontal ratlines seized to the shrouds transformed them into ladders as well, by which the hands could clamber into the tops and out upon the yards.

A long bowsprit—effectively a fourth mast—now poked out directly over the figurehead of Alexander the Great, and workmen were preparing to send up spindly topgallant masts to be fitted to the topmasts, which would be followed by even more spindly royals fitted to the topgallants. When completed, each towering mast would give the *Macedonian* a commanding sense

of height, and would be held in place by an elaborate array of
shrouds, stays, halyards, and sheets, an intricate cat's cradle of
standing and running rigging designed to support the masts,
control the yards, and provide access to the higher parts of the
ship.

In due course the captain's barge arrived to transport him
to his new ship, and shortly thereafter FitzRoy found himself
ceremoniously piped aboard to take formal command. The *Macedonian* had not yet received her full crew, so only a handful of
officers and men were present to stand at respectful attention
and witness the brief ceremonies. At their conclusion, Captain
FitzRoy took the opportunity to address a short and unusual
speech to the ship's company, the thrust of which was the importance of his hereditary title, which he emphasized was to take
precedence over his rank. With sober intensity he explained to
one and all that under no conditions was he ever to be addressed
simply as "sir," but always as "my lord." Having delivered this
important message, he disappeared into the great cabin and
shortly thereafter reemerged in workaday uniform, and accompanied by his clerk, began making his personal inspection.

For all his youth and patrician affections, FitzRoy was no fool.
He was a sixteen-year veteran of the naval service, and knew
exactly what to look for in the ship and where to find it. He was
soon poking about in every corner, from forecastle to magazine,
occasionally drawing a tape from his coat pocket to measure
something, and dictating notes as he went. He was interested
in everything. After a very long and very thorough examination,
he retired to his cabin and composed a letter to the Admiralty.
The letter, dated June 14, 1810, and addressed to the influential
John Wilson Croker, Esq., First Secretary of the Admiralty,
shows a commendable grasp of detail.

Sir, I have to request you will be pleased to solicit the Lords
Commissioners of the Admiralty to give directions that the
skids under the Booms on board the *Macedonian* may be shut
in (except near the hatchways) with 1½ inch deal and caulked
and from thence to the gangeway carling to be fitted with

gratings being fully sensible of the advantages to be gained by its being so done—

Whether it was FitzRoy's aristocratic upbringing or his long years in the navy, he has an admirably no-nonsense manner of making his requests explicit and unequivocal, and for all the politeness of the address, there is no question that his petitions are in fact orders.

That a part or the whole of one, out of three fore Hatchways on the Main Deck may be shut in, being of no use whatever as it not only prevents a passage round from the one side of the ship to the other, but having a very small space between that and the Main Hatchway.

He ends with a revealing coda:

Also, that a Bulkhead may be put up in the Cabin abaft the aftermost port on the Main Deck.

This last request was a personal one. The "Cabin abaft the aftermost port on the Main Deck" was in fact the captain's own quarters, sometimes known as the "great room," which would serve as his office as well as his sleeping area. The additional bulkhead ordered by FitzRoy created an interior wall separating the space into two rooms and providing him with a level of additional privacy commensurate with his titled standing.

This seemingly insignificant alteration in the *Macedonian*'s design, this soupçon of aristocratic elegance, was to have far-ranging consequences for the frigate, and helps explain why in future years she was so often selected as a flagship. Many a captain who followed Lord FitzRoy into the *Macedonian* was quick to appreciate his little non-regulation luxury.

As IN ALL Royal Navy vessels, there were two distinct classes of officers in the *Macedonian*: the sea officers, who, like the captain, held commissions from the Admiralty (commissioned officers); and their lesser brethren, those entrusted with the day-to-day mechanics of running the ship, who only held warrants from the Navy Board (warrant officers). Chief among this latter group was the sailing master, Mr. G. D. Lewis, who was responsible for the navigation and general handling of the ship. Lewis had a long record of service, and had only reached his present position—the highest to which a warrant officer might aspire—after many years of sea duty in a number of vessels under the command of a wide variety of skippers.

By the time of FitzRoy's arrival on board, Lewis had already supervised the laying of ballast and much of the stowage of provisions, which was an important part of his job, since the distribution of weight throughout the ship would directly affect her trim, and therefore her sailing qualities. Victuals and dry goods of every description streamed aboard under his watchful eye—water kegs and cannonballs, barrels of biscuit and hogsheads of salt beef, endless coils of rope, bundled sets of new sails, and other spare parts—and found their way into the dark interstices of the ship, each item placed precisely where the sailing master ordered, and its location recorded in his personal log. With lists in one hand and a bit of chalk in the other, he moved about everywhere, officiously marking barrels and ticking off items, supervising the workmen and attending to the endless details of getting a ship ready for sea.

There was nothing in Mr. Lewis's manner or in his previous record to suggest that he was either incompetent or a troublemaker, and his rapport with the new captain during the fitting-out period appears to have been cordial enough. Certainly there was nothing in their relationship to warn either Lewis or FitzRoy that within months each would become the nemesis of the other, and that a clash of wills between the two would eventually bring down both men in a disgraceful confrontation so queer and comical that it remains to this day unique in the annals of the Royal Navy. But as every sailor knows, such unexpected dramas have a way of flaring up at sea, where men must live in enclosed, isolated societies subject to specialized social pressures. It seems to be in the nature of ships.

* * *

AFTER THE ALMOST leisurely tempo of months, seasons, and years that marked the construction of the *Macedonian*, the fevered pace of her final fitting out must have seemed something of a scramble. There was a great deal to do, and not much time in which to do it. Sailing ships were expected to remain at sea for extended periods, far longer than modern ships, and had to be able to carry an enormous load of goods—enough food and water for three hundred men for up to six months. Each day great mountains of fresh provisions arrived on the quay, only to be annexed by Mr. Lewis's men and fed into the ravenous hold, while the master ordered up even more from the dockyard's agent victualler.

FitzRoy was anxious to get to sea, and found himself frustrated by what he saw as Mr. Lewis's delaying tactics. While the sailing master busied himself with the ship's provisioning, the captain kept his eye on the small groups of freshly recruited seamen who appeared each morning on the quay along with the supplies, and like the supplies, were ingested into the ship.

These were the men who would form the backbone of his crew, all hardened veterans, all volunteers who had signed up for the bounty, which could amount to anything up to £70 for a man with the right skills, a generous sum in Regency England. They were good men, FitzRoy knew, reliable and well trained, and he was pleased to have them in his ship. He was equally pleased to note that with each passing day their number increased.

Within a week the captain counted almost a hundred hands, more than sufficient for a skeleton crew, and decided to leave Woolwich despite Lewis's request for additional supplies. After signing a last batch of papers connected with the fitting out of a new ship, he at last gave the order to raise anchors and cast off, and for the first time the *Macedonian* caught the wind, finally leaving Woolwich behind, if only for a brief trip downstream to the naval ordnance depot at Northfleet, where she would take on the guns for which she had been built.

* * *

EVERY ASPECT OF a warship was determined by her guns; it was their size, their weight, their placement, and the number of men it took to work them that governed every detail of a warship's design. Because guns had to operate in fair weather and foul, they had to be positioned high above the waterline, where they could not be swamped by a high sea. Since such a placement made the ships top-heavy and unstable, the designers were forced to overbuild the lower parts of the ship to compensate.

Guns were labor-intensive, each one requiring as many as eleven men to load, aim, fire, and swab it out, and this meant that warships required huge crews—80 percent of the men in a man-of-war were there primarily to fire the guns—which led to further compromises, particularly in provisioning and the design of storage areas.

And finally, guns had to produce enough "hitting power" to justify the expense of the ship that carried them. Since the muzzle-loading cannon of the day were notoriously clumsy and could only be fired about once every three minutes, the only way to increase firepower was to cram extra guns into every ship, which of course called for still further design compromises.

The end result were ships like the *Macedonian*, large, bulky, and somewhat ungainly, but which carried a truly formidable firepower. Although officially rated as a 38-gun frigate, she and her sisters in fact carried considerably more cannon than that, in a mixture of large caliber and small, long range and short, distributed on the top two levels of the ship for maximum flexibility and effect.

Her principal battery consisted of twenty-eight carriage guns, ranged in two lines on either side of the main deck pointing larboard and starboard. These were long-range 18-pounders, so called because they fired cannonballs that weighed eighteen pounds each.

Above the main deck, on the forecastle and quarterdeck, the *Macedonian* carried different guns, called carronades. These were larger-caliber cannon, with short barrels that took up less space than long guns and weighed only a fifth as much, but were only effective at close range. They were known affectionately within the navy as "smashers." The *Macedonian* carried fourteen 32-pounder carronades on her quarterdeck, seven on each side. Forward, on the forecastle, she carried two more 32-pounder carronades, one 18-pounder carronade, and two 9-pounder long guns, which were mounted on either side of the bowsprit, pointing forward, and were known as chase guns, since they were used primarily in pursuit.

Her total armament came to forty-seven guns, which was about average for a ship of her size. The cannon weighed about sixty tons in all, and when the full complement were lowered on board and trussed into place at the Northfleet arsenal, the *Macedonian* sank those last few inches into the Thames and rode on the waterline for which she had been built. She was finally ready to to go to war and had only to take on the remainder of her crew.

IT WAS A sad and unpromising selection of humanity that arrived on board the *Macedonian* from the receiving ship at Gravesend, downriver from Northfleet. The shabby, crestfallen men who would make up the final two thirds of the ship's crew were in marked contrast to the robust and capable hands taken on at Woolwich, and were evidence, if any was needed, that Britain's shortage of sailors to man its ships was even more serious than its shortage of oak with which to build them. The new men, most of them glum and defiant, were ferried over to the *Macedonian* in hoys under the watchful eye of armed marines, to ensure they did not escape. (Why did Britain bother to build jails, Samuel Johnson wondered, when she had a navy?)

There was, as always, a smattering of volunteers among them, young provincials seeking adventure, and invariably, an additional contingent of men running away to sea to escape domestic problems on shore, usually relating to marriage. Most of the men were not volunteers, however, but unwilling conscripts who had been unlucky enough to be snared by the navy's press gangs, or caught up in Parliament's quota acts, which forced local authorities to raise drafts of men to fill the Royal Navy's needs. Often as not the counties used such acts as an excuse to rid themselves of undesirables, filling their quotas with convicts, rogues, debtors, and vagabonds. Inevitably, a number of such men now found their way into the *Macedonian*.

A sprinkling of well-born wastrels known as "Lord Mayor's men" made up still another category of conscript. These were young hell-raisers of the privileged classes who had managed to get into trouble with the authorities and chose to be released to the navy in lieu of standing trial.

And finally there were the foreigners, hapless strangers caught up by the press gangs with no government to protect their rights. There were over twenty thousand such men in British service at the time, about 15 percent of the total, and by far the largest number were Americans. For years the United States government had protested Britain's high-handed impressment of Americans—Royal Navy captains were in the habit of stopping American merchantmen at sea and arbitrarily kidnapping whatever men they might need—but Whitehall chose to disregard the complaints. The practice would in time goad the feeble United States into declaring war on mighty Britain, an action that would forever change the destiny of the *Macedonian*.

What thoughts might have passed through the mind of Captain FitzRoy as he stood on the quarterdeck and watched each succeeding boatload of sullen, inept crewmen bump up against the side of his new frigate and clamber onto the still pristine main deck? It is easy enough to guess. Doubtless he saw the angry, bemused, desperate men moiling about below him quite simply as the scum of the earth, a ragtaggle assortment of stupid, potentially mutinous villains, who would have to be watched constantly for signs of insubordination.

It was always possible that his officers might find a few good men among this dross—men who, given the time and training, could be turned into excellent topmen and boatswain's mates—but such gems were the rare exceptions. For the most part, the men who came on board at Gravesend were the scrapings from the barrel, and a prudent captain had good reason to treat them with suspicion and distrust, and to trust to the cat-o'-nine-tails to maintain order and keep them tractable and obedient.

The *Macedonian* remained at Gravesend for the better part of a week, while officers and men sent their last letters home and took leave of relatives. Predictably, Mr. Lewis made the most of the opportunity to bring on board whatever last-minute supplies he could find. While these details were disposed of, the boatswain and his men divided the crews into watches, helped them settle in, and introduced the bewildered landsmen—many of whom had never been in a ship or even seen the ocean—to something of the strange new life that lay in store.

Eventually the *Macedonian*'s sailing orders arrived from London, directing her to Lisbon to deliver a company of soldiers to Wellington's army in the peninsula. On FitzRoy's orders, the crew turned to at the capstan with the boatswain's cries of "All hands up anchor ahoy!" and later, "All hands make sail ahoy!" The new and untried frigate, riding on a fair tide with a following breeze and gliding silently under fresh, newly bent sails of glistening white canvas, made her way down to Sheerness, past Margate, out of the brackish water of the Thames and into the salt of the English Channel.

The *Macedonian* had found her way home.

FitzRoy

CAPTAIN LORD WILLIAM FITZROY IS CERTAINLY NOT ONE OF the better known officers in the war against Napoleon, but neither is he an historical cipher. His name and exploits crop up here and there in various histories of the Royal Navy, and he was a man of social prominence, so he turns up in the various newspapers and journals of his day. We have a sufficient knowledge of him to draw a fairly accurate sketch of his character.

He seems to have been a competent enough officer (his letter to the Admiralty indicates as much), but it is abundantly clear he was also bloody-minded and petty, excessively thin-skinned, and in the final analysis, a man of profound self-delusion. Such characteristics were not necessarily drawbacks for the captain of a wooden warship—William Bligh, of the *Bounty*, shared many of the same traits and was an outstanding commander—but FitzRoy's character flaws were filtered through such a hopelessly distorted sense of snobbery that in the aggregate they served neither his ship nor himself.

His fussy insistence on being addressed as "my lord" or "your lordship" was typical of his eccentric sense of priorities. Equally typical was the grizzly bit of theater he arranged for the *Macedonian*'s first day at sea. Before she had even passed from the sight of land, FitzRoy took the opportunity to impress upon his crew the full extent of his power over them by ordering the *Macedonian*'s first flogging.

We have an eyewitness account of the event written by Samuel Leech, the thirteen-year-old boy FitzRoy had recruited at Blenheim. Leech describes how all hands were mustered on the gun deck to witness the punishment while the officers, attired in full-dress uniform and wearing their swords to mark the solemnity of the occasion, observed the scene from the quarterdeck. To the ruffle of drums, the prisoner, who had committed "the very sailor-like offense of getting drunk," was brought on deck, where he was ceremoniously stripped to the waist and seized hand and foot to a wooden grating. Then, at a signal from FitzRoy, two burly boatswain's mates, working at a deliberate pace, began to scourge the unfortunate man with a cat-'o-nine-tails, drawing blood with almost every stroke, until, after forty-eight smartly delivered blows, his back resembled "roasted meat burnt nearly black before a scorching fire." By the end of the ordeal the prisoner was only barely conscious, and had to be half-carried below to recover as best he could, his dripping wounds leaving a trail of blood behind him to mark his passage. The young Leech marveled at the fact that an English farmer who dared beat a horse in such manner would have been prosecuted for cruelty.

Every man in the ship that day was fully aware that Admiralty Regulations limited a captain's sentencing power to a dozen lashes, and that FitzRoy had deliberately flouted the rule by ordering the prisoner to receive four times that number. The men were also aware that there was nothing they could do about the captain's flagrant disregard for their rights, which was undoubtedly the lesson FitzRoy most wished to convey.

LISBON, IN THE winter of 1810–11, proved a congenial station for officers and men alike. The Royal Navy maintained a fleet on the Tagus primarily to guard against a possible attack by French forces, but since such an attack never materialized, the crew of the *Macedonian* fell into a comfortable routine of alternately going out to sea on regular coastal scouting sorties and returning to equally regular stretches in port. Fresh food and the mild Portuguese winter did much to lift the spirits of one and all.

Captain FitzRoy had his own personal reasons to appreciate the Lisbon assignment: it provided him with the opportunity to make large amounts of money. For all his upper-class posturing, Lord William was almost totally dependent on the generosity of his relatives for anything beyond his captain's salary, which amounted to less than £20 per month. The Portuguese station offered him the chance to make a financial killing, and although the means to do so was illegal, he was quick to exploit it.

It is impossible at this late date to document the precise details of his crimes—the evidence has long since been destroyed—but we know the charge for which he was eventually convicted, which was "signing false expenses of stores," and it is easy enough to reconstruct the nature of his misdeeds. In the hurly-burly and confusion of a wartime supply depot such as Lisbon, with provisions and supplies constantly in transit and bits of paper marking their passage flying about in all directions, there were any number of ways a captain might contrive to fiddle the books and siphon money out of a ship as large as the *Macedonian*. As a captain, FitzRoy could operate without direct oversight, and it is likely that his modus operendi involved some form of skimming, with FitzRoy signing for more materials than were in fact delivered, and taking surreptitious payment from the provider. Whatever the method, it is clear that over that winter his lordship found an effective, if temporary, substitute for a rich wife.

DISCIPLINE, AND THE problem of maintaining order among the unruly mob of pressed men in the ship, was partially resolved during that Portuguese winter thanks not to so much to FitzRoy as to his first lieutenant, a Mr. Scott. Scott was something of an anomaly for his day, an officer who was an outspoken foe of flogging. It was under his calm and judicious leadership that the crowd of angry troublemakers that came aboard at Gravesend was slowly transformed and trained into a more or less efficient crew. As a result of his ameliorating influence on the captain, both the number of courts-martial and the severity of punishments handed down by FitzRoy gradually decreased.

This happy state of affairs changed abruptly when, a little before Christmas, Mr. Scott was replaced by Lieutenant David

Hope, a highly energetic officer who was also violent and sadistic, and an enthusiastic champion of the cat. Predictably, under Hope's influence, FitzRoy's rule grew more tyrannical, and once again the number and severity of floggings increased dramatically.

The wretched conditions on board the *Macedonian* were hardly unique. The life of a common sailor in the Royal Navy during the wars with Napoleon tended to be so miserable, and so characterized by harsh conditions and cruel punishments, that it is a wonder there were not more mutinies. While mutineers could expect to be hanged, such a fate seems a reasonable risk under the circumstances, and only marginally worse than remaining alive under the grievous conditions prevailing in many of His Majesty's ships. Desertion was the preferred means of redress, but in most ships this was virtually impossible. In the *Macedonian* the sailors were as much prisoners as were any convicts behind walls. Only trusted hands were allowed to leave the ship unescorted, and in many vessels men spent as much as five years on board without ever being allowed to set foot on land.

The navy provided only one means to alleviate the dreadful life of a sailor, and that was alcohol. Strong drink, usually in the form of grog, was meted out liberally to all hands on a twice-daily basis. Rum was the preferred form, but ships such as the *Macedonian*, operating off the Iberian coast, substituted local spirits, issuing half a pint of brandy to each man at noon, followed by a pint of wine at four o'clock. These were substantial amounts of alcohol. It is worth noting that a British pint is about 25 percent larger than its American equivalent.

Drink was seen primarily as a sop to the miseries of life at sea. What made it such a dynamic force on shipboard was the fact that it did not have to be consumed as soon as it was issued, and could be hoarded and used as a medium of exchange among the sailors, an accepted currency. "It is grog which pays debts, and not money, in a man of war," as one veteran explained. The result was that no matter the day of the week or hour of day, any man determined to get drunk could always find the means to do so if he could pay the price. Hence drunkenness

was commonplace throughout the fleet and the reason for most
of the courts-martial and floggings.

On holidays or other special occasions, the captain could order extra rations of drink, and this is what FitzRoy did when
the *Macedonian* lay at anchor in the Tagus on Christmas Day in
1810. "To be drunk is considered by almost every sailor as the
acme of sensual bliss," wrote Samuel Leech. He described in
vivid detail the drunken celebration on board the *Macedonian*
that lasted all of Christmas Day and well into the night. Sailors
caroused noisily throughout the ship, officers and men alike.
Men brawled and sang, argued and laughed, fought, got sick,
and lay collapsed in a stupor. In spite of all the mischief it caused,
drink was probably small enough compensation for a life that,
more than most, was likely to be nasty, brutish, and short.

AS ABSOLUTE RULER over a community of three hundred souls,
FitzRoy oversaw everything that took place in the *Macedonian*.
In the course of his daily duties, he would regularly come into
contact with Mr. Lewis, the sailing master. The two men shared
many responsibilities, and the normal business of running the
ship brought them together frequently. The two men seemed
to get on well enough, which could not have been all that easy,
given the Ciceronian hauteur of FitzRoy.

One of Lewis's responsibilities was maintaining the ship's
trim, which involved regularly shifting and rearranging the provisions in the hold, as new supplies were shipped on board, or
old ones were used up and discarded. Supervising such work
made him intimately aware of everything that had to do with
the storage of goods in the *Macedonian*, and apparently at some
point the sailing master came to realize that there was a discrepancy between what was being carried on the ship's books and
what was actually stored below decks, a discrepancy which further investigation indicated was of criminal proportions.

Later it would be recalled by members of the crew that not
long after the Christmas celebration the master's manner toward
the captain began to shift, and to take on a less deferential tone,

a change that in hindsight suggested that he now felt safe from censure, even from such a strict disciplinarian as FitzRoy.

The captain undoubtedly sensed the shift, with predictable results. The relationship of the two men, never very cordial, became increasingly acerbic, and eventually broke into open hostility in a heated but inconclusive confrontation on the evening of February 6, 1811, when the *Macedonian*, on returning from an unsuccessful search for French raiders, encountered high seas and strong winds.

The ship began rolling heavily, and the captain, coming onto the quarterdeck during the six to eight o'clock watch, observed that she was going before the wind, which had grown so strong that Mr. Lewis, who was officer of the watch, had ordered the topgallant masts struck—that is, brought down and secured to the deck—as a precaution against their breaking off in the storm.

The sails were set almost square, and the captain could see that the masts that supported them were under considerable strain. FitzRoy, standing in front of the sailing master and shouting to be heard over the sound of the storm, demanded to know of Mr. Lewis if the larboard backstays had been set up to relieve some of the strain. Lewis, who was preoccupied with handling the ship under difficult conditions, distractedly assured the captain that the larboard backstays had indeed been set up, but FitzRoy was skeptical and sent Lieutenant Hope to see for himself. Moments later the lieutenant returned to report that contrary to Mr. Lewis's assurances, the larboard backstays had not been set up.

FitzRoy exploded. He rounded on his sailing master, impugning his honesty and calling his seamanship into question. Mr. Lewis, though stung by such public humiliation in front of the men at the wheel, held his peace.

There matters stood for two days, with the captain convinced that his sailing master was an arrogant, incompetent liar, and the sailing master angry at himself for being caught out in such an insignificant error and nursing a grudge against the captain and his high-handed manner.

Two days later, on February 8, the captain and the sailing master again found themselves on the quarterdeck during the same evening watch. The ill feeling between them had in no way diminished since the incident of the larboard backstays. According to later testimony, the second confrontation began when Captain FitzRoy, noting that the quarterdeck gratings had been removed from the hatches and not replaced, ordered Mr. Lewis to put them back. Lewis bristled. Hatch grates were a matter for the ship's carpenters, and certainly not the concern of the sailing master.

He turned on the captain and, with his thumbs hooked truculently in his trouser pockets, answered angrily, "Recollect that I am the master of this ship, not a midshipman!"

FitzRoy bristled at such insolence. "Take your hands out of your pockets when you speak to me!" he demanded.

Lewis removed his thumbs from his trousers, and then cheekily placed his hands behind his back, in an act of deliberate disrespect that he knew would be understood by everyone on the quarterdeck. The sailor at the wheel and another stationed near the carronades stood frozen in amazement. Never had they seen or even heard of such a public scene between officers.

FitzRoy missed nothing of Lewis's dumbshow. He was livid, and spoke deliberately. "You will answer to a court martial for this, Mr. Lewis, but in the meantime, you will do your duty."

The captain and his sailing master then withdrew from one another, although both remained on deck. All accounts agree that somehow the gratings were returned to the hatches, although no one could remember who moved them or when.

During the hour or so after the argument over the hatch grates, the gale grew stronger. Both men remained on deck. The captain was discussing matters with his first lieutenant, and the master was standing near the wheel concerned only with sailing the vessel. Mr. Lewis decided to reef the topsails, and in a loud voice he hailed the men stationed in the tops overhead. When he received no answer, he called out again in a louder, angrier tone, which finally brought a response. After giving the topmen his orders, the master added a shouted warning: "The next time you do not answer me, I'll have you all down and give you a damned good thrashing!"

FitzRoy bristled. It might be all right for Lewis to badger and yell at the useless landsmen dragged in by the press gangs, but now he was threatening the best sailors in the ship, the topmen, on whom FitzRoy depended. Spoiling for a fight, and sensitive to the fact that it was his exclusive prerogative to assign punishment, he shouted at Lewis, "No, no you won't! I won't allow you to lift a rope's end to any man in this ship!"

"I'll take very good care to have them punished, then, my lord," Lewis growled.

"I'll be the judge of that," the captain shot back.

Lewis's anger, originally directed at the men in the tops, turned now on FitzRoy. "If your lordship will not punish the men," he said passionately, "I will have them tried by a court martial. It is no use my carrying on the duty of the ship if I am not supported in it!"

FitzRoy boiled over. "What do you mean by going on in this insolent, mutinous manner to me?"

The master recognized at last the dangerous path he was treading, and attempted to pull back. "I do not understand you, my lord," he said feebly.

But FitzRoy was not to be mollified. In retrospect, we can only wonder why some innate sense of self-preservation did not warn FitzRoy that perhaps Mr. Lewis's obduracy indicated he held a trump card of some sort, and that his lordship might be wise to moderate his anger. But caution and introspection were not in FitzRoy's nature. He turned to Lieutenant Hope. "Do you hear the insolent, mutinous manner the master is going on with to me?" he demanded. Then, directing himself to the other men on deck, the afterguard and quartermasters, he said decisively, "You are all witness to the master's mutinous conduct towards me!"

Secure in his case, he turned back to Lewis and pronounced sentence: "I will put you in irons!"

It must have been an extraordinary moment—an absolutely unparalleled moment—in the experience of every man on deck. It was one thing to place a common sailor in irons, but not even a captain could treat another officer with such impunity, particularly not an officer as senior as a sailing master.

To the astonishment of Lieutenant Hope and the crewmen on duty, Mr. Lewis, his mind in a whirl and trying desperately to think through his next move, turned stiffly on his heels and marched off the quarterdeck and down to his berth below. This was high drama indeed, and it immediately became the principal subject of speculation and discussion throughout the *Macedonian* from ward room to main top.

As soon as the ship reached Lisbon, the captain made good his threat and pressed charges against the master. But what caused the far greater sensation was that the master pressed countercharges against the captain. His first charge—that of tyranny—was expected, since it was the general opinion that Fitz-Roy had probably overreached himself by ordering the master put in irons. But totally unexpected was the second charge—that of signing false expenses of stores. The fracas between the two officers now reached beyond the *Macedonian*, and dominated the talk throughout the fleet.

The two cases were placed on the docket and scheduled to be brought before the court-martial convened aboard the ship-of-the-line *Barfleur*, in Lisbon Harbor. Here, in the presence of the ranking officers on the station, the navy would hear the evidence and render its decisions.

Lord FitzRoy's was the first case heard. The trial lasted two days, which suggests there were many witnesses and considerable evidence, but we are shy on details of what must have been a fascinating case. Virtually the entire record has disappeared, deliberately removed from Admiralty records by persons unknown. Only a single page of the proceedings remains in the yellowing files at the Public Records Office at Kew, but it is the most informative page, the cover sheet, and while it lacks the details one might wish to examine, it does provide the court's decision:

6th and 7th March 1811
The Right Honorable Lord William Fitzroy
Captain HMS Macedonian
For signing false Expense of Stores—Tyranny & Oppression
Sentence
To be dismissed His Majesty's Service.

It was a stunning decision, totally unexpected, and utterly contrary to the accepted practice of the Royal Navy, where it was well known that sons of the peerage had an automatic influence at the Admiralty, for the obvious reason that their fathers' support in the House of Lords was vital to the naval service. That a lord—the son of a duke, no less—and an officer with sixteen years service should be so disgraced was a matter of almost unparalleled sensation. Undoubtedly the case against FitzRoy was so clear, so straightforward and unequivocal, that even the most subtle and devious of admirals had found it impossible to avoid voting for a guilty verdict, no matter how hard he tried.

Having reluctantly announced their decision, the officers of the court, who were fully aware of the enormity of their action, adjourned for the dinner hour. Mr. Lewis, already aboard the *Barfleur* awaiting his own trial, must have heard the news of the court's finding within minutes, and may be forgiven a flush of triumph. But if he hoped that Captain FitzRoy's disgrace would in any way help his own case, he had not reckoned on the depth of his lordship's animosity or on the implacable arrogance of the aristocracy.

When the court reconvened to hear the case of Mr. Lewis, the sailing master was astonished to discover that he was to face a totally unexpected prosecutor: no less an adversary than Lord William FitzRoy himself! The newly cashiered captain of the *Macedonian* now stood proudly before the court, bold as brass and utterly unrepentant, ready to wreak vengeance upon the commoner who had the temerity to bring about his conviction. During the dinner break he had hastily shed his epaulets and gold braid, and appeared now in mufti, his only concession to his drastically changed circumstances.

Poor Lewis never stood a chance. Even admirals had to pay attention to lords, and now the court officers, conscious of the political gravity of their decision against his lordship, and painfully aware of how it might some day come back to haunt them, were forced to listen attentively to the arguments of the shameless FitzRoy, and to accede cravenly to his lordship's demands. Dutifully, the court found G. D. Lewis guilty of a shadowy infraction defined only as "neglect of duty, etc." He too was dismissed the service, with the added proviso that he be "rendered incapable of ever again serving as an officer in the service of His Majesty, his heirs or successors."

There is an interesting coda to the story of Captain FitzRoy that says something about arrogance, something about power, and something about the survival of large bureaucratic institutions like the Royal Navy.

In August 1811, shortly after his return to England, Lord FitzRoy was quietly restored to the navy active list with no loss of rank or seniority. (It is very likely that it was at this time that the records of his court-martial were "lost.")

Five years later, in 1816, his financial difficulties were finally resolved when he married Miss Georgiana Raikes, second daughter of the late Thomas Raikes, Esq.

For the rest of his life, Lord FitzRoy remained on the navy's active list, and half a century after the unfortunate business in Lisbon, his lordship, by this time an admiral, passed on to his reward freighted with honors and full of years.

Mr. Lewis was never heard of again.

INTERIM CAPTAIN

~~~~~~~~~~~~~~~~~~~~~~~~

T HE DAY AFTER THE COURT PRONOUNCED FITZROY'S PRECIPI-
tous downfall, Admiral Sir George Berkeley, commanding
at Lisbon, forwarded an official report of the decision to the
Admiralty in Whitehall, accompanied by a brief covering note:

> Sir—You will herewith receive the Sentence of a Court martial
> held by my order on Capt the Right Honble Lord William Fitz
> Roy, which you will be pleased to lay before their Lordships
> and acquaint them that in consequence thereof I have appointed
> the Honble William Waldegrave from the Command of His Maj-
> esty's Ship *Melpomene* to be Captain of the *Macedonian*. . . .

"The Honble" William Waldegrave. The new captain was to
be another aristocrat, albeit of a less exalted rank than the departed FitzRoy. We know little of him beyond what Samuel
Leech tells us, which is almost entirely negative. Apparently,
during his brief tenure on board the *Macedonian*, he made life
for the crew a living hell.

It is quite possible that Captain Waldegrave was not a brutal
man—the pressures of wartime conditions have probably given
British naval officers of the period a somewhat exaggerated reputation for nastiness—but he trusted the wrong man, so the result
was the same. He saw his transfer from the decrepit old French
prize *Melpomene* to the spanking new *Macedonian* as an important
career move, and was determined to make the most of it. In an
attempt to ingratiate himself with his new subordinate officers,
he made the common mistake of paying too much attention to

his lieutenants, particularly his first lieutenant, David Hope. It was an error in judgment that was to cost the ship dearly.

The sadistic Hope, who really *was* brutal, and who had already established his penchant for inflicting pain and humiliation under FitzRoy, was able to convince the new captain that an even more liberal use of the cat was the only thing needed to turn the *Macedonian* into a first-class fighting vessel. Waldegrave gave Hope his enthusiastic blessing, and under the new regime, punishment was inflicted on an almost daily basis.

Even the boys, previously protected from corporal punishment, were now flogged, often for the most trifling offenses. The crew noted with disgust that Mr. Hope and the captain took obvious satisfaction in seeing the youngest sailors writhe under the cat. Many of them were still children as young as ten years old. "Show me his backbone," Hope would urge the men with the whips. Sometimes they did.

The new stricter discipline made life aboard the *Macedonian* intolerable for many of her crew, and an increasing number of sailors chose to run away, despite the fact that desertion carried the death penalty if caught. Some escaped while on shore duty, others dropped overboard in the night and either swam ashore or drowned. Desertion in Lisbon was particularly dangerous. In England, a deserter might hope to melt into the crowd and disappear, but in this foreign place it was impossible for English sailors, who could not speak Portuguese, to disguise their identity. In consequence, they became easy targets for Portuguese bounty hunters, happy to hunt them down for a few shillings of reward money.

At one point during Captain Waldegrave's brief command, so many men deserted that he was forced to put together a press gang to search the harbor front and round up enough men to fill the roster. Among the unfortunate victims taken by the gang were a number of American merchant sailors, who were forcibly dragged back to the ship, and who complained bitterly about their unlawful kidnapping, demanding access to the American consul. It was cold comfort for them to discover other Americans in the crew who had been caught in previous presses. Needless to say, they did not get to communicate with their consul. American captains, who knew that their men had been illegally shanghaied, were equally powerless to rescue them because they rarely knew which British ship had carried off their crewmen.

In the sorry record of tyranny aboard the *Macedonian*, the story of seaman Richard Suttonwood is the only cheerful note. Suttonwood was a foul-mouthed but merry scapegrace better known as "Bloody Dick," who liked to entertain the crew with his comic songs. He would sit on the breech of an 18-pounder surrounded by scores of his shipmates, and for an hour or more sing a selection of popular favorites, both bawdy and sentimental, for the delectation of his admiring audience. But eventually even the ebullient Suttonwood found life on board the *Macedonian* intolerable, and one dark night he clambered down a cable and made off. He managed to elude the Portuguese bounty hunters, and after several close calls, eventually found a berth in an English merchant brig which had just arrived in harbor. The following morning he discovered to his horror that the brig was laden with a cargo of gunpowder specifically earmarked for the *Macedonian*, and that she was at that very moment heading directly for his old ship. It was too late to save himself, so Bloody Dick resolved to make the best of it. As soon as the brig dropped alongside the *Macedonian*, he stepped boldly on board his old ship and coolly announced in a loud voice that he was prepared to return to duty.

The humorless Lieutenant Hope was outraged at such insolence, and was all for having him flogged through the fleet, a punishment so extreme that it usually killed the victim. But Captain Waldegrave would have none of it. He was so charmed by the sailor's bravura that he cheerfully welcomed him back on board and refused to even consider punishment.

SOON AFTER THE return of Bloody Dick, Waldegrave learned that the Admiralty in Whitehall had chosen not to endorse his interim appointment and had instead selected a new captain, a man destined to be the last—and least understood—English commander of the *Macedonian*.

CARDEN

～～～～～～～～～～～

I T IS EASY ENOUGH TO RECONSTUCT JOHN CARDEN'S FIRST appearance on the *Macedonian*. We have two different eyewitness accounts of that otherwise marginally significant event. The first is that of Samuel Leech, describing the hopes the sailors felt for their new captain, and the second is Carden's own account, describing the hopes he had for his new ship.

He arrived in the ship's launch dressed in full uniform, sitting stiffly in the stern sheets, his hands resting on the hilt of the sword which he held between his legs. Moments later, to the ruffle of drums and the insistent squeal of the boatswain's pipe, he stepped for the first time through the sally port and onto the deck of the *Macedonian*, and after the traditional exchange of salutes, turned his attention first to his officers standing respectfully hand on hat, and then to the line of crewmen mustered for his inspection. The men, more curious of him than he of them, scrutinized him in return, searching for clues that might express something of his character and temperament.

He was a thin, aesthetic type, this John Surman Carden who was to be their new captain. His face was enigmatic, with narrow lips, heavy-lidded eyes, and the high, broad brow that people sometimes equate with intellect. Significantly, he was an older man than either FitzRoy or Waldegrave, and some wondered if his greater maturity might not signal a kinder, more restrained commander. Could this man Carden bring some sense of humanity and balance to life in the *Macedonian*?

The new captain drew his orders from inside his coat and read the time-honored sentences of his warrant in a loud, clear voice to the assembled ship's company. It was the third time in less than a year that the crew had heard the same words.

By the Commissioners for Executing the Office of Lord High Admiral, of the United Kingdom of Great Britain and Ireland Etcetera, to Captain John Surman Carden, Hereby appointed Captain of His Majesty's Ship *Macedonian*. . . .

The familiar phrases defined the covenant linking the Admiralty to Carden, and Carden to the crew.

By virtue of the Power and authority to us given, We do hereby constitute and appoint you Captain of His Majesty's Ship *Macedonian*, willing and requiring you forthwith to go on board, and take upon you the Charge and Command of Captain in her accordingly; Strictly charging and Commanding all the Officers and Company of said ship to behave themselves jointly and severally in their respective Employments, with all due Respect and Obedience unto you their said Captain.

Captain Carden paused for a moment to survey his audience before continuing.

And you likewise to observe and execute the General Printed Instructions, and such Orders and Instructions as you shall from time to time receive from us, or other your superior Officers for His Majesty's Service. Hereof nor you nor any of you may fail, as you will answer the Contrary at your Peril. And for so doing this shall be your Warrant.

Here he paused again, as ship's captains in the Royal Navy have ever been wont to do, to let the awesome threat of the words sink in, before he hurried through the brief remainder.

Given under our hands, and the Seal of the Office of Admiralty, this 5th day of April, 1811. And in the Fifty first Year of His Majesty's Reign.

In the respectful silence that followed, the heavy, stiff paper made a crackling sound as Carden folded it once again and returned it to his coat pocket. The boatswain piped the men down, and they returned to their duties, each man eager to share his impressions of the new captain with his mates.

"Hereof nor you nor any of you may fail, as you will answer the Contrary at your Peril."
It is almost impossible to recreate Carden's first day aboard the *Macedonian* without visions of his last day crowding in— visions of smoke and terror, carnage and dishonor. Who was this John Surman Carden, who would play such an important part in the history of the *Macedonian*, and whose name would be forever linked with hers? History has treated him harshly, but history has been known to misunderstand, and even to lie.

C. S. Forester characterized Carden as "stupid" for an action for which a court-martial judged him "brave." Who are we to believe? Samuel Leech, first chronicler of the *Macedonian*, labeled him "merciless" and "heartless," and it is true enough that he once ordered a man flogged through the fleet with three hundred lashes on the suspicion that *he might have stolen a handkerchief*. But there was another side to Carden that was capable of the warmest, most human responses. Theodore Roosevelt dismissed him airily as "a poor commander," and wrote him off for showing "bad judgement at all times." But was he really that poor an officer?

He was, first of all, a gentleman—nothing as grand as Fitz-Roy, to be sure, nor even Waldegrave, but a man of the privileged classes, a member of the Anglo-Irish ascendency, born in Tipperary into a family that was powerful enough to wangle him a commission as ensign (at the age of ten!) in the Prince of Wales' Royal Americans Corps. Such purchased commissions for juveniles were common enough in those days, but what made Carden's different was that he actually served on active duty while still a child. He was sent to South Carolina in 1781, and became a veteran of the American Revolution before his eleventh birthday. From that time on, his whole life was given over to the military. At sixteen he entered the Royal Navy and served in India, Africa, and the French blockade. In 1798, he helped put down the Irish rebellion at the famous Battle of Vinegar Hill. More recently he had held a number of temporary commands in the Baltic and off the French coast.

Poor Carden! His is a respectable enough record. Lots of sea duty, regular promotions, and the occasional mention in dispatches; but for all that, he comes down to us as a failure. In truth, he was probably quite average, which by definition means that he was better than half of his brother officers. Certainly he should have been adequate to the job of commanding the *Macedonian*.

CARDEN SEEMS TO have intuitively understood the malaise that gripped the *Macedonian* at the time of his arrival. In his memoirs he describes how he found her "wanting in much refitting & very badly mann'd," and how he decided to deal with the problem himself, since "to complain would be deem'd a Fault." Today we would probably identify the crew's disorientation and confusion as a problem of morale, but such a concept would have been entirely foreign to anyone in Carden's time.

Yet he not only understood the nature of his crew's problem but something about solving it as well. His first act specifically designed to improve life on board the *Macedonian* was simple, imaginative, and startlingly direct, and in its style and impact, inspired: he hired a band.

It happened that soon after his arrival in Lisbon, Carden learned that a Portuguese naval squadron had captured a French prize with a fine professional band of German, French, and Italian musicians on board, and he immediately arranged to hire them, paying their wages out of his own pocket. The musicians were at first reluctant to transfer to a British ship, but finally agreed on condition that they would not be subject to flogging and could be excused from any fighting.

The band made an immediate and popular contribution to life in the ship. In an age where music of any sort was a rare enough treat, the crew could listen to the musicians every day as they performed for the captain during his dinner hour. Whenever the ship entered or left port, Carden made it a point to have the band perform on deck, so that the rest of the squadron could share the enjoyment. It was a saucy gesture that quickly earned the *Macedonian* a special cachet. Until that time, she had been simply another 38-gun frigate. Now she was something special. The band gave her a personality. For the first time, the members of the crew took pride in being recognized as "Macedonians," as they styled themselves. The new captain, by this single gesture, lifted everyone's spirits and signaled his determination to make life in the *Macedonian* as pleasant as wartime conditions might allow. It was an auspicious beginning.

Carden was equally thoughtful and solicitous in the matter of women. He was sensitive to the fact that because his men could not be trusted to be given shore leave, they were deprived of female companionship. To alleviate the hardship, he followed the generally accepted Royal Navy practice of allowing women to live on board when the ship was in port. But Carden went considerably further than other captains in the squadron, and allowed the women to remain on board even when the ship put to sea. Such an accommodation was contrary to Admiralty Regulations, but Carden chose to disregard the rules for the sake of the crew's happiness.

At least one cruise that summer was positively domestic. When the ship lay at anchor off St. Michael's in the Azores, one of the *Macedonian*'s women gave birth to a baby boy, and Carden officiated at his christening. Not surprisingly, the mother chose to name him Michael.

IMPROVING THE QUALITY of life was only the first step in Carden's program to turn the *Macedonian* into a happy ship. He was also determined to whip her into fighting shape, which meant molding her crew into an efficient team by increasing the number of training sessions and simultaneously weeding out the riffraff and untrainable landsmen swept aboard by the press gangs. During his first weeks in the *Macedonian* he made it a point to personally assess every man in the crew, taking note of those who showed promise and spotting the troublemakers and the dullards. Once he determined that a man could not be turned into the kind of sailor he wanted, he arranged to get him out of the ship.

Carden would have happily given such men an official discharge, but he knew that would only encourage his good men to feign incompetency so that they too might qualify. Instead, he devised a subterfuge that quickly became an open secret aboard ship. The unwanted crewmen were designated "broomers," and were sent ashore under guard to cut straw to make the brooms used for sweeping the deck. Carden saw to it they were sent to locations beyond the watchful gaze of the Portuguese bounty hunters and were guarded by inadequate numbers of marines. Invariably, the broomers ran away. Carden made no attempt to hunt them down or to punish the responsible guards. It was as humane a method as possible to deal with a vexatious problem, and saved many a shiftless incompetent a painful and unprofitable flogging.

There was a limiting factor to this particular game, as Carden well knew, namely, that he had to retain enough men to handle the *Macedonian*'s guns. In actual practice, this meant he needed men to handle half the guns, since it was highly unlikely that the *Macedonian* would be firing from more than one side of the ship at a time. With eleven men needed to load, aim, fire, and swab out each of fourteen cannon, and six men to handle each of seven carronades, he needed at least two hundred men for the guns alone. In addition, another 60 men were needed to handle the ship during a battle, which gave him an inflexible minimum of 260 men for his crew, not counting marines, who manned the fighting tops—the overhead platforms on the masts—and formed the backbone of the boarding party. Since there were only three hundred men in the *Macedonian* when he took command, Carden knew he could not lose too many broomers without seriously diminishing his vessel's fighting capabilities.

* * *

BUT THE MOST intractable single problem Carden faced in his efforts to improve the ship centered on Lieutenant David Hope, the man who enjoyed flogging children. The captain of a frigate had such varied responsibilities that it was essential that he work closely with his officers, and particularly with his first lieutenant, but it soon became clear that Carden and Hope were so thoroughly mismatched that close cooperation between them was virtually impossible. The junior officer's preoccupation with punishment as a means of instilling discipline was forever clashing with Captain Carden's more measured and mature administrative style. Carden was loathe to stifle Hope's zeal—he recognized that his fighting spirit would be a valuable asset in an action with the enemy—and he therefore allowed Hope considerable latitude. Unfortunately, his forbearance seemed only to encourage the lieutenant's aggressive nature, and as a result, the relationship between the two officers, never strong to begin with, deteriorated throughout the closing months of 1811.

CARDEN HAD FRIENDS in high places, and in January 1812 they were able to put him in the way of an opportunity to pocket a large and unexpected windfall. The new assignment provides an interesting example of the nonmilitary use of naval vessels, as well as offering an intriguing glimpse into the machinations of international finances as practiced in an earlier, more piratical age.

A directive from Admiral Berkeley's headquarters ordered Carden to take the *Macedonian* to Norfolk, Virginia, and there to deliver certain papers for the British Embassy in Washington, and to receive in return a consignment of goods to be brought back to Lisbon. The apparently innocuous nature of the orders in fact masked Britain's most secret and most pressing wartime crisis: the Bank of England was going bust. The country was running out of cash—the gold and silver coinage known as "specie"—that was needed to pay for the provisioning of her armed forces. Without fresh infusions of specie, Britain's entire war effort stood in jeopardy. The search for new sources of cash became an issue of the highest priority.

The cabinet in London, struggling to resolve the crisis, looked across the seas to the banks of America, which were brimming with more than enough gold to supply Britain's needs. But Washington, although theoretically at peace with Britain, was hostile, and not likely to cooperate in any scheme to help the Bank of England. American animosity arose from the Royal Navy's high-handed refusal to allow freedom of the seas to American shipping, and its continuing practice of impressing American sailors.

Angered by Britain's refusal to change its ways, Congress had at last closed American ports to British shipping. The prime minister knew that if he wanted Yankee cash, he would have to resort to trickery to get it.

By presidential order, the only British ships allowed into American harbors were naval vessels sailing on diplomatic business, and it was this loophole that the cabinet decided to exploit as it put together its scheme to winkle specie out of the Yankee banks and bring it back across the Atlantic. The plan called for smuggling a large amount of financial paper into the United States in the form of bills of exchange, which were a form of promissory notes written on the Bank of England. With the bills in hand, British agents in America, working clandestinely, would plant rumors in the financial centers calculated to temporarily increase the exchange rate between dollars and pounds sterling. When the value of the pound rose, the agents would sell off the bills of exchange for specie, which would then be gathered together and shipped back to England. The British government would, in effect, write a check for the specie, payable at some later date. It was estimated that the entire operation, from the smuggling in of the British paper to the smuggling out of the American specie, would take only a fortnight.

The scheme was not exactly illegal, but it was certainly an unfriendly act; and even given the rough and ready financial standards of the period, it was clearly sharp practice, not calculated to improve the deteriorating relationship between Britain and America. The cabinet understood the danger inherent in their action. If the plan was discovered, it might lead directly to war. For that reason alone, the project called for the utmost discretion at every step.

Under a heavy veil of secrecy, an unusually large order of bills was made up in the Bank of England and forwarded to Admiral Berkeley's headquarters in Lisbon. The admiral's son-in-law and aide, Captain Sir Thomas Masterman Hardy, searched the squadron for an officer of sufficient maturity and discretion to be trusted with the precious papers. It was a lucrative assignment to bestow, because the captain of a naval vessel carrying specie was entitled to receive a percentage of the value of the specie carried. Hardy decided to give it to his friend, John Surman Carden of the *Macedonian*.

The entire operation was of such delicacy that Carden was only informed of the nature of the consignment, but not its size, which was enormous. But there was no reason to keep the ship's destination a secret, and the announcement that the *Macedonian* was bound for the United States generated considerable excitement below decks. The cruise promised a welcome change of scene for all, and for the impressed Americans on board—there were at least seven of them—it provided fresh hope that some means might be found to escape to their native land.

AFTER AN UNEVENTFUL passage, the *Macedonian* entered the Chesapeake on February 10, 1812, and took on her Hampton Roads pilot. Carden, with his large packet of "sealed dispatches" under lock and key in the great room, was anxious to interview the pilot personally, and to get some idea of what he might expect to find in the country he was now approaching. Was he likely to run into trouble? Was the mood of the public strongly anti-British? Was war imminent? The pilot was amused by Carden's inflated fears, and because he had a sense of humor and perhaps a dash of anglophobic bias, he decided to confirm the captain's anxieties. He gave Carden a highly exaggerated account of American anger toward England, painting a picture of national outrage, and warning the captain that neither he nor his officers could expect to travel from Norfolk to Washington without being exposed everywhere to danger and insult. In all probability the jesting pilot did not expect his account to be taken as literal truth, but Carden, who held the aristocratic Briton's traditional contemptuous disdain for things American, would not stay for an answer, and thereby set himself up for a highly embarrassing and painfully unprofitable confrontation.

As a direct result of the pilot's story, Carden decided to cancel his original plan, which had been to send one of his officers to Washington with the packet of "sealed dispatches." Instead, he decided to deliver them to the local British consul in Norfolk, and as soon as the *Macedonian* dropped anchor in Hampton Roads he and his clerk left the ship bearing the large and bulky packet, and upon landing, hired a man with a barrow to carry it, and headed into the little city of Norfolk. It was the first time in thirty years that Carden had set foot in America, and his arrival must have stirred long-buried anger and resentments. His beloved father had been killed by American soldiers during the Revolution, and much of the family's wealth, which had been invested in the colonies, had been forfeited in the peace that closed the war. His distaste for Americans, and his unconsidered assumption that they were at best untrustworthy rogues, was to plague him more than once during his brief stay in Virginia, and before it was over would cause him painful embarrassment.

With the help of directions from the barrow man, Carden quickly found his way down the cobbled streets to the home of the British consul, Colonel John Hamilton, who welcomed him warmly. Due to the embargo, English visitors were a rarity, and Hamilton was happy for the company and eager to be of service. Carden handed over the large packet, cautioning the consul of the dangers that the pilot had warned against. He was startled when Colonel Hamilton laughed at his fears and casually turned the "sealed dispatches" over to a servant, instructing him to send them off to the British minister in Washington by common post. Noticing the distress on Carden's face, Hamilton cheerfully assured him that the American postal system was every bit as private and reliable as that of Britain.

Over coffee, Hamilton turned the conversation to social matters, and learning that Carden planned to remain in Virginia for
at least a fortnight, began enthusiastically making arrangements
for the officers of the *Macedonian* to meet the good people of
Norfolk, and in particular the officers from the American Navy
ships wintering over in the Roads, chief among whom was Commodore Stephen Decatur, captain of the 44-gun frigate *United
States*.

With the "sealed dispatches" on their way, Carden and his
officers had little to do until the specie arrived, and were happy
to fill the days and evenings with one agreeable social function
after another arranged by the sociable Colonel Hamilton. They
found themselves the center of flattering attention on all sides,
and were pleased to discover that the citizens of Norfolk, in
spite of the troubled diplomatic situation, were eager to offer
their British visitors a warm and lively welcome.

Carden moved into a room in Colonel Hamilton's house, and
on several different occasions the two of them were guests at
the table of Commodore Decatur and his vivacious wife, Susan.
In light of later events, these meetings were to take on heightened significance. There was a deal of good-natured bantering
between all of the officers over the parlous diplomatic situation
between their two countries. With their respective governments
at loggerheads, it was possible that they might next meet as
enemies, and the prospect became the subject of joking speculation. But there was also a deal of serious naval discussion as
well. As professional sailors, the Americans held the Royal Navy
in high esteem, and were keenly interested in learning the latest
developments in marine warfare. They were also eager to show
off their own potential. Decatur, who was about ten years
younger than Carden, boasted of the size and strength of his
frigate, the *United States*, and of the destructive power of the 24-
pounder long guns she carried. Carden listened politely, and
condescended to point out that the Royal Navy had already
experimented with 24-pounders in frigates, only to find the 18-
pounders more efficient.

As the round of parties continued into a second week, Carden warmed to the Americans. He was charmed by their attention and deference, and appeared ready to see them as possibly something other than the mendacious and quarrelsome rabble he remembered from his experiences as an-eleven-year-old. But any such mellowing on his part was abruptly cut short when a shocking letter arrived from the minister in Washington, bearing the alarming news that all was lost, that the sealed packet had been publicly opened and discovered to contain bills of exchange, and that the resulting publicity now made it impossible to bid up the prices on the exchange or carry out any part of the rest of the scheme. In consequence of this disaster there would be no large freight of specie forthcoming.

Carden exploded in outrage, partly in disappointment at losing the fee for carrying the specie, but primarily in anger at the Americans for breaching the sacred privacy of the postal system. Boiling with self-righteous fury, he stormed out of Hamilton's house, and upon running into some American acquaintances in the street, immediately told them his story, expressing his anger and disgust at such unmannerly behavior. He continued to repeat the story to others in Norfolk, and to heap scorn on the postal service and by extension, the American government as well.

The reaction to Carden's angry charges is interesting. Everyone in Norfolk was shocked and mortified. Americans of the day were inordinately proud of their new country and sensitive of its honor, and liked to believe they represented a cultural gentility equal to or even superior to that of their British cousins. Carden's attack was painful and humiliating. A group of Norfolk citizens, acutely embarrassed by his charges, petitioned the local postmaster to ascertain all the facts of the incident, which if true, everyone agreed, were fully as shameful and distressing as the British captain alleged. An enquiry was despatched, and two days later a letter from the postmaster in Washington told a very different story from the account so rashly broadcast by Captain Carden.

The package had in fact arrived in Washington intact, with the seals unbroken, but the British minister, Augustus John Foster, who had come down to the post office in person to accept it, balked at paying the $39 first-class postal charge. In all innocence, he assumed that because the package was so large, it undoubtedly contained only London newspapers and other printed material, and therefore he should be charged a lower fee. The postmaster politely agreed to reduce the charge if the minister could demonstrate the truth of his assertion by opening the package in his presence. Mr. Foster accepted the offer and broke the seals, only to discover after he opened the packet in front of witnesses that he was mistaken, and that it contained neither printed material nor even sealed dispatches, but a large number of bills of exchange, with a face value of some £600,000 and more. His subsequent letter to Carden had expressed the truth, but had been short on particulars, and it was Carden who had arbitrarily assumed that the Americans had been at fault, and had then filled in the missing details with self-damning fictions.

Upon hearing this quite different version of the affair, a very much relieved Norfolk lawyer named Littleton Waller Tazewell hurried to Colonel Hamilton's house to relate the details to the still outraged Captain Carden. After hearing the story in full, the dumbfounded Carden abruptly burst out, "Then the cat is out of the bag at last." Tazewell, who was concerned primarily in restoring the good name of the postal service, and who had not stopped to consider the significance of the bills of exchange, was puzzled by Carden's apparent non sequitur. He continued to discuss the details, but it was clear that Carden was not even listening.

The captain was, in fact, totally occupied with mental arithmetic. Sir Thomas Hardy in Lisbon had explained the nature of the package he would carry across the Atlantic but not its value, and Tazewell's news now told him for the first time the colossal amount of money involved. After several minutes, unbidden and with no explanation, Carden interrupted the lawyer and stated in a hollow tone, "I shall lose £1800 pounds sterling on the blunder," that being his percentage of the specie he was to have carried back to Lisbon. It was a huge loss for Carden, equivalent to perhaps $200,000 today, a sum equal to about fifteen years of his captain's salary.

Tazewell had no idea what the Englishman was talking about. Puzzled by Carden's behavior, he left the consul's house and made it his business to seek out bankers and naval men who might be able to throw some light on the captain's enigmatic comments. It was only a matter of time before he was able to decipher Carden's strange utterances, and grasp the true nature and purpose of the visit of the *Macedonian* to Norfolk. It was now the Americans' turn to be outraged by such deception, made all the more dishonorable by the fact it had been the English mountebank himself who had been so quick to accuse the Americans of duplicity.

Never was Albion seen to be more perfidious.

Carden, publicly exposed as a charlatan and a cheat to all of those whose hospitality he had so blithely accepted, was in an agony of humiliation. He tried as best he could to maintain his patrician dignity until such time as he could make ready his departure, but by this time he was a well-known figure in Norfolk, and he discovered it was impossible to walk the streets of the little city without incurring angry scowls and bitter accusations, or worse still, knowing winks and condescending smiles. He found it too painful to remain on shore, and returned to his cabin in the *Macedonian*. Two days later, on February 28, he was at last able to give the order to up anchor and set sail for Lisbon. For the first time, his band of musicians remained silent as they left port.

Carden, like any naval captain, was a proud man, and it must have hurt him deeply to be publicly exposed as a schemer and a common trickster. But in the long run his personal embarrassment could be put behind him as the Virginia capes disappeared over the horizon. A more serious failing was his strong anti-American bias, which caused him to undervalue some superior fighting men and their equally superior vessels, simply because they were not English. While in Virginia he should have paid more heed to his host Decatur, and to Decatur's hulking 44-gun ship, the *United States*. The *Macedonian* was anchored

only a few cable lengths from her in Hampton Roads, and Carden should have made it his business to learn something of her
size, her strength, and the terrible force of her 24-pounders. She
represented one of the most interesting designs of the great age
of sail, and along with her two sister ships presented a new and
very dangerous kind of naval threat. "I see trouble for Britain
in those big frigates across the sea," Lord Nelson had observed
thoughtfully, when he first heard of them ten years before Carden's visit to Norfolk.

The history of the *Macedonian* might have been radically different had Carden paid more attention to the Yankee sailors and
their frigates.

29°N × 29°30' W

A FEW MONTHS AFTER THE NORFOLK FIASCO, THE *MACEDONIAN* lay at anchor at Spithead on the south coast of England, just off the huge Royal Navy station at Portsmouth. On her quarterdeck Captain Carden was bidding farewell to an illustrious passenger, the gallant Charles William Stewart, Marquis of Londonderry, late of Wellington's staff, who had been invalided home from Lisbon.

Young Stewart was a man of considerable influence in Regency England. His brother, Viscount Castlereagh, was the foreign secretary and one of the most powerful men in Parliament. As Stewart made his farewells to Carden and thanked him for the attentions he and his men had received on the voyage, the young nobleman inquired if there was anything he might do for the captain in the way of recompense. It was no idle offer, as Carden well knew. He would describe the scene years later: "I replied that the Command of my then Ship was all I could wish for, but that I did not like being confind to the Lisbon station, & the only possible circumstance that could add to my Ambition was, or could be, a Cruise in the Western Ocean where chances would be more favorable to my future prospects." With the ruefulness of hindsight he added, "A Proof how short sighted are the Creatures of this World."

STEWART WAS AS good as his word, and on September 29, 1812, Carden's fondest wish was realized. He received sailing orders calling for the *Macedonian* to depart from England in company with a large East Indiaman bound for the Cape of Good

Hope. Carden was to convey her on the first part of her voyage. Once safely past Madeira, the two ships would part, and Carden was then free to cruise the seas in search of prizes for as long as his provisions and water would permit before returning to England. As an added fillip, he could now look forward to a new quarry, for word had just reached London of America's declaration of war, which meant that Yankee ships, as well as French, were fair game.

The Times expressed the general British view of the new enemy, dismissing the American Navy as "a few fir built frigates with strips of bunting, manned by sons of bitches and outlaws." Carden, with his painful memories of his tour in the Carolinas during the Revolution and the more recent Norfolk embarrassment, was particularly eager to have a go at the Yankees. As the *Macedonian* passed the Needles, her little band of musicians sawing away atop the forecastle, the promise of adventure and prize money was in the air, giving the whole ship a sense of anticipation and spirit.

At the Portuguese island of Madeira, where they stopped off long enough for the *Macedonian*'s officers to purchase a supply of the island's superior wine for the ward room, the British consul had interesting news. He informed Carden that an American frigate, the *Essex*, was reported to be in the area and on the prowl for British merchantmen. It was the best news Carden could have hoped to hear. America had only six frigates, and the *Essex* was one of the smallest. She carried something like forty-six guns, but most of them were short-range carronades, which meant that if he were to run into her, the Americans would have nothing to match the range of the *Macedonian*'s long 18-pounders. Carden would have the distinct advantage.

On October 22, once again at sea, the *Macedonian* at last bade farewell to the Indiaman and set off alone into the Western Ocean in search of wealth, glory, and adventure. Carden's star would never stand higher than it did that morning. He was in command of a swift, powerful new frigate, recently overhauled and manned by a sparse but well-trained crew, free to roam the trade routes and seek out prizes, unencumbered by secondary orders or responsibilities. It was every naval captain's dream come true, and he knew in his heart that any Royal Navy officer worth his salt, including even the gouty old admirals in Whitehall, would have jumped at the opportunity to trade places with him. There were ships out there for the taking, and now the only trick was to find them.

If the *Macedonian* was to catch a prize in this vast empty ocean, a permanent watch was the first order of business, and the higher the watchmen were above the surface of the sea, the better. A man standing on deck could only see seven or eight miles to the horizon, but due to the curvature of the earth, a man standing overhead on the trestle trees could see almost twice that far. The captain gave orders to post lookouts on the highest yards of the foremast and mainmast for every hour of daylight. At night, he would make do with only a single lookout on the foreyard.

The captain's good humor was evident to all who saw him. He was in the best of spirits, laughing with his officers, joking with the men and calling up to the lookouts regularly, admonishing them to keep their eyes peeled.

Only one problem dampened his enthusiasm. His old nemesis, Lieutenant Hope, stirred by the prospect of a fight, was making a nuisance of himself, bullying the crew, browbeating the petty officers, demanding extra drill when it was not necessary, urging greater discipline and more punishment, and even subtly threatening his own captain with blackmail for some apparent lack of zeal. Carden's patience ran out. It was time for a final and definite break between the two men.

In a highly unusual private conversation in the great room, a weary Carden laid aside any pretense of an amicable understanding, and informed Hope that it was no longer possible for both of them to remain in the same ship. At the end of the cruise he would, he promised, petition the Admiralty to transfer one of them out of the *Macedonian*. Until then, he would appreciate it if the lieutenant would simply contain himself and do his duty. It was a polite form of dismissal. Both men knew that the Admiralty would undoubtedly choose to remove the lieutenant;

but if Carden hoped his talk might induce Hope to bank his fires, he was mistaken.

ON THE SECOND morning of their cruise a large shark, accompanied by pilot fish, adopted the ship and stayed with her for a number of days. Sailors usually hated and feared sharks, but no one seemed to see this particular one as an ill omen. They looked for it each morning, and hailed it as an old friend. The captain's good spirits, and the general air of optimism and excitement throughout the ship, banished dark thoughts and helped make the *Macedonian*, perhaps for the first time ever, a happy ship.

On the fourth day, soon after sunrise, Carden stood on the quarterdeck, planning out his day with one of his lieutenants. They were at the western edge of the Sargasso Sea. The subtropical sun was bright and warm upon the empty ocean, and a fair breeze blew out of the south-southeast. It was a Sunday, and as was the custom of the ship, after breakfast the men would be mustered on the forecastle deck dressed in their Sunday best, wearing blue jackets and white trousers, with brass buttons and black, glossy hats ornamented with ribbons lettered with the name of the ship. Usually the captain read a church service after muster, and the rest of the day was given over to idleness.

Suddenly the leisurely Sabbath routine was shattered by an excited call from the masthead, "Sail ho!"

Carden snapped his eyes upward toward the sound of the voice. "Mast head there!" he shouted.

"Sir!"

"Where away? What does she look like?"

"A square rigged vessel, sir," the lookout reported, pointing north.

The crew came tumbling out on deck, galvanized by the news of possible action.

"Mast head there!" Carden called again. "What does she look like?"

"A large ship, sir, standing towards us!" came the call from above.

The railing was now three deep with sailors excitedly calling out to messmates and straining to catch a glimpse of the approaching vessel.

"Keep silence fore and aft!" ordered the captain irritably, and the crew fell instantly quiet. "What does she look like?" he asked again.

"A frigate, sir!"

"All hands clear the ship for action, ahoy!" The stranger was still too far over the horizon to be seen from the deck, but Carden turned to James Walker, his sailing master, and ordered him to wear ship and stand for her.

The captain was in a state of intense excitement. Beneath the upper-class calm of his demeanor the adrenaline coursed through his system setting his nerves atingle as he readied himself for the coming confrontation. If the ship now approaching over the horizon was indeed a man-of-war, she was almost certain to be an enemy, either French or American, and the next two hours could, he knew, profoundly change his life.

For one thing, victory in a single-ship action could earn the captain a knighthood. For Carden, born into the lower end of the aristocracy, the opportunity to ratchet himself up to a higher social level on the basis of a single morning's work would have stirred his deepest ambitions.

There was also the promise of prize money. By royal edict the victorious captain in a single-ship action stood to receive a quarter of the entire value of the capture when she was brought into prize court. In the case of a frigate, that could mean something on the order of £10,000, a true fortune. It was a heady prospect.

And then there was the simple matter of honor and tradition. For twenty years, the Royal Navy had been locked in a series of naval wars, fighting practically everybody in Europe at one time or another. In those years the navy had compiled an astonishing record of single-ship victories. In battle after battle with the French Navy it had been British pluck, British daring, British determination that won the day. Only once, in 1805, when the *Milan* captured the *Cleopatra*, had the French been victorious.

As often as not, those British victories had been purchased in the face of formidable odds, as when the *Seahorse* captured the Turkish frigate *Badère-Zaffer*, when the *Astraea* captured the French *Gloire*, and when, most glorious of all, Lord Cochrane, in the gallant little brig-sloop *Speedy*, with only 50 men, overwhelmed the Spanish *Gamo*, with a crew of 320.

The names of the victorious ships and their captains were legends, not only within the navy, but in the public press as well, and every officer in the *Macedonian* was acutely aware that he now had the opportunity to join that hallowed group of heroes, and to become part of the glorious record.

IT WOULD BE at least an hour before the two ships met, and Carden needed every minute. Speaking coolly and with precision, first with Lieutenant Hope and then with Mr. Walker, his sailing master, he gave the orders that would transform the *Macedonian* into the war machine she was designed to be.

David Hope was beside himself with warlike ferocity, and for once Carden shared his eagerness. The lieutenant hurried off to execute the commands, and within minutes the tompions were pulled from the carronades and cannon on the upper decks and main deck, and the guns run out. The cookstove was doused as a precaution against fire, the greatest danger to any wooden ship. Teams of sailors, still dressed in their Sunday best, scoured the ship for non-essential items that might get in the way during the action. Extra ladders, a few sticks of furniture from the ward room, a set of worn sails, and similar odds and ends were all unceremoniously thrown over the side.

Seamen who would not have dared set foot on the quarterdeck took over the captain's personal quarters with barely a by-your-leave, knocking open the gunports on either side of the cabin and running out the 18-pounders lashed to the bulkheads. Even Lord FitzRoy's special partition, built into the great room when the *Macedonian* was still at Woolwich, was torn down and sent below.

Down in the hold, all was deathly quiet in the flickering gloom of the filling rooms adjacent to the copper-lined magazine. Here the ship's gunner carefully weighed out precise measures of gunpowder, each one enough for a single cannon shot, and tipped them gingerly into flannel cartridge bags. The powder was tricky stuff, and had to be handled with extreme care. A single spark in that cramped room, stacked to the rafters with barrels of explosives, was enough to blow the *Macedonian* sky high. The gunner worked slowly and with precision. As he completed each six-pound cartridge, he handed it through a scuttle to a waiting boy, or "powder monkey," who placed it carefully in a spark-proof carrying case and ran it up to the gun deck.

On the quarterdeck, Carden privately reviewed his tactics for the upcoming battle. He was concerned that no less than 35 members of his total crew of 301 were boys, some as young as eleven or twelve years of age, and hardly worth ship-room. It meant he had no reserves, and each man was therefore irreplaceable. The size of his crew would affect his plan of battle. He was determined to be aggressive, but because he could so ill afford to lose men, he would have to fight in such a way as to keep casualties to a minimum.

Carden's thoughts were interrupted by the arrival of his bandmaster, looking somewhat sheepish, who reminded him in halting English that he and the other musicians were not obliged to take part in the action, and would prefer to sit out the battle in comparative safety below decks. Carden started to protest, pointing out that the musicians had regularly participated in the gun drills along with the rest of the crew, but he relented soon enough when it occurred to him that reluctant musicians at the guns might be more trouble than they were worth. With an oath, he ordered the band members below to the cable tier, where they would be out of the way and safe from stray cannonballs.

His small crew, he reflected, was now reduced by eight, even before the start of hostilities.

A seaman named John Card, an impressed American, sought permission to address the captain, and after knuckling his forehead respectfully explained that he did not wish to fight his own countrymen, and should the approaching frigate prove to be American, he asked to be relieved of duty and treated as a prisoner of war. Carden angrily denied the request, and ordered him back to his station, threatening to shoot him down if he attempted to avoid his duty. Foregoing the help of eight foreign-speaking musicians was one thing, but losing an experienced English-speaking seaman was something else again.

Some sailors standing at the gun carriages in the bow called out to their mates and pointed excitedly toward a tiny dot to the northeast. Carden threw his glass to his eye and caught his first sight of the stranger, hull down and under easy canvas, with only her masts and sails yet visible. He estimated another half hour at least before the two ships would reach closing range.

It was coming up to eight o'clock.

Directly below Carden, on the gun deck, the men stood at ease by their 18-pounders. Those who had been in previous sea battles braced themselves for the hell to come. Those who only knew of battle from the tales of veterans tries as best they could to deal with the dread of the unknown. All watched in bitter amusement as Lieutenant Bulford armed each of his pimply faced junior midshipmen with a brace of pistols and stationed them on the berth deck with orders to shoot to kill any crewmen seeking to run from the action.

Each gun on the main deck was fitted with one of the new friction locks, which made them as simple to fire as a musket; but the captain did not fully trust such technical novelties, and had insisted that each gun captain carry a smoldering slow match as well, so that he could still fire the guns in the old, clumsier fashion should the friction locks fail. The precaution was typical of the attention to detail Carden had insisted upon in his training sessions.

By the time the stranger had approached to within four miles or so, it was evident even to the naked eye that she was a frigate. Her ports, like those in the *Macedonian*, were open and her guns run out, but that in itself might not indicate belligerence, only caution. The open seas were a dangerous place, and any chance meeting of ships required discretion. The stranger was heading almost directly toward the British, so they could not make out if she was displaying national colors. The *Macedonian*, which had no ensign flying, was as anonymous to the stranger as she was to them.

It was now half past eight in the morning, and as the ships began to close Carden ordered the British colors hoisted, along with the sequence of signal flags spelling out the Royal Navy's secret recognition code. It was now up to the stranger. If she was British, she would recognize the code and hoist the prescribed countercode. If she was not British, she might either hoist neutral colors, in which case Carden would insist on sending a boat to verify, or she could identify herself as an enemy, in which case a battle would ensue. Friend or foe, the time for anonymity was over.

Through his glass, he could see the officers in the other ship reacting to the signal from the *Macedonian*, and a minute later, small lashed bundles soared up to the stranger's three mastheads and to the end of the spanker gaff. When the lashings were tugged free, four bright, peppermint-striped American ensigns snapped briskly over the frigate.

A roar of pent-up excitement exploded across the upper deck of the *Macedonian*, an inarticulate outburst brought on by the release of emotional tension. So there was to be a fight after all! The shouting was quickly echoed below as the news was passed down to the main deck. Many in the crew, particularly the Americans, had hoped the stranger would turn out to be French, but in the imperative of the moment that hope was already forgotten. Each man's life was now on the scales, and the possibility of sudden death, or perhaps even more frightening, life-long mutilation, only minutes away. Now the men were shouting simply because those around them were shouting, shouting as a release from indecision, shouting to keep their spirits up, and perhaps some of them shouting to overcome the urge to keen with terror.

ON THE AMERICAN ship, the officers and men had just completed precisely the same drill as on board the *Macedonian*. Small clusters of men now stood by each larboard gun, waiting tensely for an order to fire. Their ship was the *United States*, sixteen days out of Boston and under the command of Commodore Stephen Decatur, Carden's erstwhile dinner host in Norfolk. Decatur was probably the most dashing and romantic officer ever to hold an American naval commission, and one of the most intelligent as well. He stood now, dressed in his favorite battle gear of farmer's homespun and a straw hat, his eyes fixed on the *Macedonian*, giving last-minute instructions to his officers and shouting encouragement to his men.

THE BATTLE BETWEEN the *Macedonian* and the *United States* is something of a setpiece in American naval history, and the story as it has come down to us includes so many distortions and half-truths that it is almost impossible to accommodate all the different accounts and to separate fact from fiction. To understand what actually happened that morning of October 25, 1812, it is necessary to know a little about the ship that Decatur commanded, as well as something about the mind-set of her commander.

The British officers studying the American ship that morning, looking at her through telescopes across some two miles of open water, had no way of discerning her true size. They could see that she was a frigate. Her three masts and single gun deck told them as much. But in fact the *United States* was a frigate in name only. She was in reality a super-frigate, a nautical bruiser. She was larger than the *Macedonian* by a ratio of three to two, and in terms of strength and firepower, was almost comparable to a 74-gun ship-of-the-line. She and her two sisters carried larger and more powerful guns than any other frigates in the world, and the weight of metal of a single broadside from her battery came to 864 pounds, as compared with 528 for the *Macedonian*, a 60 percent difference. Poor Carden, who was convinced he was up against the dainty little *Essex*, never had a chance.

But an even more important differential between the two ships was the vision each captain carried into battle. Carden would fight fiercely for king and country, shaping his battle plan to the traditions of his service, playing by the book, and using tactics tested and proved in a hundred enemy actions. Decatur would wage a far more unorthodox fight, and it was his course of action, played out with superb cunning, that would determine the outcome that day.

Decatur's battle plan was born out of bruised ambition and professional jealousy. Early in the month, while the *United States* still lay in Boston Harbor, he had learned, along with the rest of America, of the thrilling news that the USS *Constitution*, Captain Isaac Hull, had encountered and sunk the British frigate *Guerriere* in the first decisive naval action of the War of 1812. It was a grand victory, and in the euphoria of the moment, Stephen Decatur shared his countrymen's excitement and took unalloyed pleasure in Hull's achievement.

But Decatur was a proud and self-centered man, who made no secret of his open pursuit of glory, and there could be no question that his joy in Hull's achievement was shadowed with profound envy. His instinctive and unreasoned response to the news was immediate: he must somehow surpass Hull's achievement and bring off an even greater triumph. The light of his own glory must outshine that of any of his brother officers. If Hull had earned the nation's adoration by sinking a British frigate, then he, Decatur, would have to do something even more spectacular. He knew precisely what that meant. Even before his ship left Boston, Decatur had privately determined that if he was fortunate enough to find a British warship, he would not only defeat her, but he would *bring her home* as well. Now, a fortnight later, fate had provided him with precisely the circumstances he most desired, and he would make the most of the opportunity.

CARDEN, ON HIS quarterdeck, was almost dancing with ecstasy. He would write later, under circumstances in which he had every reason not to exaggerate, "I hailed it as the happiest hour of my life when we described the stranger to be an enemy, and in the excess of feeling could not help saying so to those around me." It was the moment every Royal Navy officer yearned for, the opportunity to fight an enemy in a single-ship action.

The powerful surge of excitement on the quarterdeck triggered by the sight of the enemy flags was abruptly cut short by the cry, "She's wearing!" The captain was standing with Lieutenant Hope and his sailing master, and all three men gazed in amazement as the American ship, which had just traveled so far to reach them, and which had so provocatively flaunted her colors, now deliberately upped helm, turned away from the *Macedonian*, and started moving off even as they watched. Carden could hardly believe his eyes. Was she actually running away? It seemed impossible. Such a maneuver was counter to everything he knew and understood of naval warfare. He ordered Mr. Walker to make sail after the retreating enemy, steering down to her starboard quarter. As the *Macedonian* turned to follow the enemy frigate, it quickly became apparent that the British had the faster ship, and predictably, Lieutenant Hope urged Carden to close on the stranger forthwith.

But Carden had no intention of closing at this stage. At the current distance, it was impossible to judge the size of the American ship, but her strange behavior convinced him more than ever that she must be the *Essex*, armed primarily with short-range carronades and carrying nothing in the way of long guns to match the *Macedonian*'s main battery of 18-pounders. At close range the *Essex*'s 42-pounder carronades would make her into a deadly opponent, but as long as Carden kept open water between the two ships, the Americans would be powerless to respond to the British broadsides. Carden would play with her at a distance, using his long 18s, and like a cat with a mouse, slowly weaken her from afar. Only after he had disabled as many of her guns as possible would he risk bringing the *Macedonian* into close action.

Such a plan, he knew, went against the conventional practice of the Royal Navy, which called for captains to close with the enemy as quickly as possible. Lord Nelson, as Lieutenant Hope angrily reminded the captain, had stated it most succinctly: "Never mind manoeuvering—go at them!" But Carden chose to ignore his lieutenant's urgent pressing for a quick closing. The discussion came as close to argument as the lieutenant dared bring it, but Carden finally cut him short, and, at about 8:45 A.M., he went down to the gun deck to give the men a little speech of encouragement. He concluded his remarks with another Nelson quote, the famous Trafalgar signal, "England expects that every man will do his duty," which was the obligatory exhortation for such occasions. The men at the guns cheered, but were interrupted by a call from the quarterdeck.

The American was wearing again!

A puzzled Carden scrambled topside in time to see the enemy once more turn round. She was now heading directly back toward the *Macedonian* and crossed her bow at a distance of a little over a mile. What was she up to? As she passed, now heading in the opposite direction from the British, her entire hull suddenly vanished in a cloud of white gunsmoke. Moments later, the dull roar of the stranger's guns rolled across the intervening space and reached the British a fraction of a second before a jagged row of white splashes in the water between the ships showed that her shots had all fallen short.

"We have crossed the Rubicon," said someone with satisfaction.

For Carden, the American broadside, harmless though it proved to be, brought with it a most unwelcome discovery. Those were not carronades on the American ship, but long guns, and judging from the distance of the splashes they were at least 18-pounders, and possibly 24-pounders. In either case they were equal or superior to the *Macedonian*'s battery. Whatever ship it was that he was facing, she was not the *Essex*. Suddenly and abruptly, his plans for a long-distance cannonading made no sense at all. He would have done better to close immediately, as Lieutenant Hope had urged.

There was a ragged paradiddle of three or four shots from his own larboard guns up forward.

"Cease firing!" he shouted angrily. "You are throwing away your shot!" Almost in the same breath, he ordered the master to wear ship and close in on the enemy.

The mistaken identification of the American ship as the *Essex* had cost Carden dearly, but not irreparably. He still had the wind with him, he reflected, and he would put it to good use. The two ships were now both under fighting sail, that is, with their royals taken in and lower sails clewed up to provide greater visibility for the sharpshooters in the tops, and as a precaution against a fire started by a stray spark. They were running in the same direction on almost parallel courses, separated by less than a mile. The American was slightly in the lead, but the faster *Macedonian* was steering for the stranger's larboard quarter and closing.

The captain and his first lieutenant, previously so much at odds, were now in accord as to the course of action, and both felt absolutely confident that within an hour they would have their prize. Their ship was faster, and their crew well trained. They had every reason for confidence, as they saw it. With enough courage and enough audacity, the day would be theirs.

But slow as she was, the American ship continued her elusive ways. Carden found her shyness inexplicable, now that he knew she was carrying guns at least equal to those of the *Macedonian*. Was she really trying to evade battle? If so, why had she turned and fired?

It was now up to Mr. Walker, the sailing master, to find a means of bringing the *Macedonian* alongside the enemy. Because he had the faster ship, the temptation was simply to up helm and point the *Macedonian* toward the enemy, to "go at them," in Nelson's words. But Walker understood the risks of such a maneuver. It would expose the *Macedonian*'s bow to the Yankee guns, and the bows and sterns of wooden warships were notoriously weak and difficult to defend. The best way to close with the enemy and at the same time protect the *Macedonian*'s bow was to ease her across the intervening space at a slight angle, while the gunners maintained a steady cannonading with her main-deck battery. It would take longer, but it was safer and would in the end accomplish the desired goal of bringing the *Macedonian* alongside the enemy.

And so the battle proper began, with both ships sailing toward the morning sun, still three quarters of a mile distant from each other, and slowly, very slowly, closing. It was almost precisely the situation that Carden had originally planned, and now so fervently regretted. His crew had moved over to the opposite side of the ship and cast loose the guns, and when Carden judged the Americans had come in range of his 18-pounders, he ordered the starboard battery to open fire. Within a matter of seconds all fourteen guns erupted one after another with nerve-shattering bangs, sending shock waves ricocheting through the confined space of the gun deck and setting the gunners' ears to ringing, a ringing that in some cases would continue in their heads for weeks. As each gun fired it caromed back upon its crew, threatening to crush the unwary, and momentarily suffocating them with thick waves of choking white smoke.

Carden watched his shots hit the water and was pleased to see a few rounds fall on the far side of the American ship. His men had the range.

The American answer was immediate. Once again her hull disappeared behind a cloud of smoke, but now, with the ships much closer, the deep boom of her broadside arrived sooner, and the odd whistling sound overhead, along with some holes in the *Macedonian*'s canvas, gave evidence that the Yankee guns had overshot their mark.

Coughing and half blinded by the smoke, the men on the main deck got round in front of their guns and began the cumbersome business of reloading. A man wielding a long tool called a worm, which looked like an oversize corkscrew, thrust it into the muzzle and twisted it about to dislodge any smoldering detritus from the previous shot. As he withdrew his tool, another man, working from the other side of the gun, pushed a wet swab down the barrel to douse the burning embers left in the gun and to cool the chamber so that it could accept a fresh cartridge. Still a third man took the new charge from the powder monkey and pushed it down the muzzle and into the breech with a rammer, after which a fourth man forced down a plug of wadding to hold it in place. Another heaved a cannonball into the gun mouth, and a sixth man, the same one who had previously brandished the worm, secured the cannonball with another plug of wadding to keep it from rolling onto the pitching deck. And now, with the cannon loaded, the gun captain supervised a team of four or five sweating men who pushed the gun once more into the port and then, squinting along crude sight bars, pried it into a position calculated to give him the best chance of actually hitting the target.

He thrust his priming wire into the vent atop the breech and ran it down smartly until he felt it pierce the flannel cartridge. Then carefully measuring a quantity of powder into the breech, he set the friction primer on its spring. Everything now depended on timing. Stepping back and holding the lanyard easily in hand, he waited until the roll of the ship presented the most advantageous angle for firing the gun. With the target in motion on the sea, and his gun moving up and down in concert with the ship, it was an exercise in mental calculus to judge the precise moment to fire. When the gun captain decided that moment had arrived, he yanked the lanyard, and the cannon jumped and exploded with an ear-splitting roar, a devil set free, and the ball shot off to whatever destiny had in store. One after the other, in no particular order, fourteen different guns, with fourteen different crews, each working as quickly as it could under uncomfortable and dangerous conditions, went through the same cumbersome drill, trying mightily to make holes in a ship they could not see and to spread misery and death among a crew they did not know.

And then the enemy found the range.

Young Samuel Leech, serving as a powder monkey on starboard gun Number Five, describes looking up at one point in the action and seeing a man's hand simply disappear from the end of his arm. No sound, nor warning, no indication that anything had struck the man. Suddenly his forearm becomes a squirting fountain of blood, pumping rhythmically to the beat of an unseen heart, and painting the deck, gun carriage, and bulkheads bright crimson.

One of the boys hurrying to the filling room for another cartridge was hit in the ankle by grapeshot, and a burly York-shireman carried him below to the cockpit where the surgeon, after making the poor wretch swallow half a pint of rum, sawed off his foot.

Another boy, hit in the leg by a ball, had it amputated above the knee.

Still another, a Portuguese lad, whose country had no quarrel with America, was running with a fresh cartridge when the powder caught fire in a single blinding flash and burned all the flesh off his face. The agonized boy, reeling and in shock, lifted his hands imploringly over his head when a cannonball merci-fully cut him in two.

The Americans were firing langrage, dismantling shot made up of old knife blades, nails, iron bolts, and other scrap for destroying rigging and sails. Lieutenant Hope suffered a minor injury when he was hit by a fragment. As he went below to have it dressed, he shouted encouragement to the men. In the best of times they had wished him dead. Now they could actually look forward to the possibility.

Despite the increasing horror, or perhaps because of it, the jollity and the cheering continued. The men at the 18-pounders pulled off their jackets and shirts and called for more powder and more shot. The gun deck was a raging, deafening corner of hell on earth, spewing out deadly shot as fast as human will and muscle could manage, while overhead on the quarterdeck, the gun crews could only stand over their silent carronades, looking across at the unbridgeable distance that was beyond the range of their guns.

There was a moment of high excitement when a ball from the *Macedonian* cut away the stranger's mizzen topgallant mast, but the cheering was quickly muffled when their own ship suffered a far more serious loss. A Yankee shot cut away her gaff halyards mizzen topmast, which fell into her maintop, tangling her sails and rigging. Soon the main topsail yardarm was shot away, the jib halyards and stay, and the topgallant ties and sails were cut to pieces and rendered useless.

Captain Carden, supervising the action from near the wheel,

sensed that his ship was getting the worst of it and urged the master to steer closer. The damage from the Yankee guns was serious, and the *Macedonian*'s sailing capacity so impaired she was no longer the superior sailer.

A midshipman clambered up from below to report that the surgeon had been forced to move from the cockpit to the steerage to accommodate the mounting number of wounded. Carden nodded. He would, when there was time, care mightily for his crew, and weep bitter tears on their behalf, but that would come later. Right now there was a battle to be fought. Such were the fortunes of war.

The shouts and moans, the urgency of the work, the roar of guns and the crack and splintering of wood gave an impression of continuous and mounting horror, but in fact the cadence of the battle was almost leisurely, with each gun firing every three minutes or so. It seemed to everyone that the shots were coming in at a faster rate than they were going out, but it was impossible to be sure.

By now it was almost ten o'clock, and the two ships had been at each other for almost an hour. They had not changed relative position, although the *Macedonian* had crept steadily closer, with the result that both ships were firing with greater accuracy. The carnage wrought by the enemy gunfire was so frightful that Carden found it difficult to ignore. It took an act of will to concentrate his mind on an assessment of the damage the *Macedonian*'s guns must be inflicting on the stranger. Presumably she was giving as good as she got.

The battle gave each man his own unique death. The boatswain's head was smashed in by a ball while he attempted to trim sail. The ward-room steward was run through by a four-foot splinter of oak, and died waiting for the surgeon to get to him. The schoolmaster, whose job it was to teach navigation and arithmetic to the midshipmen, was killed trying to lift a wounded gunner. Even the poor goat, kept by the officers for her milk, did not escape. Her hind legs were shot off and poor Nan was thrown overboard.

A man named Aldrich received a shot from a cannonball that tore open his gut and spewed the contents across the gun deck. As he started to fall, he was caught by two men who saw immediately that he could not survive and threw him, still alive, over the side. Ironically, his probable cause of death was drowning.

And then, after an hour of ceaseless cannonading and with the distance between the two ships narrowed to about three hundred yards, the American ship abruptly stopped running, and backing her mizzen topsail came to the wind, as if finally bowing to the British insistence on close action. Carden and Hope felt a momentary rush of triumph, but it was quickly tempered by the somber discovery that all but two of the *Macedonian*'s starboard carronades—the guns they would need for close fighting—had been knocked out by enemy fire and were useless.

And so began the endgame.

The two ships, now side by side within fifty yards of each other, so close that the men in one ship could see the faces of the men in the other, hammered away at each other in a titanic contest of iron and gunpowder. The crew of the *Macedonian* fought fiercely and with magnificent valor, but the British ship paid heavily for the action she had so long sought.

The enemy guns, now firing from two decks, were methodically taking the *Macedonian* to pieces. Her heavy-caliber carronades sprayed a curtain of grape and cannister across the quarterdeck and forecastle, forcing those not hit by the murderous fire to seek shelter below, where the enemy's main-deck battery was spreading equal devastation and mayhem. The Americans were also firing small cannon from each of their three fighting tops, which made it still more dangerous to remain on deck, but Carden and the other men on the quarterdeck chose to ignore the peril.

If any questions remained about the American guns, Carden knew the answers by now. They were superior to his long 18s, and there seemed to be twice the number of them, although he knew such could not be the case.

Fifteen minutes into the point-blank action the terrible climax

arrived when the *Macedonian*'s main topmast came crashing
down into the foretopmast, tearing it from its place, and the
two masts fell to the deck in a tangle of rope and splinters.

In the heat of the moment, the wreckage seemed just another
inconvenience—serious but not fatal—but in truth the tangled
pile of wood, rope, and canvas confirmed the fact that the *Macedonian* was barely more than a hulk. By now all the running
rigging was shot away, and most of the standing rigging as well.
The hull was riddled with shot—later they would count ninety-
five cannonballs in it—and the stubby remains of her three masts
held only two pieces of sail—a ripped and fluttering foresail,
clewed up awkwardly, and an almost useless forestay.

If the situation appeared bleak, the demeanor of the officers
gave no hint of it. The captain, who had taken personal command of the carronades, sent a messenger down to the gun deck
to make sure the men on the 18-pounders were firing canister
and grape as well as ball. Lieutenant Hope started organizing a
boarding party armed with pikes and cutlasses, and was in the
act of dividing it it into groups for a final hand-to-hand attack
on the Yankees when suddenly, without warning, the American
ship, which seemed almost unscathed except for some holes in
her sails, pulled ahead and crossed the *Macedonian*'s bow.

For an agonizing moment, it seemed the end had come. The
enemy frigate, in perfect control of the situation, now stood in
a position where no British guns could bear on her, yet his entire
larboard battery bore on the fragile bow of the *Macedonian*, ready
to blow her out of the water. The British were totally at the
mercy of their opponent. All activity came to a standstill. The
Macedonian lay helpless to defend herself. For a moment, no
one spoke. The men trying to clear the wreckage from the two
working carronades stepped back, awaiting the inevitable broadside.

And then this strange American frigate, this ship that had so
puzzled Carden for almost two hours of hell, had one more
surprise to offer. She held her fire, and simply sailed away.

There was a low, almost inaudible grunt of incomprehension,

a vaguely hysterical gurgle in the back of someone's throat, and then, simultaneously, from every side, a loud, uncontrolled, triumphant cheer went up from the survivors on the *Macedonian*. Lieutenant Hope was almost beside himself with relief and joy and pride in his ship.

What had happened? Why, at this apparent moment of her triumph, had the American ship withdrawn? Lieutenant Hope had little time for speculation, but was convinced that there had to be a good reason why she held fire from such a favorable position. Perhaps she had suffered as much or more than the *Macedonian*, or perhaps a lookout on one of her mastheads had spotted unfriendly sails over the horizon. No matter the cause. What counted with Hope was his conviction that the enemy did not mean to renew the action. His naturally aggressive nature responded eagerly to what he perceived as a fresh opportunity. If the Yankees would not close, then it was up to the *Macedonian* to do so. The battle was far from over!

Lieutenant Hope's blind determination to continue the action in spite of devastating losses seems almost farcical in retrospect, and was certainly irrational; but both he and his men were in a maddened state brought on by almost two hours of unrelieved physical and emotional strain, and their reactions under the circumstances were quite normal. Such apparently foolhardy zeal and bravery is a familiar aspect of battle accounts throughout history, and goes to the heart of esprit de corps.

There was a frenzy to clear the confusion of wreckage from the deck. The jungle of spars and rigging was so thick and impenetrable that it was impossible to move about, and with the enemy ship already well beyond boarding range, Lieutenant Hope's pike and cutlass teams were detailed to cutting away the wreckage and throwing it into the sea.

Clearing the deck became enormously difficult, for without her sails to steady her, the *Macedonian* was at the mercy of the heavy swells that now pitched her from side to side, causing her to roll drunkenly, at times dipping so far over that her gun ports shipped water. Carden, with a cautious glance at the still

retreating American ship and an encouraging word to the men
struggling with the wreckage, took the opportunity to go below
to see how the rest of the ship was faring.

He had heard reports of heavy casualties, but nothing in a
quarter century of life at sea had prepared him for the scene of
carnage that met him when he reached the foot of the companionway. The gun deck was crimson from one end to the other,
and the sickly sweet, slightly metallic odor of blood overlay the
smell of gunpowder that permeated every quarter. Great red
spatters on the bulkheads marked the places where men had
been hit, and bloody handprints showed where they had struggled to hold on. Smears of blood on the white pine deck traced
the paths where fallen men had been pulled along to the surgery,
or in case of death, simply dumped overboard. He could hear
men struggling with the pumps, indicating that the ship was
taking on water.

There was a semblance of order on the larboard side of the gun
deck, where the 18-pounders had only briefly been employed in
the opening moments of the action. The guns stood now in a
neat row, each one at the ready, squared off before its open
port, evenly spaced and well secured, ready to be cast loose and
run out should the occasion arise. But to starboard, where the
action had been heavy and unceasing, the scene was one of
utter confusion. Enemy batteries had chopped gaping holes in
the wales and had splintered timbers, turning pieces of the ship
into jagged wooden shrapnel more deadly than the iron rounds.
One gun, now totally disabled, was canted crazily against a
wooden knee, and another, missing a trunnion, lay broken
athwart its carriage. The other twelve starboard guns, the ones
that were still operable, were standing at odd angles, as close
to their ports as the men could keep them, but threatening with
each roll of the ship to break loose and career about the deck or
hurl themselves through one of the ports.

The crew, blackened by the smoke and powder, and deafened
by the constant explosions, lay slumped over the trucks, each
man's countenance weary and drained of emotion. They looked
up at their captain as he moved down the battery, making only

the slightest attempt to show him deference. There were so few men, Carden thought. Surely there will be more when the fighting recommences? But he knew the answer even before he got to the lower deck.

Here in the gloom, illuminated only by the faint sunlight that passed down from the gun deck, Carden's terrible suspicions were confirmed. Bodies lay about in groaning heaps, almost every one of them incomplete in some vital element. The smell was fierce, the now omnipresent odor of blood mixing with sweat and the foul stink of men's innards. So many wounded, and such grievous injuries!

A wrenching bellow from the ward room told Carden that the surgery had been moved still again. Fortunes of war, he reminded himself. He decided not to interrupt the surgeon, but said a few words he hoped might cheer the groaning casualties lying on the deck, and returned topside.

It was undeniably a relief to get out into the open air again. The men had not progressed very much in their struggles to clear the wreckage. He could see that the enemy ship had now hove to about a mile distant where, presumably, the Americans were dealing with their own wounded and repairs. Carden was proud of the fight his men had shown. They gave as good as they got, no question there. But then he contemplated the stranger's masts and rigging, which were still almost totally intact, and wondered how she had escaped damage while inflicting so much on the British.

He looked at his remaining sails—the forlorn single fore stay-sail and the awkwardly clewed up foresail that would be all they could depend upon to get them close to the American should the opportunity arise.

From his position near the wheel, Carden discussed the situation with Lieutenant Hope. Both men had at first interpreted the enemy's withdrawal as a permanent disengagement, but the fact the she had remained in the area, just beyond gunshot, now convinced them she planned to renew the action, and might do so at any moment. Carden and Hope jointly decided to take the initiative while the Yankees were still otherwise occupied. They would mount a boarding party and take the enemy by storm. They called over Mr. Walker, and were on the verge of conferring with him on the best way to employ the two remaining sails to get the *Macedonian* close to the enemy when the American ship, having completed whatever it was she was doing, wore round and tacked toward the British.

Carden, reacting quickly, ordered a number of men down to the gun deck to help with the main battery, and set the rest scrambling to clear more wreckage. There were shouts, and some cheering as the *Macedonian* prepared once more to do battle. But hardly had the men taken up their stations when all human sound was overwhelmed by a great shuddering, wrenching groan from the *Macedonian* herself, as the remaining stump of the mizzenmast, weakened earlier by a direct hit, slowly toppled over the taffrail and slithered into the sea, dragging tons of shrouds and yards and rigging with it.

It was the end. The great ball of wreck became a sea anchor, totally immobilizing the ship. The *Macedonian* could no longer answer to her helm. She was now no more than a log in the water, totally helpless. The awkward foresail, now irrelevant, flapped mockingly in the wind.

The American ship stood for the British ship's larboard bow and then hauled off to take up position off her stern, once again out of harm's way and perfectly positioned to send the *Macedonian* to the bottom. Carden could see her decks crowded with men apparently unworried about exposing themselves to the fire of the moribund *Macedonian*. His ship had even lost her power to intimidate.

There comes a point where bravery becomes hollow bravado, and Carden understood that he had now reached such a crisis. He called all his officers aft to discuss something he could barely find words to describe: the surrender of a Royal Navy frigate.

That he should be the captain of that ship was almost beyond his ability to comprehend. That his name should go down in history as the first and assuredly only British frigate captain to surrender to an American was a cause of indescribable pain. In a calm, subdued voice calculated to cover the anguish he was at that moment feeling, Carden detailed their helpless condition and asked gravely if there were among his officers any who would wish to propose a course other than surrender. Predictably, Lieutenant Hope urged his captain to fight on, and if such were not possible, then surely the choice of death was preferable to that of dishonor. Sink the *Macedonian*! Put a torch to the magazine and blow the ship to pieces! If Carden had not felt responsibility for the men under him who had fought so bravely, and who had in no way dishonored themselves, he would have gladly taken precisely the action his first lieutenant implored him to.

But Lieutenant Hope stood alone. The others, cognizant of the fact that the responsibility fell solely on Carden, grudgingly agreed that there was no acceptable alternative to surrender. Having received their answers, the captain gravely asked the same question again, and received the same answers.

Then he asked the question a third time, and there was an identical response.

With a heart now as heavy and overflowing with grief as two hours earlier it had been filled with joy, Carden gave the order to strike the colors. The actual duty fell to a seaman named Watson. With shaking hands and tears streaming down his face, he struggled momentarily with the halyards and then haltingly, reluctantly, pulled down the British ensign. At first he made an attempt to catch it up as it came within reach, and bundle it into a great wad, but then, overwhelmed by the enormity of his act, he simply let it fall to the wreck-strewn deck.

The American frigate moved closer, and the British soon saw her lower a launch manned by two rows of oarsmen, with an officer in the sternsheets. As the launch swept solemnly toward the *Macedonian*, Carden went below to gather up the official documents in his possession, including the logs and the tables of secret signals used by the entire Royal Navy. He would just have time to jettison these precious papers in their lead-weighted box before dressing himself in a fresh uniform, as spotless and shiny as he could manage. Then he would for the last time strap on the sword which he must by tradition surrender to the Yankee captain. It would be the most dreadful, the most shameful experience of his entire life.

NEVER, AT ANY time during the battle or even in the years that followed, did it ever occur to John Surman Carden that the American ship he so doggedly tried to bring to close action, and which behaved in such a puzzling, unpredictable fashion, was in fact following a well-conceived, brilliantly executed battle plan, and that from first to last the *Macedonian* was the mouse, never the cat.

DECATUR

~~~~~~~~~~~~~~~~~

A HEARTSICK CARDEN, DISTRACTED AND CONFUSED, WAS politely but firmly ushered into the American longboat and rowed across to the *United States*. The enemy ship rode serenely and confidently in the rolling sea, her unmanned guns still trained on her vanquished foe. The crippled *Macedonian*, lying dead in the water, listed unpredictably with every wave.

As they came up alongside the American ship, Carden, in spite of his nervous exhaustion, was still alert enough to take note that she seemed to have suffered little damage. Her hull was almost unscratched, a fact that might have surprised him more had he not been overwhelmed with his own thoughts, which kept returning to his men. So many dead and dying and permanently crippled, so many who had paid such a terrible price for such an ignoble outcome. He must arrange for their care, he reminded himself, but first he would have to get through the disagreeable business that lay directly ahead.

As he stepped stiffly through the sally port, barely conscious of the boatswain's whistle, he found himself momentarily disoriented. He had expected to find a chaotic scene much like the one he had just left in the *Macedonian*, but to his bewilderment, he found the American ship virtually untouched. Guns were lashed up and secured, all wreckage cleared away, and a large crew mustered in his honor. Where were the blood-stained decks? The splintered yards and tangled rigging? Why was he not assaulted by the moans of the dying, the shrieks of the wounded? He felt a welling up of panic. What sort of frigate was this?

A vaguely familiar figure dressed in homespun and a straw hat stepped briskly toward him, his hand outstretched. He was obviously in command, despite his strange attire, and Carden, striving to keep control of himself in this moment of personal shame and agony, unsheathed his sword and presented it.

The man in the straw hat airily waved the sword away. "I could never accept the sword of a man who had so nobly defended the honor of it," he said, grinning. He introduced himself as Commodore Stephen Decatur, and reminded Carden of their previous meetings in Virginia. The Englishman looked at him blankly, frowning slightly as he tried to concentrate. At last he understood, and returned the sword to its scabbard.

"I am an undone man," he said with dignity, straining to mask his mortification. "I am the first British naval officer that has struck his flag to an American."

Decatur, all bonhomie, grasped Carden's hand and pumped it with great fervor, saying comfortingly, "May I inform you sir, you are mistaken. Your *Guerriere* has been taken." When Carden seemed not to understand, Decatur explained gently. "The flag of a British frigate was struck before yours." Carden could not decide whether the news relieved him of an onus or gave him fresh reason for despair.

As soon as Decatur could gracefully get away from the shattered Carden, he left his English prisoner in the *United States* and had himself rowed across to inspect his new prize—for prize he was determined she would be. His old shipmate Isaac Hull, having captured a rotting and leaking *Guerriere*, chose to put her to the torch and sink her rather than patch her up and bring her home in triumph. Decatur would make no such mistake. He understood public sentiment intuitively, and because he conscientiously courted it at every opportunity, he knew the powerful effect it would have on the American people if he could bring home a captured British warship. He was determined to get the *Macedonian* into an American port in one piece, no matter what the cost.

It was for this reason that he had adopted the tactics that so mystified Carden and Hope—the deliberate withholding of fire on two different occasions when he had the *Macedonian* at his mercy. But the battle had been so fierce and the effect of the *United States*'s guns so conclusive, that despite all his efforts to limit the damage, Decatur could see from his own quarterdeck that the *Macedonian* was now only barely afloat.

He put his first officer, Lieutenant William Allen, in charge of saving her, and gave him a large contingent of crewmen from the *United States* to help. When they reached the vanquished ship, they found their first job was to disarm and pacify the surviving British crewmen, who had broken into the spirits locker and were now fighting drunk and ready to continue the battle. With the British safely under guard, the Americans were able to turn their attention to saving the ship, which was not going to be easy. She already had seven feet of water in her hold and was likely to sink before nightfall unless something could be done about staunching her wounds. Her pumps were working, but because of the large number of holes below the waterline, the sea was still coming in faster than the pumps could flush it out. With so much free water in the hull, the *Macedonian*'s center of gravity was shifting with every roll of the sea, aggravating an already difficult situation.

The first order of business was to fother the leaks. Fresh sails were commandeered from the *United States* and hurridly suspended from the *Macedonian*'s remaining yards and masts. Clew lines from the two lower corners of each sail were run under the keel, and while one group of sailors hauled in on the lines, another group slacked off on the upper corners, and slowly the sail was drawn down and over the ship's bottom to cover the holes. With water pressure holding the canvas snugly in place, carpenters—working from inside the hull—fitted fresh planking over the holes as best they could, sealing the seams with oakum and pitch. Within a few hours Allen and his men had stabilized the ship, although as night fell her chances of survival were still impossible to predict. Lieutenant Allen suggested the possibility of jettisoning the *Macedonian*'s cannon to lighten ship, but Decatur refused to consider such a step except as a last resort. He wanted his prize to have teeth in her when he brought her in. By the following morning the ship was beginning to empty out and right herself, and she and her guns were saved.

Decatur's original plan had been to tow her home, but an inspection topside showed that given time and some spare parts from the *United States*, it would be possible to jury rig the *Macedonian* so that she might make the voyage to America independently. This was an infinitely preferable solution, both as a practical matter and for its psychological impact on the public. Using block and tackle mounted on the stubs of the old masts, the men were able to step new masts, hang yards upon them, and then cinch them into place with fresh coils of standing rigging tightened to the necessary tension at the capstan.

For two solid weeks Decatur remained hove to directly in the path of British shipping, with the risk of discovery by enemy squadrons a real and constant threat, while his men—who were eventually joined by their new friends, the *Macedonian's* own crewmen—patched and pulled their ship together and made her ready for the dash to the American coast.

It took Captain Carden almost a full day on board the *United States* to appreciate the enormity of his defeat. His ship and crew had suffered mightily, and all for nothing. As he inspected the *United States*, it became increasingly evident that he had never had a chance against the American ship, which, despite some superficial damage inflicted by British guns, was so much stronger, so much more powerful, as to be a different class of vessel. The *Macedonian* had taken almost a hundred cannonballs in her hull, many below water, where they did terrible damage, while the American's hull had only been hit five times. There could be little doubt American gunnery was both faster and more accurate, as well as being devastatingly more powerful with 24-pounders against his 18s.

The American small-arms fire was even more effective. Of the fifty-two officers and men who had stood on the *Macedonian's* quarterdeck, Carden reckoned that only he and eight others had

escaped death or serious wounding. At the surrender ceremonies, Decatur had jokingly chastised his Marine Corps sharpshooters, pointing to Carden and saying, "You call yourselves
rifle men, and have allowed this very tall and erect officer, on
an open quarterdeck to escape your aim. How was it that you
let such a figure of a man survive unscathed?"

Three days after the battle, John Carden sat down at a desk
in the *United States* to write the most painful letter of his life,
addressed to the Secretary of the Admiralty:

> . . . It is with the deepest regret I have to acquaint you for
> the information of my Lords Commissioners of the Admiralty
> that His Majesty's late Ship *Macedonian* was Captured on the
> 25th Instant by the U.S. Ship, *United States*, Commodore Deca-
> tur Commander, the details as follows . . .

After sketching in the action, Carden came to the painful
circumstances of the surrender.

> . . . [W]hen having the mizzen mast shot away by the board,
> Topmasts shot away by the Caps, main yard shot in pieces,
> lower Masts badly wounded, lower rigging all cut to pieces,
> a small proportion only of the Foresail left to the Fore Yard,
> all the Guns on the Quarter Deck and Forecastle disabled but
> two, and filled with wreck, two also on the Main Deck disa-
> bled, and several shot between wind and water, a very great
> proportion of the Crew Killed and wounded . . . being a per-
> fect wreck, and unmanagable Log . . . I deemed it prudent
> th'o painful extremity to surrender His Majesty's ship, nor
> was this dreadful alternative resorted to till every hope of
> success was removed even beyond the reach of chance, nor
> till I trust their Lordships will be aware every effort has been
> made against the Enemy by myself, my brave Officers, and
> Men, nor should she have been surrendered whilst a man
> lived on board, had she been managable . . .

Each detail in the mournful recital must have added a new
level of anguish to his personal misery. But no part of the letter

could have been more difficult than the awful reckoning in human life:

> I am sorry to say our loss is very severe, I find by this days muster, thirty six killed, three of whom linger'd a short time after the Battle, thirty six severely wounded, many of whom cannot recover, and thirty two slight wounds, who may all do well, total one hundred and four. The truly noble and animating conduct of my Officers, and the steady bravery of my Crew to the last moment of the Battle, must ever render them dear to their Country . . .

Carefully he skirted the fact that English losses had been nine times that of the Americans, whose total killed and wounded was only thirteen.

Finally, in the only truly disingenuous part of his letter, Carden described the ship that had won the day, using a mixture of envious and self-serving comments. The tone, if not the substance, almost implies that the American ship was somehow unfair:

> On being taken onboard the Enemys Ship, I ceased to wonder at the result of the Battle; the United States is built with the scantline of a seventy four gun Ship, mounting thirty long twenty four pounders (English Ship Guns) on her Main Deck, and twenty two forty two pounders, Carronades, with two long twenty four pounders on her Quarterdeck and Forecastle. Howitzer Guns in her Tops, and a travelling Carronade on her upper Deck, with a Complement of four Hundred and seventy eight pick'd men.

Even the American crewmen were bigger and stronger. Tough, tall, strapping fellows, all volunteers, all able seamen, without a landsman in their number. The *Macedonian* could not boast a dozen such specimens.

Having signed his name to this most onerous of letters and sealed it with wax supplied by the obliging Americans, it only remained to find some means of getting it to its destination at Whitehall. Fortuitously, a Swedish merchantman appeared on the horizon bound for Europe, and Decatur allowed Carden's purser to take passage in her so that the letter might reach London as quickly as possible. He was as anxious for the British to hear the bad news as he was for his own countrymen to hear the good.

ONE MORNING, a week or so after the battle, when the two captains were together on the quarterdeck of the *United States*, Carden pointed toward two of the 24-pounders and asked why the words VICTORY and NELSON were painted over their gun ports. Decatur laughed and explained that those were the affectionate nicknames the crews gave their guns, and that the men on the first gun had all served aboard Nelson's flagship of that name, and those on the second gun had served in the admiral's personal barge. Carden was incensed to find Royal Navy veterans fighting on the American side, and denounced them as traitors, choosing to overlook the fact that their connection to the Royal Navy was no indication that they were British. A vast number of the men serving in British warships were in fact foreigners, including many thousands of Americans.

Decatur, for all his elation, was genuinely concerned by Carden's low spirits, and tried to comfort him by pointing out that the superior size and firepower of the *United States* undoubtedly influenced the battle's outcome. He could afford to be open and generous with his defeated enemy, but such candor on Decatur's part was limited strictly to his private discussions.

When committing himself to paper, he was careful to choose his words, and to imply that his battle with the *Macedonian* was a fight between equals. His motive for such deceit was not vainglorious, but practical, and stemmed from his close familiarity with the rules governing prize money. Congress had stipulated that if the captured vessel in a sea battle was weaker than the victor, then the conquerors would be awarded only half the value of the capture, but if the captured vessel were equal or more powerful than the victor, the winners would receive the full value of the prize. Decatur was determined that he and his crew should take away as much money as possible for their morning's work, and he was not above employing a little harmless disinformation to double their prize earnings. He was undoubtedly guilty of bending the truth, but then, the sort of man who wins victories is the sort of man who takes advantage of opportunities wherever he finds them.

Five days after the battle it was Decatur's turn to draft a report, this one addressed to the American Secretary of the Navy. His opening paragraph includes a carefully crafted obfuscation calculated to serve his ends:

> Sir, I have the honour to inform you that on the 25th Inst. being in the Lat. 29 N. Long. 29° 30 W., We fell in with, & after an action of an hour & a half, captured his Britannic Majesty's ship *Macedonian* commanded by Captain John Carden, and mounting 49 carriage guns. . . . She is a frigate of the largest class—two years old—four months out of dock, and reputed one of the best sailers in the British service.

Decatur is gilding the lily a bit here—most of the Royal Navy frigates were indeed smaller than the *Macedonian*, but that did not make her "a frigate of the largest class"—but he is more deliberately playing fast and loose in his enumeration of the *Macedonian*'s guns. He was quick to recognize that the best means he had of confusing the differences between the two ships lay in carefully doctoring his definition of the two ships' armament.

Wooden warships always carried more guns than indicated by their rating. Thus the *Macedonian*, rated for thirty-eight guns, actually carried forty-nine, just as Decatur's own *United States*, which was rated for forty-four guns, actually carried fifty-five. But Decatur, in his report of the action, and in the months to come, would unfailingly define the *Macedonian* as a 49-gun ship, and the *United States* as a 44, clearly implying that the *Macedonian*, with its five "extra" guns, was the more heavily armed vessel, and by extension, the more powerful, which was a significant distortion of the facts.

His letter then went on to describe the battle and its outcome, concluding with another self-serving exaggeration, by maintaining that the damage sustained by his *United States* "was not such as to render her return into port necessary, and had I not deemed it important that we should see our prize in should have continued our cruise." In fact, the *United States* had taken at least one shot below the waterline and was leaking enough to require her to be pumped out every watch—a quite sufficient reason to "render her return into port necessary."

DECATUR'S GOOD FORTUNE held. Throughout the long fortnight needed for repairs, no enemy vessel showed herself above the horizon, and he had the ocean to himself with the exception of the innocuous Swedish merchantman already mentioned. His luck continued to hold after the *Macedonian* was finally judged fit to sail. The two frigates, traveling slowly and haltingly in concert through waters infested with Royal Navy vessels, proceeded unnoticed and without incident in a northwesterly direction until, on December 3, 1812, thirty-nine days after their initial encounter, they raised Montauk Point on the eastern tip of Long Island.

Decatur decided to put in at New London, on the Connecticut shore, but the *Macedonian*, still sailing sluggishly due to her jury rig, lost him in the fog and failed to make it into Long Island Sound. Lieutenant Allen, after a shouted conference through the fog and a hurried conference with his pilot, headed eastward for Newport, where they arrived the following day.

EVEN TODAY, AS one reads the delirious newspaper accounts of the *Macedonian*'s arrival in America, one can almost sense the seismic ripple of excitement that must have raced outward across the country from New London and Newport as the news spread of Decatur's spectacular capture. Here was cause for rejoicing indeed—not only did our gallant sailors give John Bull another magnificent boot in the backside, but this time they brought home the prize for all to see!

And what a sight she was. Decatur, writing to his old business partner John Bullus, almost purred as he described her as "a beauty, a look at her will be good for sore eyes."

At Newport, where the *Macedonian* remained for several days while shipwrights sought to improve her condition and the authorities dealt with her wounded, Commandant Oliver Hazard Perry, who within a year would become as famous as Decatur, could only agree. "This day has been a most gratifying sight for us," he wrote to a friend, "this beautiful frigate mooring as a prize in our harbor."

The Newport *Mercury* proudly proclaimed "ANOTHER BRILLIANT NAVAL VICTORY." "[W]ith emotions of heartfelt pride and pleasure, we place before our readers another proof of the superior skills and bravery of our officers, seamen and marines which will secure to them the unanimous applause of a grateful country."

Overnight, a minor industry arose, manned by local calligraphers and dedicated to the creation of an almost endless production of ornately worded Civic Welcomes, Corporation Endorsement, and Public Proclamations lauding Commodore Decatur and his worthy men for having written still another glorious chapter of heroism and accomplishment into the national record.

Amid all this flattering attention, Decatur learned that a naval ball was scheduled to be held in Washington less than a week hence, at which the flag of HMS *Guerriere* was to be presented to Dolley Madison, wife of the President. It was too good an opportunity to miss, and with his flair for the dramatic, Decatur ordered Lieutenant Archibald Hamilton of the *United States*, who happened to be the son of the Secretary of the Navy, to ride south as quickly as possible to announce the news of the capture of the *Macedonian* at the same levee.

THE DRAMA OF the occasion must have been breathtaking: a grand military ball at Tomlinson's Hotel on Capitol Hill attended by the entire glittering assemblage of Washington society, with cabinet members, congressional leaders, and Supreme Court justices in attendance, the ballroom dominated by the battleflag of the *Guerriere* festooned across one wall, with the orchestra playing a festive air beneath it, when, with a flurry of excited voices and ladylike chirps and gasps, the attention of the entire room is suddenly directed to a young man in a lieutenant's uniform, exhausted and still covered with the dust of the road, standing in a doorway and carrying an immense bundle. The dancers stop. The musicians, sensing the significance of the moment, put down their instruments expectantly. The voices rise as the young man is recognized as the son of the Navy Secretary. The senior naval officers being honored that night rush to his side, and the crowd gives way before them as they escort the young man and his large package toward the First Lady, standing in the center of the floor. Stooping before her, the young man opens the bundle and unfurls another British battle flag upon the floor, as large as that of the *Guerriere*. There is a rapturous shout of triumph and the ecstatic guests burst spontaneously into "Hail, Columbia."

Never, for the rest of their lives, would any of the onlookers that night forget the name *Macedonian*.

GALLATIN

~~~~~~~~~~~~~~~~~~~~~~~

T HE NEWS OF THE *MACEDONIAN*'S CAPTURE REACHED LONDON
only a fortnight after it reached Washington, and as might
be expected, it produced a degree of anguish and distress equal
in intensity to the delight and pride occasioned by the arrival of
the news in America. *The Times*, bemoaning the fact that the
news followed so hard on the loss of the *Guerriere* to the *Constitution*, wailed, "O, miserable advocates! In the name of God, what
was done with this immense superiority of force?" And a few
days later that most belicose of English papers returned to the
same distressing subject. "Oh, what a charm is hereby dissolved!
What hopes will be excited in the breasts of our enemies!"

The Pilot, Britain's leading naval journal, spelled out the astonishing facts and lamented in disbelief,

> Can these statements be true; and can the English people hear
> them unmoved? Anyone who would have predicted such a
> result of an American war this time last year would have been
> treated as a madman or a traitor. He would have been told,
> if his opponents had condescended to argue with him, that
> long ere seven months had elapsed the American flag would
> be swept from the seas, the contemptible navy of the United
> States annihilated, and their maritime arsenals rendered a
> heap of ruins. Yet down to this moment not a single American
> frigate has struck her flag. They insult and laugh at our want
> of enterprise and vigour. They leave their ports when they
> please, and return to them when it suits their convenience;
> they traverse the Atlantic; they beset the West India Islands;

they advance to the very chops of the Channel; they parade along the coast of South America; nothing chases, nothing intercepts, nothing engages them but to yield them triumph.

In truth, only Britannia's ego had been bruised, not her ability to make war. With a fleet of a thousand ships, the loss of the *Macedonian* diminished the Royal Navy by about one tenth of 1 percent. But what had been a small loss for Britain was a monumental gain for America, which had a total fleet of eighteen vessels, of which only the six largest were frigates. The addition of the *Macedonian* to the United States Navy—and no one doubted she would soon join that service—increased America's effective seapower by almost 18 percent. This was a significant increment, and the fact was not lost on a grateful nation.

By the time Decatur brought the *United States* and the *Macedonian* down Long Island Sound and into New York Harbor on New Year's Day of 1813, the number of newspaper articles, public proclamations, and party invitations celebrating the capture had reached blizzard proportions.

The city was thrilled with its newest novelty. It became the rage for members of polite society to be rowed out to where the *Macedonian* lay at anchor and hoisted on board in a boatswain's chair—no simple matter for the ladies, given the fashions of the day—to get a first-hand look at the navy's most recent acquisition. Young Samuel Leech, who was still on board the *Macedonian* as a prisoner awaiting repatriation, earned generous tips by acting as a guide for the curiosity seekers, showing visitors around the ship and retelling the story of the battle. After several days of profitable lecturing, the young entrepreneur amassed enough money to finance his escape, and one evening he quietly jumped ship and lost himself in the immigrant hordes of the teeming city. Like thousands of others before and after him, he became an American overnight. He would not see his native land again for thirty years.

The Corporation of New York, anxious to honor the new heroes, weighed in with a sumptuous dinner for Decatur and his officers, as well as a gala naval ball, and then, in a fit of patriotic fervor, provided another dinner for the crewmen of the

United States, replete with illuminations, fireworks, parades (led by Captain Carden's band, which had been recruited by Decatur to his own command), and theatrical performances, with the entire evening awash in wine and spirits. Not to be outdone, Philadelphia announced it was ready to offer the gallant commodore an equally glamorous affair as soon as he could arrange to get there, and the prestigious Society of the Cincinnati voted to induct him into its august and politically powerful circle.

For all the excitement, Decatur never lost sight of the serious business of the day, namely, the matter of prize money. Both he and the U.S. Navy were eager to settle the issue quickly, and the commodore's prize agent, the Virginia lawyer Littleton Waller Tazewell, journeyed to New York to attend the prize court and to personally present Decatur's case, viz., that, despite all evidence to the contrary, the *Macedonian* was in every sense the fighting equal of the *United States* and therefore Decatur and his men deserved to receive her entire value in prize money.

A curious argument supporting Decatur's claim to the full amount of the prize money was presented by one of his own junior officers in an interview in *Niles' Weekly Register*:

> I am aware it will be said, she [the *Macedonian*] is a little ship, with five guns less than you, and a hundred men less, and carries lighter metal, &c.—well, all this is true—she is inferior in all these—but she is just such a ship as the English have achieved all their single victories in—'twas in such a ship that Sir Robert Barlow took the *Africaine*—that Sir Michael Seymour took the *Brune*, and afterwards the *Neiman*—that Captain Milne took the *Vengeance*, Captain Cook the *La Forte*, Captain Lavie the *Guerriere*, Captain Rowley the *Venus* and God knows how many others; she is, in tonnage, men and guns, such a ship as the English prefer to all others. . . .

In other words, the *Macedonian* was indeed inferior to the *United States*, but since that was the way the British chose to fight, the battle was therefore between equals.

* * *

THE AMOUNT OF prize money would depend specifically on how much money the government was willing to put up to buy the *Macedonian* into the navy. Throughout the first days of the new year, a team of evaluators crawled all over her, examining every detail, checking through her stores, and measuring everything from the length of her yards to the depth of her hold, in order to establish her value. (One important element of her manifest had long since been removed. The wine that the *Macedonian*'s officers had purchased at Madeira for their ward room had been purchased by the officers of the *United States* for *their* ward room.) In due course, the evaluators determined her total worth at $200,000, a liberal sum, but not out of line for an English frigate less than three years old.

Now it was the turn of the prize referees to determine the relative strength of the two vessels, and they quickly agreed, with nary a wink or a nudge, that *mirabile dictu*, the two ships were of equal force, and therefore the entire purchase price should go to the captors. Given the public's excitement over the capture, and the national adoration of Decatur, it would have taken a remarkably detached team of judges to reach any other conclusion.

Their official decision meant Decatur's personal share would come to $30,000, an immense sum, equivalent to at least $600,000 in today's money. He promptly dispatched the decision to the Secretary of the Navy in Washington, who on February 3 wrote an unambiguous reply:

> . . . I have received your letter of the 29th ulto. accompanied by the decision of the Referees, as to the relative force and value of the frigate *Macedonian*, which gives to the captors the whole of the vessel—and values her at Two Hundred thousand dollars—It now only remains for you to name the agents to whom you wish this sum to be paid, in order that it may be immediately paid over & distributed according to Law.

By return mail Decatur informed the Secretary that he was instructing his father-in-law, Luke Wheeler, of Norfolk, to act as his agent to accept the entire amount—$200,000 in gold—on behalf of the captain and crew of the *United States*. There matters stood, and since it appeared to be a settled issue, the interested parties turned their attention to more pressing concerns. And then, just short of two months later, when the money was scheduled to be transferred, fresh complications arose. On the morning of March 22, Decatur's agent, Luke Wheeler, arrived at the office of the Secretary of the Navy at a little after ten o'clock. By prior arrangement it had been agreed that it was on that date and at that hour that he was to actually to receive the money, and he was in a cheerful and optimistic mood.

While Wheeler waited in an anteroom to be announced, he was surprised to see the Secretary himself hurry in from elsewhere in the building. On spotting Wheeler, he appeared flustered and embarrassed, and with suspicious apologies explained that some urgent piece of business had just come up which he had to discuss with President Madison, and would Wheeler be pleased to come back at one o'clock in the afternoon.

Wheeler returned at the appointed hour and was again asked to wait. Eventually the Secretary, apparently even more upset than in the morning, popped out of his office, asked Wheeler to be patient still a moment longer, and disappeared again. During the next quarter hour, Wheeler, now very much concerned by what he perceived as an ominous turn of events, observed a good deal of hustle and bustle in and out of the Secretary's door, and was eventually treated to the sight of the Secretary of State, James Monroe, and the Secretary of the Treasury, Albert Gallatin, hurrying in. Wheeler was immediately on the alert, divining that all the high-level activity was closely connected with his own specific mission. His suspicions were confirmed when, a half hour later, as Monroe and Gallatin took their leave by one door, the Navy Secretary called Wheeler in by another, and apologizing still again, explained rather breathlessly that unfortunately the money would not be forthcoming that day because there had not been time to complete the proper requisition forms for the Treasury Department, and that Wheeler would have to return the next day.

At this point, Wheeler, who was still very much in the dark but suspicious that parties unknown were dragging their heels at the prospect of taking such a large sum of money out of the government's reserves, politely pressed for an appointment in the morning, and after some hesitation the Secretary of the Navy agreed.

That night Wheeler dashed off a long and excited letter to Decatur's lawyer, Tazewell, in which he described the events of the day. He made no bones about the nature of his suspicions. "We are indeed in bad luck. You must indeed go to Congress, if it be for but one session to trim the lamps of these damned Secretaries particularly the Genevian [Gallatin was Swiss born] who I now more than ever, believe is at the bottom of our delays. . . ."

The next morning Wheeler dropped by the navy accountant's office on his way to the Secretary's office, and was relieved to learn that the Secretary of the Navy had arrived particularly early that morning to prepare everything relating to the delivery of the prize money, and to ensure that all was in order. The accountant then gave Wheeler an official note for $200,000 made out in his name as agent for Decatur. By itself it meant little— it was not legal tender—but it suggested strongly that matters were back on track. Wheeler proceeded to the Secretary's office, was relieved to find him "with considerable complacency of countenance & affability in manner," and was advised he would get the money within an hour or two. "[P]erceiving the Secretary was beset with numerous calls, letters & so forth," Wheeler reported, "I observed that I would retire to the accountants room below—& there wait his leisure."

Wheeler's sense of well-being increased a few minutes later when he saw the accountant dispatch a messenger to the Treasury Department with a note requesting the $200,000, but he was considerably distressed when the same messenger returned in less than half an hour with a written reply from one of the Treasury clerks stating that there was no money on hand at the disposal of the Navy Department, and that Secretary Gallatin rarely arrived at his office before one o'clock, but that he would undoubtedly turn his attention to the subject as soon as he arrived.

Wheeler had no choice but to cool his heels for another two hours, which then stretched to three. He was growing ever more apprehensive and angry. His patience exhausted, he finally stalked out of the Navy Department Building and was making his way back to his lodgings on foot when he was overtaken by the accountant on horseback begging him to return as they were just now in receipt of information from the Treasury.

A smoldering and suspicious Wheeler returned and was met at the door by a distraught Secretary of the Navy, who informed him that Mr. Gallatin had placed him in a most awkward position. By way of explanation he handed over a note from the Secretary of the Treasury.

> I read through the note [Wheeler reported in another of his feverishly composed letters to Tazewell], it was from Gallatin stating explicitly his objection . . . to the award that had been made in the case of the *Macedonian*, "a vessel inferior both in Caliber & number of Guns, as well as . . . men; but adding, that he had placed 200m Dollars at the Disposal of the Secretary of the Navy if he chose to apply it"—meaning no doubt on his own responsibility if he did so. . . .

Albert Gallatin, generally conceded by historians to be one of the truly great Secretaries of the Treasury, was also a commissioner of the Sailors' Pension Fund, and since it was the pension fund that would have received the other half of the prize money had the decision called on it to be split, he was using his fiduciary responsibility as protector of the pension fund to thwart the large, and in his view, blatantly unfair award.

The note confirmed Wheeler's worst fears, and when the Secretary begged him to accept the first hundred thousand dollars and leave the matter of the second to further adjudication, the agent knew his cause was in even more serious trouble than he had at first imagined. It was clearly time to take off the kid gloves.

He brusquely refused the Secretary's offer point blank, and then, returning to the decision of the prize court, stated: "I am persuaded, sir, that there is not a court of justice competent to the decision which would not decide the principle that a first rate British frigate is, in all points of a national view, equal to a first rate frigate of any other nation of the world." This appeared to be a restatement of the earlier curious argument in *Niles' Register*, and was immediately followed by a veiled threat.

Wheeler alluded to the fact that it would be an awkward matter for any naval officer to sue the government, and that he supposed that Commodore Decatur and his lieutenants in the *United States* would prefer to suffer indignity and gross imposition rather than bring this tawdry matter into the public eye, but that he did not see that the same consideration ought or could influence the petty officers and men in the ship, and that since he was acting as their agent, too, he wanted the Secretary to know that he was prepared to make a very public case of the prize money on behalf of these men.

The Secretary was visibly taken aback by the threat of a lawsuit, and Wheeler's further promise that should he fail in court, he would take the matter to Congress, and from there to the general public if needs be. To a politician sensitive to the power of a popular hero, these were strong threats. But Wheeler had an even stronger one. "It was at my tongue," he reported to Tazewell, "to tell him I would attach the Ship, but I choked myself there." Like a good field commander, Wheeler understood the wisdom of using his ammunition sparingly.

Wheeler's obstinacy brought matters to a head, and by the following morning the field of conflict had broadened to include the office of the Secretary of War, who along with the Secretaries of Navy and Treasury comprised the commissioners of the pension fund. The three men met to discuss the impasse, and the minutes of their meeting make clear that Gallatin won over the Secretary of War to his side. The minutes begin with an objection to the original prize court, claiming it to be illegally constituted. None of the commissioners had a quarrel with the valuation of the *Macedonian* at $200,000, but neither the Secretary of War nor the Secretary of the Treasury was prepared to admit the fact that she and the *United States* were of equal force, and therefore the commissioners refused to be bound by the court's decision. Finally, they recommended that until such time as the case could be judged in a properly convened court, the captors should be awarded the first hundred thousand dollars, with the promise of the second hundred thousand should the court decide in their favor.

When the matter was again put to Wheeler, he was forced to decide whether to settle for half a loaf now and keep on fighting for the rest, or to continue to insist on the findings of the original prize court, and thereby risk the very real possibility that the entire two hundred thousand might disappear mysteriously into the coffers of the Treasury without a trace. Reluctantly, he decided to take the money and run. In his final, rueful report to Tazewell, an exhausted and dispirited Wheeler gave the Secretary of the Navy credit for trying his best against an implacable Gallatin, who was determined to deny Decatur his full prize.

> I should like much to see the Genevian foiled, very much indeed—I have no doubt however, but he, who never Sleeps, has already handed out his notes of instructions to the U.S. Attorney—with directions, if need be, to appeal to the Supreme Court.

Stephen Decatur, the nonpareil at sea, had met his match across the conference tables of Washington.

THERE WAS ONE unequivocal winner in the imbroglio: the United States Navy. Over time, the government would come to recognize that the $200,000 paid for the *Macedonian* was a bargain price, and that the prestige she imparted to the navy, and to the United States, was worth many times that figure.

United States
~~~~~~~~~~~~~~~~
Frigate
~~~~~~~~~~~~~~~~
Macedonian,
~~~~~~~~~~~~~~~~

36 guns

NEW LONDON

~~~~~~~~~~~~~~~~~~~~

IN JANUARY 1814, THE *MACEDONIAN* WAS ONCE AGAIN MOORED in a river called the Thames. It was not the river into which she had been launched, but another Thames, this one in Connecticut, where the local people pronounced the name the way it was spelled, rhyming it with "games," rather than "gems."

Just upstream lay the sloop-of-war *Hornet*, and a cable's-length downriver, Decatur's *United States*. The three vessels were anchored off a place called Gales Ferry, just north of the little city of New London.

It was early morning and bitter cold. Sea smoke drifted off the water's surface, and the newly risen sun reflected prettily off the snow-clad countryside. Captain Jacob Jones, standing on the deck of the frigate, his tall, lanky frame wrapped in a heavy cloak, surveyed the scene gloomily, and thought ironically of the blue-green seas and lush foliage of the Caribbean.

Then the captain turned, and grasping the railing for support, stepped gingerly over the icicled side of the *Macedonian* and down into the launch waiting for him below. With a grunt he settled into the boat, and turning wordlessly to the boatswain's mate, nodded in the direction of the *United States*. As the men at the sweeps pulled him away from his ship, he had time to ponder the bitter lot he shared with his fellow captains: prisoners in their own country.

Jacob Jones's long, saturnine face and hunched posture perfectly expressed his black mood. The euphoria of the previous winter—that winter of victories, of banquets and congressional

medallions, that winter of endless brave plans for the future—
now seemed almost beyond the reach of memory.

Back in February 1813, the newly promoted Captain Jacob
Jones had torn open the letter from the Secretary of the Navy
to discover his fondest dream realized:

> You are hereby instructed to repair to New York, take charge
> of the *Macedonian* frigate, whose repair & equipment you will
> direct and superintend, regulating your orders in that respect,
> by what may be necessary to render the ship perfectly efficient
> in all respects in the shortest possible time & with the most
> moderate expenditure.

Never had his future seemed so bright or offered such promise. The most sought after ship in the navy was to be his! Such
a command, coming so soon after his victory over the *Frolic* in
the gallant little *Wasp*, might have turned the head of a younger
man; but Jones was older and more mature than most of his
fellow officers, and at forty-five had long passed the age where
vanities counted for much. He had trained originally as a physician, and only gave up his practice to go to sea in his late twenties
when he realized the navy offered him a better opportunity to
exercise his restless and wide ranging intellect, his abundant
energy and purposeful drive.

THE WEEKS FOLLOWING his appointment to the *Macedonian*
had been a whirl of activity as he and the other naval captains
in New York sought to get out of port before the British blockade
locked them in for the duration of the war. Jones was to take
the *Macedonian* to the West Indies, where her presence would
force the Royal Navy to dispatch at least a half dozen frigates
from the blockade to search out the raider. Such a move would
not only weaken the blockade, it would set British ships in pursuit of one of their own vessels, an irony that delighted President
Madison and would not be lost on English newspaper editors
and their readers. It was precisely the sort of news item likely
to provoke awkward questions in Parliament.

The *United States* and the *Macedonian* would be sailing under different orders and bound for different parts of the world, but it was agreed they should leave New York together, since their combined strength would increase their chances of overcoming any British forces lurking outside the harbor.

It was a good idea, but like so many wartime plans, it came to naught. In late May of 1813, the two frigates set off in company with the *Hornet*, Captain James Biddle, and on the first day of June, as they attempted to round Montauk Point and gain the open Atlantic, they were stopped cold by a powerful British squadron and were forced to scramble to safety in New London, where they took shelter under the port's guns. The big British ships-of-the-line, with their deep drafts, made no attempt to follow them into the river, and were content to post a permanent guard off the Connecticut coast, making escape impossible.

Now, half a year later, the three landlocked ships—representing a third of the entire American Navy—remained at anchor, powerless to challenge the British squadron patrolling the coast in plain sight under the watchful command of Commodore Sir Thomas Masterman Hardy. "Here we are," a disconsolate Decatur wrote to a friend, "John Bull and us, all of a lump."

DECATUR GREETED JACOB Jones warmly as he entered the great cabin of the *United States*. Captain Biddle of the *Hornet* was already present, standing close to the small stove that warmed the room. As always, the taciturn Jones brightened in the presence of Decatur. He felt an almost fatherly fondness for the commodore, and wondered what fresh surprise he might have in store.

Throughout the months of their enforced confinement, Decatur had never lost heart. He had concocted one scheme after another to get the American ships past the British and out to sea—some practical, some audacious, and a few blatantly harebrained. With the help of his friend the inventor Robert Fulton, Decatur furnished local patriots with high-explosive sea mines called "torpedoes," and instructed them on how to create distractions that might divert the enemy long enough to allow the

American ships to slip away. When the plans misfired, Decatur worked out a scheme to kidnap the British commander, Sir Thomas Hardy, hoping to ransom him in exchange for their liberty. The venture, commanded by one of Jones's midshipmen named Abraham Ten Eyck, came a cropper, and the men were fortunate to get back with their skins intact. Undiscouraged, Decatur convened a meeting with Fulton and his captains to study the inventor's plans for a strange new steam-powered catamaran designed specifically to destroy the New London blockading fleet. Fulton called her *Demologos*, Greek for "voice of the people." She was under construction in New York—the first steam-powered warship in history—and for all her novelty, *Demologos* was an eminently practical proposal, save for the fact that no one could say when she might finally be ready to attack the British.

It was clear to both Jones and Biddle that Decatur was now eager to impart the details of still another scheme. As soon as the three men were alone, he sat them down and described the unexpected opportunity he had fortuitously stumbled upon the previous day.

The commodore described how he and a small party from the *United States* had spent most of the day in New London on ship's business, and having completed their work, decided to stop for dinner before returning to Gales Ferry. They were dressed in civilian clothes at the time, and went unrecognized when they entered the chophouse and sat down. As they ate, their attention was drawn to an adjoining table, where a cheerful and somewhat boisterous group of men was celebrating the return of one of their number. During the course of the meal the navy men learned that the man being fêted was a local sea captain named Nicholas Moran, who had been captured by the British while attempting to run the blockade. The enemy had confiscated his vessel and cargo, but since Moran and his crew were civilians there was no point in keeping them prisoner, and they had been released that morning.

Decatur listened with growing interest as the recent prisoner described being taken on board HMS *Ramillies*, flagship of the blockading squadron, and introduced to Commodore Hardy and Captain Henry Hope, of the *Endymion*. Mr. Moran related how, in the course of conversation, Captain Hope had referred disparagingly to the American vessels anchored up the river, and wondered in mocking tones whether Decatur and his men would ever dare come out, implying that if they were looking for a fight, it might be arranged.

The eavesdropping Decatur leaned forward excitedly. He was familiar with every ship in the blockading fleet, and knew the *Endymion* to be a large frigate similar in size and strength to his *United States*. A duel to the death between the two was everything he could ask for—and it offered the possibility of freedom.

Captain Moran then described how Commodore Hardy picked up Hope's challenge and remarked that he was less interested in a contest between Hope's *Endymion* and the *United States* than he was in the possibility of a single-ship action between the *Macedonian* and the British frigate *Statira*, Captain Hassard Stackpole, which had recently joined his squadron. The two were sister ships, Hardy pointed out, both *Lively*-class frigates, built from the same Navy Board plans, and were therefore virtually identical. A fair battle between them might go a long way toward addressing the questions of the relative courage, skills, and fortitude of the two opposing navies. Hardy made it clear that such a challenge could not come from the British side; but should it arise by some other means, he would be happy to guarantee that such a battle would be fought without interruption from other warships.

Decatur could not let such an opportunity pass him by. Stepping over to Moran's table he introduced himself, and after clarifying certain details of the master's story, left the eating house in a state of high excitement.

Both Jones and Biddle listened to Decatur's account with ever-increasing enthusiasm. Perhaps here at last was a way out of their seemingly hopeless predicament: twin duels—*Macedonian* versus *Statira*, *United States* versus *Endymion*—two separate contests, arranged with all the formality of sporting events, matching a pair of American frigates against their British equivalents.

If there was something unreal about the proposed challenge, the three men chose to ignore it. What interested them was the possibility of freedom, which was worth almost any conceivable price.

Eagerly the men set about preparing a letter for Decatur's signature that would provide Commodore Hardy with the challenge he wanted. Of necessity, the letter went into considerable detail on the relative strength of the four ships, and it is those details that hold particular interest. They touch on specific differences between the vessels, which was a particularly sensitive point for Decatur, who was still involved in prize money negotiations in Washington over the relative force of the *United States* and *Macedonian*. It was important that in fashioning his proposal for the British, he not make any direct comparisons between his own two frigates which might compromise his case against Secretary of the Treasury Gallatin.

17 January 1814

. . . the *Endymion* I am informed carries 24 pounders and mounts 50 guns in all—This ship [the *United States*] also carries 24 pounders and mounts 48 guns beside a 12 pound carronade, a boat gun—The *Statira* mounts 50, the *Macedonian* 47—metal the same—so that the force on both sides is as nearly equal as we could expect to find—If Mr. Moran's statement be correct, it is evident that Captains Hope and Stackpole have the laudable desire of engaging with their ships the *United States* and *Macedonian*. We, sir, are ready and equally desirous for such meeting forthwith. . . .

The letter closed with obligatory compliments for the two enemy captains, in keeping with the formalities of the period:

At the same time we beg you will assure Captains Hope & Stackpole that no personal feeling towards them induced us to compose this communication—They are solicitous to add to the renown of their Country—we honour their motives—

The little War of 1812 does not lack for bizarre incidents, but the exchange of letters between Decatur and Hardy concerning the quadruple ship challenge must rank as one of its more curious occurrences. The idea of battling out of New London harbor under some sort of Marquis of Queensberry rules, and of defining an act of war in terms of a gentlemen's agreement, provides an almost whimsical example of how wars were sometimes fought in an earlier age.

The two commodores saw themselves not so much as enemies but as fellows in a sort of freemasonry of the seas. They might have been members of rival clubs, challenging one another to a tennis match. The fact that men on both sides were certain to die terrible deaths as a result of the challenge, and that others would suffer dreadful wounds, did not seem to weigh much in the scheme of things. If anything, the mortal danger added an element of excitement to the prospect. Nor was the cavalier attitude toward death and dismemberment limited to the officers. It was matched by the crews who would do most of the fighting. In all four ships, British and American, the men cheered lustily when informed of the negotiations. Hundreds of young men, with too much testosterone and too little outlet for their energies, were more than ready to put their lives on the line, just to break the monotony.

James Biddle, whose sloop *Hornet* would not be involved with the challenge, carried the letter to the blockading squadron under a flag of truce, while Jones and Decatur prepared to make ready their ships.

The following morning brought Hardy's carefully worded reply, and the three Americans met once again in the great room of the *United States* to study it.

> . . . I have the honour to acknowledge the receipt of your letter of yesterdays date by Captain Biddle, signifying a desire on your part, and that of Captain Jones, as Commanders of the United States Frigates the *United States* & *Macedonian*, to meet his Britannic Majestys ships *Endymion* & *Statira* . . . and

in reply I beg to inform you I have no hesitation whatever in permitting Captain Stackpole of the *Statira* to meet the *Macedonian*—as they are sister ships, carrying the same weight of metal and number of guns. . . .

So far, so good. Jacob Jones was delighted to see that his ship was going to be allowed to fight.

But as it is my opinion the *Endymion* is not equal to the *United States*, being 200 tons less and carrying 26 guns on her main deck and only 32 lb Carronades on her Quarter Deck & Forecastle, when I am informed the *United States* has 30 guns on her main deck and 42 lb Carronades on her Quarter Deck & Forecastle I must consider it my duty (though very contrary to the wishes of Captain Hope) to decline the invitation on his part. . . .

Hardy closed with the same sort of obligatory compliments to the Americans that Decatur had directed to the British.

The Captains of His Britannic Majesty's Frigates under my orders, as well as myself, cannot too highly appreciate the gallant spirit that has led to the communications from you Sir and we are equally convinced that no personal feeling towards each other can ever influence a laudable ambition to add to the Naval Renown of our respective Countries. . . .

Enclosed was a letter from Captain Stackpole:

. . . Captain Sir Thomas M. Hardy Bt and Commodore off New London has this afternoon handed me a letter from you—expressing the desire that the United States Ship *Macedonian* commanded by Captain Jones, should meet His Majesty's Ship *Statira* under my command . . . I shall confine my reply to your obliging letter, as to the future acts of His Majesty's ship I have the honour to command—It will afford her Captain, officers & crew, the greatest pleasure to meet Captain

Jones in the *Macedonian*, tomorrow—next day—or whenever such a meeting may suit his purpose—let him only be pleased to appoint the day, and place, say six or ten leagues south of Montuck point or further if he pleases—my only object for selecting this distance from the shore is to avoid any interuption. . . .

Stackpole closed with a chauvinistic flourish.

. . . In accepting this invitation, Sir, it is not to varnish, or in the most trifling degree to enhance my own professional character. . . . The honour of my King, defence of my Country engaged in a just & unprovoked war added to the glory of the British flag, is all I have in view. . . .

Decatur and Jones sat with the two letters before them, weighing their options. The original scheme, which had appeared to offer significant promise when it involved four ships, looked quite different when it involved only two. Hardy's reasoning for denying a battle between *Endymion* and the *United States* seemed dubious—the disparity of guns was a simple matter to rectify, and the imagined 200-ton difference between the two ships was a somewhat suspect statistic and, even if true, largely irrelevant. Was it worth reopening the issue and suggesting changes in armament to redress the balance? Or should the Americans pin all their hopes on the *Macedonian*?

Jacob Jones argued forcefully for the opportunity to bring the *Macedonian* into action, with or without Decatur's ship in attendance. He was eager. His officers were eager. His crew was eager. But Decatur demurred. If the Americans committed two ships, there was good reason to believe that at least one would win her contest and escape. Such a gamble was worth the risk. But with only one ship, the odds shifted dramatically. If Captain Jones won the day, all well and good. He would be off to the West Indies or elsewhere to lick his wounds and fight again. But if he lost—and here, for the first time, they addressed the question of the importance of the *Macedonian* to the prestige of the U.S. Navy—if he lost, the damage would be little short of catastrophic. For the Americans to have won so great a trophy as the *Macedonian* only to lose her again would create a symbolic resonance far outweighing any strategic value. Such a loss would be humiliating, but more than that, it would diminish Decatur's original victory, implying, inevitably, that the *Macedonian* was inherently a loser, no matter who manned her.

Inexorably, under the pressure of decision making, Jones and Decatur were forced to recognize that the *Macedonian* was worth far more as a trophy than as a warship, and was simply too valuable to risk in such an enterprise.

The three captains, drafting an answer for the commodore's signature, put as good a face upon it as they could:

> . . . The proposition for a contest between HBM Frigates *Endymion* & *Statira* and this Ship and the *Macedonian* was made by me in the full belief that their force was equal, but this has been declined in consequence of your entertaining a different opinion on this Subject from my own—I do not think myself authorized to comply with the wishes of Captains Jones & Stackpole for a meeting in the ships *Statira* & *Macedonian*— This squadron is now under orders from the Government and I feel myself bound to put to Sea the first favorable opportunity that may occur. . . .

Decatur, in closing, could not resist a final swipe at Captain Stackpole's assertion of superior rectitude:

> Whether the war we are engaged in be just and unprovoked on the part of Great Britain, as Captain Stackpole has been pleased to Suggest, is considered by us as a question exclusively with the Civilians, and I am perfectly ready to admit my incompetence & unwillingness to confront Captain Stackpole in its discussion. . . .

The next morning, a final answer from Hardy closed the episode on an amicable diplomatic note.

. . . I have the honor to acquaint you, that I will communicate
to Captain Stackpole, your letter of the 19th Instant, I this
morning had the honor of receiving by Capt. Biddle and I have
nothing farther to offer in addition to my former letter. . . . I
beg to assure you Sir I shall wait with pleasure the return of
an amicable adjustment of the differences between the two
Nations. . . .

It was the Americans' last feeble act of defiance. With every
passing month the British blockading fleet grew increasingly
stronger and more impregnable, and by early spring even the
most optimistic observer could no longer envision any possibility
of the American ships escaping from New London, with or without the help of Fulton's *Demologos*. In April 1814, Jones and
Decatur ordered the dismasting of the *Macedonian* and the *United
States*, and landed almost all the guns, hauling them down to
the forts overlooking the harbor entrance. They left Biddle in sole
charge of the squadron, and departed for other, more promising
theaters of war, Decatur and his men to New York, and Jones
and the crew of the *Macedonian* to Lake Erie.

TUNIS

~~~~~~~~~~~~~~~~~~~~~~~~~

T HE INCIDENT THAT FINALLY DROVE HOME THE *MACEDONIAN'S* unique significance to the U.S. Navy took place on July 26, 1815, in the city of Tunis, on North Africa's Barbary Coast. The principal naval figures involved were once again Stephen Decatur and Jacob Jones, although neither was present at the epiphany.

FOR CENTURIES THE Barbary pirates, operating out of the armed city-states of Algiers, Tunis, and Tripoli, ran roughshod over merchant shipping in the western end of the Mediterranean. No one was safe from the ravages of these bold and ruthless outlaws, who roamed the seas with impunity, capturing vessels, ransoming or enslaving their passengers and crews, and growing rich on their stolen cargoes. The only means of curbing the rapacity of these corsairs was the payment of tribute, and even the most powerful maritime states, Britain included, paid huge annual contributions in gold to the pirates to ensure the safety of their merchantmen. It was a protection racket on an international scale, and enormously effective.

The United States, as one of the leading traders in the Mediterranean, maintained an edgy relationship with the Barbary powers, at times cravenly paying the tribute demanded, while at other times defying the pirates under the proud motto, "Millions for defense, but not one cent for tribute!" It was during one of America's defiant periods, in 1803, that Stephen Decatur first came to public attention when he and his men, in a daring raid, blew up a Barbary frigate in Tripoli harbor.

That incident had the desired effect on the pirates, and they quickly agreed to a treaty which protected American shipping. Things quieted down until the United States went to war with Britain in 1812, at which point America could no longer protect its merchant vessels, and predictably, the pirates once again started preying upon them, committing the usual indignities and atrocities against captured American citizens. When at last the war with Britain came to an end, a furious Congress, much relieved to have got out of a war against a vastly superior power and delighted to find an enemy small enough to conquer, declared war on the pirates and sent a punitive expedition across the Atlantic commanded by the American the pirates knew best, Stephen Decatur.

EARLY IN MAY 1815, Decatur, in his spanking new flagship *Guerriere*, 44 guns, led a flotilla of nine vessels through the Pillars of Hercules. It was the largest squadron of American warships ever assembled, and he had made sure that it included his prize, the *Macedonian*. Within forty-eight hours of his arrival in the Mediterranean, he managed to capture a large and powerful Algerian frigate, the *Mashouda*, killing her captain in the process. It was a spectacular beginning to what was planned as a voyage of intimidation. Days later, Decatur swept down on the *Mashouda*'s home port of Algiers, and with his guns leveled at the governor's palace, negotiated a peace treaty under which the Algerians promised to behave themselves.

FLUSHED WITH SUCCESS, the commodore ordered his squadron eastward to Tunis, where he arrived on July 25, 1815, to continue his nautical blitzkreig. The sudden appearance of so many American ships off that city created a sensation and deeply alarmed the authorities. The American consul at Tunis, a man named Mordecai Noah, Esq., sailed out to confer with Decatur, and upon arriving on board the *Guerriere*, received the American demands, which not only called for a promise to refrain from further attacks on American ships, but also insisted on the payment of $46,000 in reimbursement to American merchants for

the cost of shipping and cargo previously captured. If the Bey
did not agree to these terms within twelve hours, Decatur told
Noah, he would immediately attack.

The consul returned to shore and was promptly granted an
interview with the Bey, or governor, of Tunis. Noah was ushered
into a large room where a group of turbaned officials stood in
a cluster around the Bey, a tough and worldly old pirate with a
long white beard, half-reclining on a pile of large, overstuffed
cushions strewn upon the marble floor. It was an exceedingly
hot summer day, and through the open casement windows overlooking the Mediterranean, Mr. Noah could see Decatur's squadron lying at anchor.

The Bey's vizier demanded an explanation for the presence
of such a large and hostile squadron, whereupon Mr. Noah
delivered Decatur's ultimatum. The Bey and his advisers listened
carefully as an interpreter translated the American demands,
and then broke into an animated discussion among themselves
as to how they should answer it. Eventually the interpreter informed Noah that the Bey was willing to refrain from further
attacks on Yankee shipping, but he was loathe to part with
$46,000 worth of gold, which he protested was a very large sum
of money.

"Tell your admiral to come and see me," the Bey told the
consul through the interpreter.

The consul shook his head regretfully. "He declines to come,
your Highness, until these disputes are settled."

"But this is not treating me with becoming dignity," the Bey
protested. Mr. Noah could only sympathize and point out that
Commodore Decatur was a very stubborn man.

The Bey suggested a delaying action, but Mr. Noah gently
but firmly explained that the matter was not subject to further
negotiation, adding that Commodore Decatur was an impulsive
man not known for his patience. He politely reminded the Bey
of Decatur's heroics against the Bashaw of Tripoli in 1803, and
the Muslim leader nodded noncommittally. Discussion slowed
to a crawl and threatened to stop altogether. A bombardment
appeared inevitable, until the consul resolved the impasse.

Mr. Noah knew that the single foreign institution the Barbary pirates respected above all others was the Royal Navy. As seagoing warriors they appreciated the size, skill, and superb organization of Britain's maritime power. Knowing of their respect for the British naval tradition, Noah pointed out casually that most of the important ships in Decatur's squadron had been forcibly taken from the Royal Navy during America's recent war with Britain. The claim was in large part a lie, but it has the desired effect on the pirates.

"You Americans do not speak the truth," said the Bey with a show of disbelief, but it was a question as much as a declaration.

With due deference, Noah stepped to the windows overlooking the waterfront and pointed toward Decatur's flagship. "Do you see that tall ship in the bay, the *Guerriere*? Taken from the British."

The Bey trained a telescope on the frigate in question. Mr. Noah's claim was not quite a lie, but close to it. He was gambling that the Bey, who may well have heard something of Hull's defeat of HMS *Guerriere*, did not know that the British ship had sunk, and that the vessel he now examined through his glass was an American-built namesake, constructed in Philadelphia and only recently launched.

Noah pointed to another frigate. "That one near the small island, the *Macedonian*, was also captured—and by Decatur himself!" This of course was the simple truth. The Bey moved his glass and proceeded to examine the *Macedonian* with the same interest he had given the *Guerriere*. He was undoubtedly counting gun ports and estimating weight of metal.

"The sloop near Cape Carthage, the *Peacock*, was also taken in battle," Noah concluded with finality. Such a claim was a total fabrication, for the vessel in question was in fact the American sloop-of-war *Ontario*, built at Baltimore in 1813, and had no connection with the British sloop-of-war *Peacock*.

At this point, according to published accounts of the discussion, the Bey, in a thoughtful mood, "laid down the telescope, reposed on his cushions, and with a small tortoise-shell comb set with diamonds, combed his beard."

An American Navy that threatened to bombard the city might
or might not be a problem. But an American Navy that could
with such impunity capture warships from the Royal Navy had
to be taken very seriously indeed. It was clearly a time for reflection. After a suitable period of discussion with his advisers, the
Bey reluctantly agreed to Decatur's demands.

Months later, when Mr. Noah's report reached Washington, the significance of the incident in Tunis was not lost on
America's leaders. The consul had perhaps exaggerated his own
cleverness in his efforts to coerce the Bey, but his story touched
on an important truth: While the *Guerriere* and the *Ontario* were
at best only pseudo-prizes of war, the *Macedonian* was the real
thing. More than that, with the fall of Napoleon at Waterloo,
she was not only the sole Royal Navy prize frigate in the American Navy, she was *the sole Royal Navy prize frigate in any navy
in the world*—an unequaled trophy and a powerful means of
impressing foreigners with the strength and will of the American
Navy.

In Ordinary

~~~~~~~~~~~~~~~~~~~~~~~~

From November 1815, when she returned from the Barbary Coast, until April of the following spring, the *Macedonian* was in ordinary at the Boston Navy Yard. The term "in ordinary" corresponds to the modern "in mothballs," and simply meant that the ship was decommissioned but remained afloat. Significantly, throughout that period, she was under near-continuous repair.

In April, she was ordered on a brief cruise to the Caribbean, under the command of Captain Lewis Warrington, and in July, on her way back to Boston, she proved to be in such poor condition that Warrington was forced to put in at Annapolis to step new fore and mainmasts, as well as to overhaul the bracing blocks and re-rig the lower yards. When she finally found her way back to the navy yard in August, Warrington's report on her condition raised disturbing questions. The navy yard constructor, Josiah Barker, after a quick survey of the frigate, confirmed Warrington's dour assessment. She needed a complete overhaul.

In the course of examining the *Macedonian*, the constructor made a surprising discovery—her bottom was planked with what appeared to be pine, rather than oak. The yard officers were incensed, remembering the British slur about America's "fir built frigates." But building materials aside, the rundown condition of the ship strongly suggested that the *Macedonian* required something more elaborate than simply another refit.

Hull outlined the problem in a sobering letter to Captain John Rodgers of the Board of Naval Commissioners in Washington.

. . . Were it not that she is the only frigate we possess, taken from the enemy, I should pronounce her not worth repairing, for we cannot, after having given her the most thorough repair, calculate on her lasting more than five or six years, her timbers being of common oak and many of them already beginning to decay.

But by 1816 the *Macedonian* had become too important to lose, and the Board was not willing to consider anything short of a complete repair. Over the following year she underwent extensive work that Hull estimated equaled the cost of a new ship, and in August 1817 she was hove out, coppered, and once again put in order for sea service.

By July 1818, when the *Macedonian* was selected for a three-year cruise to the west coast of South America, Commandant Hull was able to send a considerably more sanguine report to Rodgers.

. . . She is admired by everyone that goes on board, and I think very justly so, for, in my opinion, she is the handsomest ship we have, and her accommodations are not less comfortable and convenient. . . . Indeed, she is the first ship that I ever fitted that the commander, when ordered to her, could not discover something to find fault with.

For the moment, the navy could rest easy. But the inherent weakness of the "Danzig Oak" which had so concerned the Master Shipwright at Royal Woolwich Dock Yard was beginning to reveal itself.

STORM

~~~~~~~~~~~~~~~~~~~~

C APTAIN JOHN DOWNES SPRAWLED EASILY IN HIS LARGE, COM- fortable cabin below the quarterdeck of the *Macedonian*, enjoying a moment of solitude aboard his crowded ship. The date was Saturday, September 26, 1818, and he and his ship were six days out of Boston, proceeding in the general direction of the Cape Verde Islands, there to pick up the trade winds for her voyage south.

The *Macedonian* was bound on an extended cruise expected to last three years, and she carried a large crew to handle the variety of circumstances she was liable to encounter over such a lengthy period away from home. With a complement of over four hundred men squeezed into a ship designed to hold three hundred, even the captain found it difficult to arrange for moments of privacy, and he had already discovered that Lord Fitz-Roy's specially commissioned partition provided an agreeable retreat.

His orders from the Secretary of the Navy called for him to stop off at Rio and Buenos Aires for a little diplomacy and some quiet snooping before running south to Cape Horn, from whence he would point out into the Pacific and up the coast of Chile to Valparaiso. The timing of Captain Downes's departure from Boston, as well as his visits to Brazil and the Argentine, were keyed to the month of January, when the dreaded Horn, universally recognized as the most dangerous stretch of water on the globe, could be expected to be at its most benign. He would have to make his westward passage during the high southern summer, or risk the possibility of months of dirty weather trying to force his way around that murderous corner of the sea. Downes was no stranger to the Horn—he had doubled it twice in the *Essex* and the *Essex Junior*—but he knew it had defeated better sailors than he. No less a mariner than William Bligh, trained by Captain Cook himself, had battled the winds and currents of Tierra del Fuego for endless weeks, only to be forced at last to turn his *Bounty* eastward and take the easier but far longer route around Africa.

The three-year time frame of the *Macedonian's* cruise accounted not only for the large number of men on board, but also for the tons of extra stores and provisions stowed below decks, which caused her to lie deeper in the water than was probably good for her. Downes and his sailing master, after conferring with experts at the navy yard, had taken great pains to ensure that she was trimmed to the head, a configuration which raised her stern slightly higher than her bow, and which caused the ship to "plow" through the water. Now that she was at sea, both men remained concerned as to how the extra weight and its distribution might affect the ship's sailing behavior. So far, the weather had been fair and unexceptional; yet even under these favorable conditions the *Macedonian* evidenced a certain sluggishness, an inability to respond to the wheel as quickly as might be wished. In rougher weather, Downes recognized, this could well become a problem. The temperature of the waters through which they were now traveling was 74° Fahrenheit, which put them well inside the Gulf Stream, where at this time of year they could expect sudden storms and squalls.

DOWNES WAS A large, amiable man, with little of the starch and formality of his brother naval captains. He came from humble Massachusetts stock, and had grown up with few of the privileges and none of the snobbism that characterized so many of America's naval officers at the time. Although in no way an abrasive man, his manner was blunt and his language often crude. He could swear a blue streak, and often did. In an era that prized high diction and elegant phrasing, Downes's lack of gentility was a matter of considerable distress to him; he blamed it on a lifetime in the company of sailors.

His first sea duty was as a boy in the *Constitution*. Later, at the age of sixteen, he was appointed an acting midshipman, and from there he had moved up rapidly to captain, carried forward by his outstanding skills as a leader and seaman, along with the modicum of good luck that is always a necessity for naval advancement. His crews worshipped him, and loved his sense of humor and penchant for practical jokes.

Now, at the age of thirty-four, Downes had every reason to look forward to a promising future. He had his own independent command, a totally refitted ship that was bandbox new, freshly rigged, painted, and caulked, with new sails, new pumps, and a new, hand-picked company of officers and men.

His assignment was to open up the Pacific to American trade, and to accomplish this laudable goal, he was taking his ship and crew on an extended cruise that would begin with a 6,000-mile run to the west coast of South America, and would proceed from there as circumstances might dictate. It was an expedition that promised adventure, enhanced prestige, and for Captain Downes, the opportunity to make money—possibly a great deal of money. This last item would have loomed large for a man with no source of income beyond his modest salary.

Since leaving Boston the ship had proceeded smoothly on her course, until this day, the 26th, when shortly before noon, the fresh breezes that had carried her eastward died away. By the time the sun touched the meridian, the *Macedonian* lay motionless, wallowing in a dead calm, rocked gently by a heavy swell from the southeast.

Four hours later, the ship still lay becalmed. The sails hung lifeless on the yards, and a boatswain's mate, with nothing better to do, leaned out through the shrouds and tried to whistle up a wind. The bright September sun, hanging in a clear sky, reflected on a glassy sea, and an odd quietness hung in the air. Downes, who was now supervising activities from the quarterdeck, was aware that no windsong sang through the rigging, no murmur of water marked the passage of the ship through the sea. The only sounds were man-made. Footsteps on the forecastle carried all the way aft and echoed on the quarterdeck. The ring of the carpenter's hammer reached into the tops. The men, conscious that their voices would carry, spoke quietly among themselves.

The captain knew well enough that there was nothing to be done but to wait patiently for the breeze to pick up and get them on their way again, but patience was not one of his virtues. He felt the need for some sort of useful activity, and if it was not a good day for sailing, it was at least an excellent day for monitoring the mysterious and ever-changing element on which they spent their lives. Downes ordered the stern boat lowered, and sent the master and one of his lieutenants to test the currents. When they returned and reported a current setting southeast at half a knot per hour, the fact was duly noted in the record, and another tiny datum that might some day help sailors understand the ocean's dynamics was added to humanity's store of maritime knowledge.

THE COLOSSAL MECHANISM that creates and governs the weather on our planet was not even vaguely understood by John Downes and his contemporaries. The elegant, self-governing, almost Newtonian relationship of various tides, currents, air streams, and weather systems around the world would not reveal itself to human beings even in its broadest manifestations until an age when aircraft, space satellites, and instantaneous global communication finally made it possible to discover the intricate way that different systems interacted with each other over thousands of miles of the earth's surface.

During the long, hot summer of 1818, for instance, excessive heat generated on the steppes of Russia and the prairies of North America had migrated south to the tropics. There, trapped by the rotation of the earth and the resulting mirrored weather systems of the two polar hemispheres, the heat piled up at the equator, with no place to go. The earth's atmosphere, an immense regulating heat pump, automatically began developing a means of returning the excess heat to the northern regions from whence it came.

Some three weeks prior to the departure of the *Macedonian* from Boston, at a location thousands of miles east of her present position, in the vicinity of the same Cape Verde Islands toward which she was now moving, a number of seemingly unrelated atmospheric conditions—a few innocent-looking clouds, a bit of wind, some rising temperatures—had quietly come together and coalesced into a partnership so tenuous as to be imperceptible to even the most sensitive of instruments. Yet even in its earliest stages this elemental confluence constituted a nascent weather system, and over a period of the next ten days or so it increased in girth and strength to such an extent that it transformed itself into a nasty tropical storm, easily measured by even the crudest meteorological device. A day or two later it changed again, this time into a great, living monster of satanic proportions, a contained fury that soon began advertising its awesome energy level by wheeling about in a measured and menacing counterclockwise dance, spreading itself slowly over an ever-increasing stretch of ocean.

Once set in motion, the tropical storm born in the first days of September began sucking in oceans of moist tropical air, which it transformed into raw energy to stoke the terrible, chaotic force of the evolving tempest. In the process it became the means by which the excess heat building up in the tropics would be returned northward. By September 20, the day the *Macedonian* departed Boston, this angry, immeasurably powerful weather system, raging in widdershins fury around a dead quiet center now fifty miles in diameter, became unstable, and could no longer hold its position. Losing its grip, it lurched crazily westward, haphazardly north. By the 26th, it had reached a point somewhere northeast of Bermuda, on the edge of the Gulf Stream.

LATE IN THE afternoon of the 26th the breeze freshened at last, bringing new life to the sails and quickening the ship. The *Macedonian* began to move directly into the path of the storm.

By sunset the fresh breezes had grown stronger still, creating nine-foot waves and whipping the crests to foam; and near midnight, when the *Macedonian* reached the outer edge of the storm, she encountered near-gale force winds that heeled the ship far over to leeward and caused the braces that held the sails to squeal at their belaying points.

For the rest of the night, the wind howled out of the southeast, and the following morning, dark and heavily overcast, found the *Macedonian*, its sails ballooning and rigid under the press of wind, plowing through high, thirteen-foot seas streaked with foam. Every man on deck was soaked through, and the wind held so much moisture it was impossible to tell whether it was raining or not. At the meridian the cloud cover made it impossible to take a bearing, but by dead reckoning the master positioned them somewhere near latitude 35°36′ North and longtitude 55°42′ West.

In the afternoon the wind grew more violent still, and great carpets of torn spindrift covered the towering seas, now measuring up to eighteen feet from crest to trough. The captain ordered lifelines riven fore and aft, so that sailors might have something to cling to as they moved about the deck. The gale blew so fresh the captain ordered the men aloft to furl the square sails, and reduced the ship's canvas to storm staysails, the small triangular sails that ran fore and aft between the masts. A little after five o'clock, one of the top men, a young sailor named William Wilkins, high on the mizzen topmast, was struggling to grasp a flapping sail when the corner of it was torn from his hands and knocked him overboard. The cry went up, and a crewman on the quarterdeck swiftly cut a life buoy from the stern davit and threw it into the raging sea, but it fell short of Wilkins and he was unable to reach it. Frantically the men tried to lower the stern boat, but the gale raged with such violence and the sea was so high that it was impossible even to swing the boat out on its davits. In mesmerized horror they watched the helpless man struggle against the waves for several minutes before finally going under barely fifty yards from the ship.

The topgallant masts, unsecured by shrouds, were bending under the force of the wind and threatening to snap. Shouting to be heard over the shriek of the wind and gesturing toward the topgallants, the captain ordered them housed. Working desperately, clinging with bleeding fingers to whatever rigging they could find high over the pitching deck, the men carefully detached the topgallants, lowered them to the level of the topmast below, and secured them as best they could. This effectively reduced the height of the masts by about a third. The light yards, which normally carried the upper square sails, were brought down, and the storm staysails, made of a stout Russian linen, were set in place between the masts.

At sunset, the *Macedonian*, now powered only by her staysails, was moving sluggishly on the starboard tack, her profile lowered, her rigging well set up, everything tied down that could be tied down, all staunch and strong. If there was to be heavy weather, she was as ready for it as it was possible to make her.

At ten o'clock that night the ship moved into the inner wall of the huge wheel-shaped storm, and ran into a hurricane of appalling violence. By midnight all of the brand new storm staysails were either split or blown away. The rigging had been so pulled and stretched by the wind it was slack and worse than useless. When the *Macedonian* rolled to leeward, the lee rigging would hang off in curved lines, while the rigging on the weather side would tighten with a surge that threatened to tear out the chain plates.

From below came the terrible news that the loose rigging was causing the masts to surge. These enormous poles, which pierced the ship to the bilge, were now rising and falling with each shift in the ship's position, battering the keelson like triphammers and sending shock waves through the great timbers that held the ship together.

It was the water, not the wind, that did the most damage. A cubic yard of seawater weighs a ton, and each mountainous wave, invisible in the blackness, was battering the *Macedonian* with the force of thousands of tons with every sledgehammer blow, twisting her oaken frames and causing her timbers to moan and shriek as the pressure of the water strained and contorted the heavy wood.

At half past two in the morning, with an explosive sound that could be heard over the noise of the storm, the mainmast cracked badly in several places, worn out by its own motion and the constant surge of the slack rigging. As the men struggled to contain the damage, they were almost swept overboard when the starboard quarter whaleboat was blown bottom up against the mizzen rigging, where it wedged itself in the hammock rail and resisted all attempts at getting it inboard. It finally had to be hacked to pieces with an ax. Around four o'clock, the mizzenmast cracked, and when the master pronounced it unsalvageable, Downes ordered it jettisoned. The crew set about cutting away the stays, braces, and lanyards that held the mizzen in place, and in a few minutes, the mast, after making several doubtful movements, fell over the larboard quarter, carrying away the stern and larboard quarter boat.

Now the foremast was also sprung, and the yards of the two remaining masts were surging about with tremendous violence. The only means of saving the lower masts lay in cutting away the topmasts, a task as dangerous as it was difficult. Two midshipmen, John Heron and Richard Pinckney, as well as a quartermaster named Collins and a seaman named Thompson, volunteered. The men divided into two teams and moved to their respective masts. To cut away the topmasts, they first had to climb the rigging to the main tops, cautiously inching up the ratlines while the ship rolled to windward, then grasping a shroud with arms and legs as they felt the rigging slacken to avoid being hurled out to sea like a pebble in a gigantic slingshot when the shroud snapped taut. All of this in the pitch dark, buffeted by shrieking winds and numbed by water.

Moving gingerly upward into the blackness, each man carrying a sharp hatchet slung to the right wrist, they at length reached the futtuck rigging, and clinging there, cut away the lanyards of the weather topmast shrouds. Freed of the constraining rigging, the masts, carrying the topsail yards, instantly snapped off at the caps and hung suspended to leeward in a hopeless tangle of rope, wood, and hardware. Whenever the ship rolled to windward, the wreckage smashed violently against the lower rigging, and it became imperative to cut the lanyards of the lee topmasts' rigging, an even more perilous assignment than cutting the topmasts. Almost miraculously, the two parties of brave men managed to complete the work and return to the deck without loss of life.

Meantime, the eighty-four-foot-long main yard parted its slings and lifts and came crashing down across the gangways, knocking loose the two boats stowed amidships, which threatened to plunge into the sea taking a half dozen sailors with them, until they were finally captured and secured under the direction of a junior officer. About the same time, Midshipman Heron, working on the foremast, cut away the foreyard, which fell to the forecastle, where deckhands quickly secured it.

Below decks it was a watery shambles. Seawater was pouring into the ship from all sides, soaking the stores and provisions and flooding the companionways. The battering pressure of the waves, the great force of the wind, and the torque of the storm that was twisting and bending every part of the wooden hull, had all combined to force out the oakum from between the planks, leaving long gaping gashes in the hull and turning the outer skin of the ship into a sieve. The pumps—the brand new, untested Baker's Patent Elliptical Pumps so recently installed at Boston—were kept working without let up by teams of exhausted seamen, who traded places at regular intervals with equally exhausted replacements.

The dim light of dawn let the men finally see the size and nature of the ocean they were fighting. Mountainous spume-covered waves of forty feet and more towered over them, higher than the remaining masts, threatening to overwhelm the ship at any moment. The *Macedonian*, with only her bowsprit and the stubs of her fore-and mainmasts, lay naked and helpless against the mindless anger of the sea. Not a rag of canvas could be set. The loss of the mizzenmast forced the ship to fall off into the trough of the sea, where she was in imminent danger of foundering. In an attempt to bring her head to the wind, the captain ordered a makeshift sea anchor made from a remaining fragment of the mizzenmast and a 900-pound kedge anchor attached to a hawser led out from one of the forward weather ports. The makeshift worked briefly, bringing the bow about four points into the wind before the violence of the storm parted the line, and the ship was pushed back into the trough with a sickening shudder.

Despite the jettisoning of the topmasts, the lower sections of the two remaining masts continued to pound relentlessly on the keelson, sending shock waves down the keel and into every timber of the ship. Captain Downes, who feared that the repeated hammering would tear the ship apart even before she had a chance to founder, called for extreme measures, and actually ordered the ship's carpenter to cut away the mainmast. Surprised but obedient, the carpenter had actually made five or six cuts with his ax before the captain countermanded his own order and came up with an alternative idea. A team of men working in a large circle around each of the two violently surging masts passed hawsers around the slack rigging that was supposed to be holding the masts in place, and then brought the hawsers to the capstan, where they were set taut. This had the desired effect of temporarily stopping the surging, but the captain knew it was only a matter of time before the wrenching force of the storm would stretch the rigging still more, and bring on more mischief.

At noon the sea still raged, but the *Macedonian* had moved out of the worst of the storm, and it was possible for the hands to start clearing the general wreckage and setting the ship to order. By late that afternoon the captain could feel assured that they had survived the hurricane, and in celebration for their deliverance he ordered the cookstoves relit and a hot meal prepared. The next day brought moderating gales, and by the evening of September 29, the exhausted ship's company was treated to a proper sunset.

By this time the crew had managed to set up a jury rig that included even a mizzenmast of sorts to replace the one lost in the storm, and Captain Downes, with all thoughts of Rio, Cape Horn, and Valparaiso long since abandoned, set course for Norfolk, Virginia, where the *Macedonian* could undergo the inspection and repairs she now desperately required. On October 3, when they sighted Bermuda on the horizon, Downes weighed the possibility of seeking the shelter of the British dockyards, but felt confident enough of his ship's seaworthiness to decide against it and continue on to the Virginia capes. When they reached the navy yard at Norfolk on October 10, the local officials, proud of their ability to identify all American naval vessels, had to send out a boat to ask for identification.

NAVAL FREIGHT

~~~~~~~~~~~~~~~~~~~~~~

IN JANUARY 1819, FOUR MONTHS AFTER SURVIVING THE HURRI-cane off Bermuda and three months after completing a re-fitting and resupply at Norfolk, Captain John Downes finally managed to take the *Macedonian* around the Horn and into the Pacific. While at Norfolk he received new orders from the Acting Secretary of the Navy, John C. Calhoun, canceling his proposed visits to Rio and Buenos Aires, and calling on him to establish a permanent station for the U.S. Navy on the west coast of South America, in what was at the time one of the most remote corners of the civilized world. It was likely to be a difficult task, complicated by the fact that the entire area was caught up in a great war of liberation.

Throughout Latin America, armies were rising under the banners of liberty to throw off the Spanish yoke, battling fiercely over the last remnants of an empire that had once been the richest in history. Captain Downes's sailing orders noted that such rebellions, with their inherent lack of established rule, could be dangerously unpredictable, even for neutral onlookers, and cautioned discretion in dealing with both the Patriot leaders and the Spanish Royalists.

Had Downes been a more circumspect officer, he might well have taken the Secretary's advice to heart, but caution was not his style. He was by nature an adventurer and a gambler. Cooler heads might concern themselves with the perils inherent in an unstable political situation, but he was more interested in what he saw as an opportunity—a once-in-a-lifetime opportunity—to make a lot of money.

As it turned out, there *was* money to be made in South America—a great deal of it—and in his twenty-six months on station, John Downes managed to collect his share. The story of how he blithely used his official position and the American naval vessel under his command to build a personal fortune underscores the remarkable freedom of action routinely bestowed upon naval captains in the age of sail, particularly those captains posted to distant stations, beyond the range of normal communications.

The exact size of the fortune he amassed in South America will never be known, because the captain kept very private books, but we know that it was substantial, and that his success did not come without a price. His single-minded pursuit of money managed to outrage the entire diplomatic community, including the American consul at Santiago. It also seriously compromised his country's position throughout the region and came within an ace of sabotaging certain delicate aspects of American foreign policy, with incalculable results. From the perspective of our own day, the captain's rapacious shenanigans seem almost comical, but it is unlikely that his contemporaries, particularly American government officials, would have agreed.

The captain's zealous quest for personal gain was so blatant, and carried on with such disregard of the potential dangers inherent in a revolutionary war zone, that he was bound to get into hot water at some point. In John Downes's case, the moment of truth came on a November afternoon in 1820, outside the loyalist harbor of Callao. The chain of events leading up to that confrontation can be traced back almost two years, to January 28, 1819, the day the *Macedonian* first dropped anchor at Valparaiso, the day when Captain Downes and his men, after a wearisome but uneventful seventy-nine-day journey from Cape Henry, Virginia, suddenly found themselves in surroundings as wild and wooly as any gold rush boom town.

Valparaiso, a city of about ten thousand inhabitants, was in the hands of rebel forces, and heavily armed soldiers of the Chilean Patriot army, often drunk and invariably ineffectual, roamed the streets in a pretense of maintaining civic order. Poverty and disease were rife, and a stranger wandering into the barrios could expect to be murdered for the clothes on his back. Visiting sailors fortunate enough to escape death were likely to run up against the press gangs that roamed the waterfront, searching out unwary foreign seamen and offering copious drafts of the local spirits and huge bribes to persuade them to jump ship. Many such a stranger awoke the following morning with a throbbing head in the dank brig of a Chilean warship, the latest recruit in the glorious patriotic war for independence. John Downes observed the general conditions during his first visit to town, and on his return to the ship regretfully canceled all shore leave, not an easy decision to relay to men who had just endured three months at sea.

"I should like to know," complained the melancholy Charles J. Deblois, the captain's homesick clerk, writing in the privacy of his personal journal, "what made our Government send the *Macedonian* to these seas?" It was a good question. Why indeed should the United States, facing east across the North Atlantic, and with an entire continent at its back door ripe for exploitation, go to the trouble and expense of sending a large warship to the other end of the hemisphere to cruise the Pacific coast of South America?

Officially, the answer was that America's emergence as a global commercial power required a naval presence in that part of the world. Even in those early days, the Pacific basin was taking on a distinctly American character. There were seventy American whalers operating in the area, as well as about forty American trading vessels. There were Yankee sealers, Oregon fur trappers and others involved in the China pelfry trade, as well as a sizable cadre of American merchants operating out of every port from Guayaquil to Honolulu. Each of these different groups welcomed the presence of a powerful enforcer to support and protect their interests.

But there was also a secret reason behind the cruise that was considerably less straightforward and which concerned an issue much closer to home: the future of Florida. President Monroe was willing to go to almost any lengths short of outright war to wrest control of Florida from Spain (and even the possibility of military action was seriously considered more than once). The strategic significance of the Spanish-held peninsula was becoming every day more evident to the government in Washington. But Madrid, once again under the rule of the Bourbons, who had "learned nothing and forgotten nothing," refused to even consider an American offer of purchase, and stubbornly stonewalled every effort to negotiate. When that same Bourbon intransigence sparked the rebellions of Bolívar and San Martín in Latin America, the White House thought it saw a new opportunity to advance the Florida question. The President reasoned that should Spain lose all of its other American colonies, it would have little reason to hold on to Florida, and his government might then be able to force a takeover. Hence the presence of the *Macedonian* in the Pacific. She was not there to take sides with the rebels—Washington was not willing to go that far out on a limb, and insisted that Downes maintain a strictly neutral stance—but to see to it that the Patriot forces did not lose.

ALMOST EVERYONE IN Washington agreed that the most suitable candidate to send out on such a politically sensitive mission was John Downes, the ambitious thirty-four-year-old war hero who had served as first officer in the little frigate *Essex* during the war with Britain, and who was therefore already intimately acquainted with the "South Seas," as that part of the Pacific was commonly known. Downes was a gregarious officer, diplomatic and shrewd, and his crews loved him. Significantly, his superiors on the Board of Naval Commissioners judged him to be particularly well endowed with *thalassophilia*, a quality much prized in naval circles of the day. It was a Greek word that simply meant "love of the sea," but as used by navy officers the term implied other characteristics as well—aggressiveness, a sense of adventure, a thirst for glory, and the sort of wild streak that could embolden a man to muster his crew and lead them fearlessly across boarding planks, throwing themselves like maddened tigers into a wall of heavily armed enemy sailors. Downes had consistently demonstrated such inspirational qualities during the war, which was sufficient recommendation for the commissioners in Washington.

If Downes was precisely the right man for the job, the *Macedonian* was precisely the right ship. The navy had several newer, larger, and more powerful warships available for the duty, including ships-of-the-line, but the *Macedonian*'s provenance as a British prize spoke eloquently of America's fighting spirit, and in the eyes of the Board, her propaganda value made her the equal to a ship of twice her force.

IMMEDIATELY UPON HIS arrival at Valparaiso, Downes set about lining up suppliers, arranging for warehousing, and attending to the thousands of details involved in establishing a permanent base for his ship and the other American warships that would follow her in the years to come. It was also a time to renew old ties from his days in the *Essex*. After a quick trip inland on horseback to the capital at Santiago to present himself to the leading figures of the *patria vieja*, he returned to the coast to begin his own tour of duty on the new station.

His most immediate goal was to get to know the one man who was likely to have a greater impact on his mission than anyone else in the Pacific, the redoubtable Admiral Lord Thomas Cochrane. Cochrane was a legendary seadog, a doughty veteran of the Royal Navy who had come out from Britain to run the Chilean Navy. He had arrived in Valparaiso only weeks before Downes, and in his short period on the coast had already organized the Patriot navy into a superior fighting machine. Almost all his officers were Royal Navy veterans, and all orders were written in English. Cochrane's name and exploits were well known to every naval officer the world over, and his reputation for daring and cunning was second only to Nelson himself.

Downes was aware that Cochrane had a dark side as well. His lordship could be headstrong and reckless, and was famous for his violent temper. Some believed him to be mentally unbalanced. Downes recognized that if he wanted to operate freely along the South American coastline, it was vital that he establish himself personally with the Scottish nobleman, and if possible,

The last remnant of HMS *Macedonian*, her Alexander the Great figurehead, dating from her Woolwich launch in 1810, remains on public display at the Naval Academy at Annapolis.

John Surman Carden, the last British captain of the *Macedonian*. Although he never received a subsequent sea command, he remained on the Royal navy's active list and eventually rose to the rank of admiral. (*Author's collection*)

The battle between the *Macedonian* and the *United States* was a standard subject for popular prints for many years. This engraving depicts a climactic moment towards the end of the action when the *Macedonian's* main topmast fell. (*Philadelphia Maritime Museum*)

Lieutenant William Henry Allen, Decatur's first officer, was designated prize master of the newly captured *Macedonian*, and as such was her first American captain. (*Franklin D. Roosevelt Library*)

A female sightseer is lifted to the deck of the *Macedonian* soon after the ship's arrival in New York in January 1813. The illustration is from Samuel Leech's *Thirty Years from Home*. (*Author's Collection*)

Stephen Decatur, already a hero to the public, added fresh laurels to his reputation when he brought home the *Macedonian* as a prize of war, but he soon found himself in direct conflict with the Secretary of the Treasury. (*U.S. Naval Academy Museum*)

The *Macedonian* under jury rig, following the hurricane of 1818. The fore-yard appears to be intact with a full foresail bent, although the mainsail and fore topsail would seem to be spare topsails bent to the smaller jury yards. The main topsail appears to be a spare topgallant. (*National Archives*)

John Downes, after surviving a hurricane in the *Macedonian*, went on to amass a personal fortune during his subsequent three-year tour of the Pacific. (*U.S. Naval Academy Museum*)

James Biddle used the *Macedonian* as his flagship on two different cruises, first in the Caribbean and later on the Brazil Station. (*U.S. Naval Academy Museum*)

John Rodgers, as chief of the Board of Naval Commissioners, was primarily responsible for the successful rebuilding of the *Macedonian*, despite strong opposition from the Secretary of the Navy and others. (*U.S. Naval Academy Museum*)

Matthew Calbraith Perry took the *Macedonian* to Africa, purportedly to hunt down American slave traders, with a singular lack of success. (*U.S. Naval Academy Museum*)

George Colman De Kay became the only civilian ever to command the *Macedonian*, when he borrowed her from the Navy Department in 1847 to carry food to the starving Irish. (*Collection of the New York Historical Society*)

The news of the *Macedonian's* arrival in Ireland in 1847, as reported in *The Illustrated London News*, reawakened British memories of the War of 1812 and prompted her last English captain, John Carden, to write his memoirs justifying his actions in the battle with Decatur's *United States*. (*Illustrated London News*)

Commodore Perry's steam frigates arrive at Odawara Bay, February 1854, where the *Macedonian* (right background) has grounded on a reef. (*Narrative of the Expedition*)

船將 アーボット

Joel Abbot, captain of the *Macedonian* and vice commodore of Perry's expedition to Japan in 1854, as depicted by an anonymous Japanese artist. (*Chrysler Museum*)

The *Macedonian* departing Hong Kong for Boston in 1856, carrying the remains of Joel Abbot home for burial. The engraving shows the ship's razeed configuration. The Navy now considered her a sloop-of-war rather than a frigate, but her purser—and the Attorney General of the United States—did not agree. (*Franklin D. Roosevelt Library*)

The controversial Uriah Phillips Levy, the last commodore to use the *Macedonian* as his flagship. In his hand he holds a scroll that reads, "Author of the Abolition of Flogging in the Navy of the United States." (*U.S. Naval Academy Museum*)

By 1866, when this picture appeared in *Harper's Weekly*, the *Macedonian* (center) was queen of the Naval Academy squadron, which by that time also included the yacht *America* (far left) and various steamers. (*G. W. Blunt White Library, Mystic Seaport Museum*)

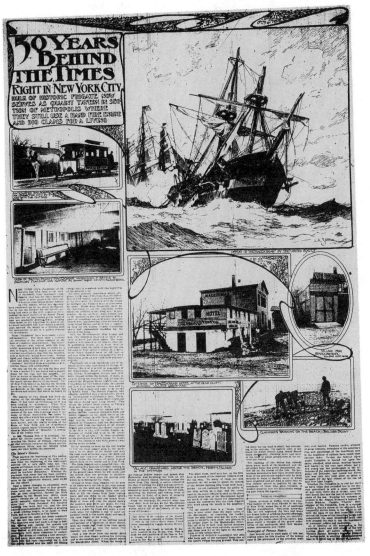

"HULK OF HISTORIC FRIGATE NOW SERVES AS QUAINT TAVERN" headlined a story in the New York *Herald* in 1902 featuring the Macedonian Hotel in the Bronx and including a scene of the 1812 battle. The article reported that "The main room, used as a bar, on the first floor, is framed by the heaviest timbers from the old ship. To many of them are still fastened the old hooks to which the sailors of the British fighting ship hung their hammocks." (*New York Public Library*)

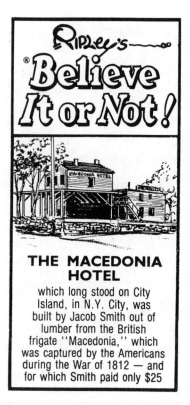

THE MACEDONIA HOTEL
which long stood on City Island, in N.Y. City, was built by Jacob Smith out of lumber from the British frigate "Macedonia," which was captured by the Americans during the War of 1812 — and for which Smith paid only $25

A syndicated newspaper item in 1983 managed to condense the entire history of the *Macedonian* into a single panel, and seemed to suggest that the most noteworthy detail of her 113-year career was the relatively low price of her used timbers. (*Ripley Entertainment Inc.*)

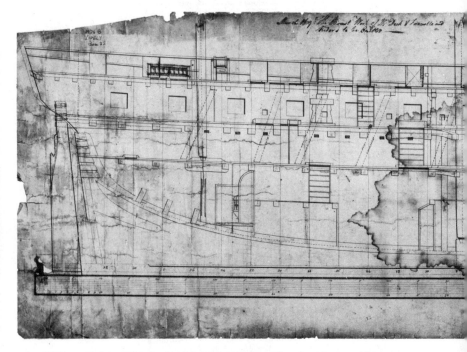

Sir William Rule's 1809 draft of the *Macedonian*. The descriptive title over the forward section of the ship has been amended to show that shortly after work commenced on the *Macedonian* a second frigate (HMS *Crescent*) was ordered built from the identical plans. (*National Maritime Museum, London*)

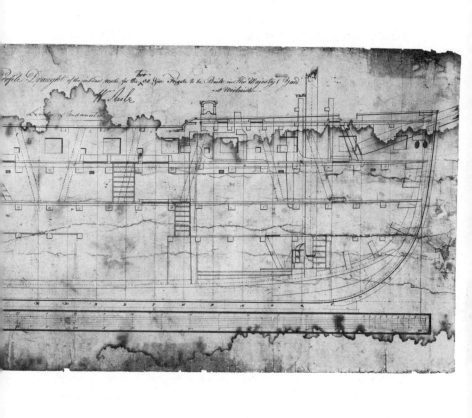

Profile Draught of the inboard works for the 32 Gun Frigate to be Built in His Majesty's Yard at Woolwich

ingratiate himself. Unfortunately for his plans, Cochrane was off at sea when Downes returned from the interior, and the American captain was forced to settle for an introduction to his lordship's wife, the young and beautiful Lady Katherine. She and the captain hit it off famously, and Downes quickly became a regular visitor to the Cochrane mansion. When Lady Katherine confided that she and the admiral were much vexed by their inability to find workmen in Valparaiso competent to carry out the extensive renovations he wished to make in his home, Downes saw an opportunity to do Cochrane a favor in absentia, and dispatched a team of carpenters from the *Macedonian* to do the work gratis.

Downes also arranged for a grand ball to be held on board the *Macedonian* in honor of George Washington's birthday, hoping that Cochrane might return in time to attend. But when her ladyship showed up alone with apologies for her still missing husband, Downes was all courtesy and took it upon himself to serve as her escort for the entire evening. The captain's clerk, the dour Deblois, confided in his diary his suspicions that Downes and Lady Cochrane were romantically involved, but it is highly unlikely that even such an ambitious gambler as John Downes would jeopardize his entire cruise for the sake of the lady's favors.

The gala was a huge success. With the single exception of Cochrane, all the leading figures of Valparaiso were present. Under the matched flags of Chile and the United States, couples danced on the quarterdeck to the strains of the large and proficient ship's band which Downes had brought out from Boston. Later, the guests partook of a dainty supper on the gun deck. Downes made sure there was sufficient alcoholic refreshment on hand, and Lieutenant Gauntt, his fifth officer, has left us a vivid description in his journal of woozy Chilean dignitaries weaving about unsurely under "a full press of sail," until the party finally broke up at five o'clock in the morning.

During those first hectic weeks on station, Downes found time to start developing his own money-spinning schemes, as well. His plan was simple: he would offer to serve as a banker to the various merchant captains plying the coast. Trading vessels from Mexico to Chile were raking in fortunes in the newly opened markets of Latin America, sailing up and down the coast and doing business with both sides. Because of the primitive commercial conditions, their buying and selling was all done in cash—gold and silver coins, for the most part, known as specie. Because there were no convenient places to deposit their working capital, every vessel had to carry its own specie and protect it as best it could, which made the little ships tempting targets, not only for the cutthroats and brigands operating along the coast, but for Cochrane's naval vessels as well. Patriot warships routinely captured any merchantman remotely suspected of trading with the enemy and claimed it as a legitimate prize of war. The value of the ship and her cargo (including, of course, her specie) would be split between those responsible for her capture, and Cochrane and his men were making fortunes.

Downes planned to offer the merchants who owned the ships protection against such hazards by providing them with the one thing they could not purchase elsewhere: security. For a fee he would lock up their specie in the hold of the *Macedonian*, where no pirate or Patriot naval officer would dare set foot. It was perhaps the safest spot for private money in the entire Pacific. For this service Captain Downes planned to charge his customers a percentage of the total amount of specie shipped, a fee that he would pocket personally.

There was no question that his plan would provide a much-needed service. The more specie a private merchant was forced to carry, the more tempting he became as a target for both pirates and Patriots. What may be a little more surprising, at least to some modern readers, is that his scheme was sanctioned by the American government and was perfectly legal, despite the fact that Downes would be using government property for his own personal gain. The percentage he charged was known as "naval freight," and it was a fairly common practice in most navies during the age of sail. It was undeniably useful, and was justified on the theory that the captain who protected his countrymen's money was thereby encouraging the national economy. (Captain John Surman Carden had hoped to profit from a similar scheme on his ill-fated visit to Norfolk in the *Macedonian* in 1812.)

By regulation, in the U.S. Navy the decision to accept such freight was solely at the discretion of the captain. Importantly, he was specifically limited to carrying the specie of American citizens only, and even then it was further limited to specie that was consigned for delivery to banks in the United States. If a captain chose to accept such freight, he was allowed to charge a fee, which could not exceed 2.5 percent of the total value of the specie shipped, all of which he could keep. Any other arrangements or interpretations were expressly prohibited, a small point that John Downes chose to overlook.

Downes was fortunate in having the enthusiastic support of Henry Hill to help spread the news of his new banking service. Hill was the American vice-consul in Valparaiso and himself a merchant, and he saw Downes's scheme as an important step toward improving the prosperity of the entire region. He seemed to know everyone who was at all active in the coastal trade, and he used his position and connections to advertise the new service to the maritime interests in the port. It was he who introduced Downes to John Murphy, master of the British brig *Thomas*, the man who would become Downes's first customer. The deal that Downes struck with Murphy gives us a measure of the captain's willingness to interpret government regulations in a highly selective manner.

Over dinner in Valparaiso, Murphy cheerfully admitted to Downes that he was not in fact a trader in the accepted sense of the word, but rather a smuggler, who shipped his cargoes clandestinely, thereby avoiding the heavy tariffs charged by both Patriot and Royalist governments. He made no apologies for his profession, but pointed out that the problem of handling large amounts of cash was even more perilous for him than it was for the more orthodox merchants, since he worked so completely outside the law. Downes wanted to know how much trade he did. It turned out Murphy was talking serious money. He esti-

mated that the amount of specie he wanted to ship with Downes would range between $100,000 and $500,000.

It was an impressive figure, but the question remained as to whether John Downes had the legal right to accept Murphy's money. Murphy was neither an American citizen nor even a legitimate trader. Nor, for that matter, did he plan to consign any of the cash to American banks. Downes could see that it would be extremely difficult—in fact impossible—to make a case for shipping Murphy's specie within the guidelines of the regulations governing naval freight. Countering these factors, however, was Henry Hill's enthusiastic endorsement of Murphy's proposal. The vice-consul urged Downes to accept the offer, arguing that there was a natural affinity between American and British interests in the Pacific, and suggesting that the scheme conformed to the spirit of his orders, if not to the letter. The vice-consul's argument was pure flimflam, but Downes chose to find it persuasive.

With the question of legality neatly sidestepped, the two captains entered into some friendly bargaining, and quickly reached an agreement. Rather than the prescribed fee of 2.5 percent of the total value carried, Murphy agreed to pay the American a whopping 6 percent. This meant that if Murphy's estimate of his expected traffic came anywhere near the mark, Downes's personal share could amount to anything up to $30,000. American naval captains of the day received a monthly salary of one hundred dollars, which meant that Downes could look forward to making a sum equal to twenty-five times his annual income.

The decision to accept the smuggler's patently illegal proposal seems out of character for a man with an otherwise unblemished record for straightforward dealings, but then, the times were unique. The huge profits being made in South America would soon disappear with the return of peace. Besides, who would know? The Naval Commissioners in Washington were so far away that it took six months to exchange messages. John Downes was unlikely ever again to experience such an opportunity, combined with such an unparalleled freedom of action.

When his own very human inclination to accept the offer was supported with such enthusiasm by the American vice-consul, the decision virtually made itself.

John Downes was no plaster saint, but neither was he a fool. He had to be aware that despite his every effort to keep the matter quiet, his alliance with Murphy was bound to surface eventually, and it could irreparably complicate his position to be publicly revealed in league with a smuggler who was playing a criminal game against both belligerents, with potentially disastrous consequences both to his country and himself. At the very least, the bargain he drew up with Murphy put him in line for possible court-martial charges upon his return to America.

On the other hand, it is likely that a man with such a healthy *thalassophilia* would almost surely have found some means to justify such a rewarding temptation, no matter what the arguments to the contrary.

A FEW DAYS after Downes's meeting with Murphy, the *Thomas* cleared customs at Valparaiso and put out to sea, ostensibly bound south to double the Horn for Rio, but in fact heading north to the deserted beaches of Arica, on the Chilean border with Peru, where most of the smuggled goods for the entire coast were put ashore. Shortly thereafter, the *Macedonian* also departed Valparaiso, following the same route north. On May 5, 1819, her log shows that she hove to off Arica, out of sight of land, and waited for Murphy to show up. Not long after dark the *Thomas* appeared with an angry and frustrated Murphy on board, but no specie. Some problem had apparently arisen on shore, he explained, and Downes would have to stand by. The same circumstances were repeated several days running. Murphy would go into the coast each night under cover of darkness and return the following morning, sometimes with a few bags of gold, sometimes with nothing. In the meantime, the *Macedonian* remained hove to.

His ship had no legitimate business in the area and Downes was concerned that he might be discovered by one of the belligerents under highly compromising circumstances. His fears were

confirmed a little after midnight on May 8 when the Patriot frigate *Andes* appeared over the horizon and came up alongside, and a voice with an English accent demanded identification. A nervous Downes, expecting the worst, ordered all fires doused and the guns cast loose, but the rebel ship, on learning that she was the *Macedonian*, sailed off without incident. It would only be a matter of days, Downes knew, before Admiral Cochrane learned that the *Macedonian* had been found hove to off a notorious smugglers' landing under suspicious circumstances.

After more than a week of waiting off Arica, Murphy finally came on board with the last of the money. The total amounted to only $66,000, considerably less than anticipated. Still, it was enough to provide Downes with a tidy sum for a week's work. It was a beginning, and as it turned out, there was a lot more to come.

CAPTAIN DOWNES'S ORDERS called for him to keep his eyes open, show the flag, and not to take sides. Over the next eighteen months he cruised the 3,000 miles of coast between Chile and Mexico, first north and then south, now and then dipping into a harbor, either Royalist or rebel, to sort things out between some American captain and the authorities, before once again continuing on his way. As the *Macedonian's* presence in the Pacific became more widely known, her captain's personal client list grew progressively longer.

It was a seller's market, and Downes had no trouble drumming up business. Many of the shipments of specie were of considerable size. In December 1819, at Callao, he shipped $480,000—part of it to be delivered to Panama, part to an American trading brig in Mexico, and part for deposit in the United States. Two months later, he picked up another $490,000.

His rate for American merchants remained the regulatory 2.5 percent, and for neutrals such as Murphy, 6 percent. He established still another rate for a third group that now sought his services—Spanish merchants and members of the Royalist government, anxious to smuggle out some last remnant of Inca treasure before the end came. By accepting the trade of these belligerents, Downes was clearly taking sides in the war, and to compensate himself for the added risk, he undoubtedly charged an even higher rate, probably around 10 percent.

The principal record we have of the naval freight John Downes took on board the *Macedonian* comes from his own deliberately sketchy and vague report to the Secretary of the Navy, written long after the events, which was designed to justify his activities and is therefore not to be accepted at face value. Both of the shipments listed above come from that accounting, but it is likely that Downes only reported the consignments that were so large they were difficult to hide.

It would have been impossible to keep secret either of the two large shipments mentioned in the captain's letter to the Secretary of the Navy. Each amounted to almost half a million dollars, and each would have weighed at least a ton, and possibly much more, depending on the amount of silver coinage mixed in with the gold. It would have required several men to manhandle such a load onto the deck and to get it down the companionways and stowed below in the magazine. There was also a lot of time-consuming paperwork involved in either shipping or landing specie. Each shipment would have to be carefully sorted and weighed, with all principals in attendance, so that there might be no later misunderstandings, and duplicate bills of lading made out showing Downes's acceptance of the freight. Such a process was likely to take several hours, during which the captain's absence from other duties would be difficult to hide.

But not all shipments of specie needed be so obvious to the officers and men of the *Macedonian*. A more discreet shipment of $25,000, for example, particularly if it were pure gold, could be transported by hand and hidden under a cape. Even a shipment of $100,000 would fit in a single cask weighing only a little over three hundred pounds, and would not have been interesting enough to cause talk among the crew or engage the interest of Cochrane's spies. Yet for all their dainty size, such freight, particularly if it came out of the viceroy's treasury in Lima, would have earned Captain Downes many thousands.

Unquestionably, he took on board a great deal more freight than he ever admitted to.

Ironically, the major reason for Captain Downes's increasing prosperity lay in the energetic activities of Lord Cochrane, who was busy pursuing his own profit-making schemes. His Patriot navy had by that time virtually cleared the remnants of the Spanish fleet from adjacent waters, leaving him free to concentrate on hunting down purported "blockade runners." Toward the close of 1819, he and his officers were capturing merchant vessels of every description and sending them in to prize courts, where their cargoes were impounded and their crews sent to work in the mines. Cochrane, as the commander in chief, took a percentage of the prize money awarded for every vessel condemned by the rebel-run court, and the money poured in. The specter of Cochrane's kangaroo courts haunted every trader on the coast, and the need for a safe place to put their money became increasingly imperative. Captain Downes was there to oblige.

OVER TIME, IT became increasingly evident to Downes that Cochrane had more on his mind than simply taking prizes. He and his men were also practicing a high degree of selectivity in their choice of victims, pulling in far more American merchantmen than British. Cochrane's long-range goal, Downes realized, was to secure the Chilean markets for British merchants. He dashed off an angry letter to Chile's supreme director Bernardo O'Higgins, complaining of Cochrane's favoritism. "The partiality which he extends to his countrymen and his extreme hostility to the Citizens of the United States are too glaring not to be perceived by everyone," Downes wrote testily, demanding that Cochrane's navy provide the same protection to American traders.

It was a brash and impertinent letter to send, considering Downes's highly illegal operations, but apparently the captain never saw any conflict between his activities as an officer of the United States and his activities as an entrepreneur.

On June 13, 1820, the *Macedonian* arrived at Valparaiso and discovered the entire Chilean fleet at anchor, and for the first time in a year and a half on station, John Downes had an opportunity to deal directly with Admiral Cochrane. What happened is instructive.

Downes, in his position as the commanding American naval officer of the Pacific Ocean, dispatched his first officer to Cochrane's flagship, the *O'Higgins*, with an offer to salute Cochrane's flag with the requisite seventeen guns, provided that the salute was returned gun for gun by the *O'Higgins*. Such an exchange, highly significant in the elaborate etiquette practiced between naval powers, would establish the two commanders as equals, which was, of course, Downes's purpose.

Cochrane sent back a message that he would be willing to answer gun for gun if the American commander would give him assurance that an even exchange was always required by United States ships regardless of the relative ranks of the commanders. Downes was outraged. His lordship had neatly punctured his attempt at diplomatic oneupmanship. Cochrane was clearly trying to belittle him, and by extension, the United States. Downes was about to cancel any salute whatsoever, which would have caused a public scene, when his friend Henry Hill, the vice-consul, persuaded him to give Cochrane such an assurance simply to maintain the peace. It was sent off to Cochrane's flagship, and in due course the two ships boomed away at each other, gun for gun.

The only face-to-face meeting between the two men took place a month later, when Lord Cochrane paid a formal visit to the *Macedonian* on July 26 in the course of his duties as commander in chief of the Chilean Patriot navy. Both he and Downes were governed by the strict protocol of the occasion, and deliberately limited themselves to the polite small talk devoid of content that can prove so useful at such times. Still, the meeting gave each man an opportunity to gauge the other at first hand, and to make the sort of character judgments that are apt to be useful in later confrontations.

*   *   *

In August, the *Macedonian* was still at anchor in Valparaiso harbor when the city awoke from its winter torpor to exciting news. Simon Bolívar had marshaled his forces and embarked on a westward march across the top of South America, and would soon be in a position to attack the Royalist strongholds in Peru. It was the news the Chilean forces had long anticipated. With Bolívar attacking from the north, and the Chilean Army attacking from the south, it would at last be possible to rid the continent of the remaining vestige of Spanish rule. The town changed overnight into a noisy, excited military supply depot, as the Patriot army and navy girded up for a major land and sea assault.

Captain Downes watched the busy preparations from the quarterdeck of the *Macedonian*, and turned his mind to the American merchant ships he knew to be anchored at Royalist-held Callao, directly in the path of the Patriot army. The vessels were likely to become pawns in a dangerous game, either held in check by a Royalist embargo or trapped by the Patriot blockade. Either way, they would be in need of protection, the kind of protection only the *Macedonian* could provide.

Shortly after General San Martín's forces left for the front, Downes gave orders to up anchor and square away for the north. Traveling by sea, he would reach Callao long before San Martín's soldiers, and with any luck have matters in hand before their arrival. It would be at Callao that John Downes would have cause to wonder, perhaps for the first time, whether he had not pursued his fortune-hunting activities too far.

When, a fortnight later, the *Macedonian* slipped past San Lorenzo Island and into the roadstead at Callao, Downes's suspicions concerning the imperiled American vessels were confirmed. Six Yankee merchantmen lay at anchor in the harbor, potential sacrificial lambs in the fighting to come. Their masters and crews, made anxious by the rumors of the impending offensive, greeted the American frigate with loud cheers and salutes. Even as the *Macedonian* let down her bower anchor, the smaller vessels began gathering alongside her for protection, like chicks with a brood hen.

They were still there the following month, when Cochrane's navy, now greatly enlarged to twenty-three sail, arrived off the coast in October and took up blockading stations, in the opening stages of the rebel offensive. San Martín's army, marching overland, was not due for some time, and Downes took the opportunity to leave the ship and head six miles inland by mule train to Lima, to finish up some business with the viceroy, turning the command of the *Macedonian* over to his first officer, John Maury. The captain reckoned to be back long before any actual fighting broke out, but he had not taken into account Lord Cochrane's penchant for the unexpected. Shortly after Downes's departure for the interior, the harbor of Callao became the setting for a clandestine attack by Lord Cochrane of such breathtaking boldness and panache that it continues to be studied in naval academies around the world to this day.

On the moonless night of November 5, 1820, a small Patriot naval force, transported in open boats under the personal command of Cochrane himself, detached itself from the blockading squadron and swept silently into Callao under muffled oars. After traversing virtually the entire length of the harbor without being noticed by the sentinels in the fort, the boats arrived just below the 40-gun Royalist frigate *Esmeralda*, the last remaining Spanish naval vessel of any consequence in the Pacific.

On a silent signal from the admiral, his men scrambled over the sides of the enemy ship and after a bloody hand-to-hand battle, captured her from her sleepy and bewildered crew. Throughout the action, the hand-picked British raiders were careful to make as little noise as possible, so even after they had lost the element of surprise, it was impossible for bystanders peering through the dark to know what was going on. Some men in the *Macedonian*, caught up in the excitement, leaned silently through the ratlines straining to hear the sounds of battle, no more than a cable's length distant. At one point, the Spanish frigate, which had been cut loose from her mooring by the raiders, drifted so close to the *Macedonian* that the cries of the wounded could be clearly heard, and spent pistol balls landed on the American warship's deck. The Royalist troops in the fort overlooking the harbor were too far away to even suspect foul play, and for a long time took no action. When they finally woke up to the reality of the situation and opened fire, it was too late. Cochrane and his men, now in full control of the *Esmeralda*, managed to make sail and clear the harbor. The following morning, the captured frigate was plainly visible from the shore, the newest addition to Cochrane's blockading squadron, saucily sporting Chilean colors.

History has enshrined Cochrane's daring raid on Callao as one of the great cutting-outs of the age of sail, but his Spanish victims were hardly in the mood to admire the admiral's daring, and could feel nothing but shame and anguish in the aftermath of the action. When the mortifying details of the capture became known the following morning, the entire population of Callao rose up in a rage, determined to find scapegoats for their communal humiliation. Perhaps because Cochrane's navy was made up almost entirely of English-speaking officers, a rumor spread that the Americans had somehow been part of the scheme. When the *Macedonian* sent in her regular supply boat, clearly displaying her American flag, to purchase fresh produce, the crew was attacked and fired upon by the angry mob. Two American sailors were killed outright and six more were wounded. The rest were lucky to escape with their lives.

Reaction was equally strong inland, at Lima, and several foreigners were murdered after the story reached the capital. Events got out of hand again two days later in Callao, when the Yankee schooner *Rampart* was fired upon by angry Spanish soldiers, who attacked with such force that the crew had to abandon ship.

Captain Downes hurried back to the coast from Lima, protesting these acts of aggression against neutral Americans in a sharply worded letter to the viceroy, and was somewhat nonplussed when in reply, instead of the usual letter couched in soothing words expressing diplomatic contrition, he received only cool and noncommittal answers. The viceroy, it appeared, suspected the mob was right, and was uncharacteristically blunt in voicing his suspicions.

Downes recognized that it was useless to protest his innocence. The fact that he had been absent from Callao at the time of the attack, and that his interests conflicted with those of Lord Cochrane, meant nothing in the heat of the moment. The Royalists were not to be assuaged by rational argument in their eagerness to find scapegoats for their shame. It was clearly time for the *Macedonian* and her brood of merchantmen to leave Callao and seek some safer haven.

Downes now found himself cornered in the kind of trap that diplomats dread above all others: in escaping one unpleasant situation he was likely to find himself facing a worse one. Leaving Callao would be easy. The problem was going to be in getting past Cochrane and his blockade.

Blockades were tricky things, and often of dubious legality. Downes did not usually worry about them. But the circumstances of this particular blockade were unusual, and what made them so were the bags of gold locked below decks in the *Macedonian*, gold in the amount of more than a million dollars, with bills of lading attesting to the ownership of every ounce. And Cochrane, through his network of spies in every port along the coast, knew all about the gold.

Under normal conditions, Downes could assume that Cochrane would let him pass through the blockade unchecked, rather than risk an unwelcome confrontation with the neutral United States, but conditions were not normal, thanks to the specie in the hold. Downes had compromised his neutrality, and by the rules of the game, Cochrane could legitimately seize the *Macedonian* in the name of the government of Chile, and personally claim a large share of the gold on board. The United States would certainly object most strenuously at the seizure of one of its warships, but Cochrane had only to display Downes's bills of lading to prove that the *Macedonian* was illegally carrying Spanish specie, and the American case would fall apart. Would Washington go to war with far-away Chile to defend the honor of an officer publicly shown to be a cheat? Even the ebullient Downes found such a prospect unlikely.

And there the matter stood. Not a great moral dilemma. Not even a delicately balanced issue demanding much subtlety of intellect. Rather, it was an open and shut case of an overly ambitious American officer who, for reasons of personal greed, placed his ship, the honor of his country, and the lives of his men in jeopardy. At least, such was the case Cochrane could make, and undoubtedly would, should he decide to attack.

In those last hectic days in Callao, as his officers hurried to get the convoy of merchantmen ready for the dash to safety, is it likely that John Downes experienced some twinge of regret for the personal avarice which had brought him to this point? Should we imagine even a hint of remorse creeping into Downes's private thoughts?

In a word, no. Men of his stripe do not regret. Waste of time. They live in the present, and what undoubtedly concerned John Downes at that moment of confrontation was the grand game of bluff that was about to begin, the contest of wills between two intense, ambitious naval officers who enjoyed taking chances, and knew how to live with the consequences.

Just possibly it may have occurred to him that of all the American naval vessels to send to the South Seas, the *Macedonian* may not have been the best choice. Flaunting a British prize in the face of such a zealous veteran of the Royal Navy as Lord Cochrane was not likely to induce a spirit of cooperation in the man. But of course putting such thoughts in Downes's mind is only conjecture.

On November 21, Downes played the only card in his hand, and signaled his departure from Callao. The *Rampart* was still undergoing repairs from the Spanish attack, and would remain at Callao, but the five other American trading vessels, as well as three English brigs, chose to accompany the *Macedonian*. If Cochrane wanted to fight, Downes knew his little convoy could not possibly survive against such odds, but he would not make it an easy victory. He ordered the *Macedonian*'s guns run out and her decks sanded in preparation for possible action.

The flotilla nosed cautiously out of the anchorage, sailed into the shadow cast by San Lorenzo Island, and then abruptly plunged directly into the sunlit ocean and the line of ships on blockade. They found themselves suddenly in the middle of the full force of the Chilean Patriot navy—the *San Martín*, the *Chacabuco*, the *Independencia*, and any number of brigs and cutters. And there in the midst of them, Cochrane's flagship, the *O'Higgins*. Downes stood tensly by the wheel, searching for clues to Cochrane's intent. But the Chilean gun ports were closed, and the sailors in the Chilean ships ignored the *Macedonian* and her brood. There were no signals, no acknowledgment of their presence. An able-bodied seaman, a cheerful captain of the top, leaned out from the main topgallant mast of the *O'Higgins* and waved his cap in a friendly greeting.

Cochrane made no move. Why? Perhaps he recognized in the brash young American captain a kindred soul—two men with perhaps a little more *thalassophilia* in their makeup than was probably good for them. Perhaps he simply felt the game was not worth the candle. John Downes would never know why Cochrane let him go. All he knew for certain was that he left Callao that day with over a million dollars in contraband specie in his ship, and Lord Thomas Cochrane looked the other way and allowed him to pass.

JOHN DOWNES AND the *Macedonian* remained on station another half year after the escape from Callao, and by that time his brazen pursuit of money through naval freight had become so notorious that the American agent on the coast, John B. Prevost, sent letters to Secretary of State John Quincy Adams deploring the practice and urging Washington to do something about it before it caused a rupture with the Patriot government. Prevost went directly to Downes, and personally begged him to desist. Downes threatened a duel, and the agent backed down.

On May 13, 1821, with the *Macedonian* safely back round the Horn and halfway home, John Downes stopped off at Rio de Janeiro and with considerable ceremony landed one million dollars in specie, for deposit to various banks. The remaining money (the actual amount was never disclosed) he brought back to the United States, again for delivery to various banks and financial houses, and of course including a generous donation to his own account. In his official report, he admits to carrying two million dollars during his tour of duty in the Pacific, but the true figure was probably twice that.

Even if we accept his figure, and estimate an average carrying charge of 5 percent, the captain's personal earnings over the course of the cruise came to at least $100,000, or eighty times his annual salary. In today's money, perhaps two million dollars.

Tax free.

TWO VISITORS

〰〰〰〰〰〰〰〰〰

O N MARCH 15, 1821, SHORTLY BEFORE THE *MACEDONIAN* departed Valparaiso for home, two separate visitors arrived on board, setting up one of those curious crosscurrents that can momentarily bring together totally unrelated strands in the fabric of history.

The first visitor was in way of being an old acquaintance, Commodore Sir Thomas Masterman Hardy, the famous hero of Trafalgar and flag officer to the late Admiral Lord Nelson, the man still known to posterity as the one to whom Nelson addressed his dying words, "Kiss me, Hardy." The commodore had just arrived in Chile to take command of the Royal Navy's Pacific Squadron, and the fact that the Admiralty saw fit to send such a symbolically important officer to the remote west coast of South America was evidence that Britain shared America's growing interest in the region.

Hardy was no stranger to the *Macedonian*. In Lisbon in 1812 it was he who selected her for the ill-starred scheme to spirit specie out of the United States, the incident that caused poor Captain Carden such acute embarrassment. Two years later, while in command of the British blockade of New London, it was Hardy who first suggested a duel between the *Macedonian* and her sister ship *Statira*, only to withdraw the challenge when Decatur started complicating matters. Now he sat in the captain's cabin exchanging pleasantries with John Downes, and cementing the bonds of Anglo-American friendship which would help both countries' navies deal with the troublesome Lord Cochrane.

The other visitor to the *Macedonian* that day was in no condition to exchange pleasantries. He was an American named Owen Chase, the first mate of a Nantucket whaler named the *Essex*, and he was resting below on the berth deck. Chase and his companions had been the victims of a bizarre and terrifying incident in the Pacific, when a sperm whale deliberately attacked their ship and sank it. The survivors spent three desperate months at sea in open whaleboats, living at first on the few crumbs of bread hastily rescued from the sinking ship, and eventually eating the bodies of their dead companions. The last members of the crew finally reached the coast of Chile, and the American agent in Valparaiso arranged for them to take passage home in the *Macedonian*.

Owen Chase would write an account of his harrowing adventure, entitled *Narrative of the Most Extraordinary and Distressing Shipwreck of the Whale-Ship* Essex, *of Nantucket*. Years later a young seaman named Herman Melville would read the book on board the whaler *Acushnet*, and the story of Owen Chase would become the genesis for his masterpiece, *Moby-Dick*.

BLADENSBURG

O N MARCH 22, 1820, WHILE THE *MACEDONIAN* WAS STAND- ing off the Mexican coast at San Blas, and Captain John Downes was contemplating his cut of the $490,000 in gold he had just shipped on board for delivery to Panama, an incident took place on the other side of the continent that would reverber- ate and influence American naval affairs for decades to come, and directly shape the future of the *Macedonian*.

At nine o'clock on a chilly morning in a Washington suburb, two former friends faced each other on the dueling grounds at Bladensburg, Maryland, each with a loaded pistol in his hand. At a signal from one of the seconds, they solemnly raised their pistols and fired. The two shots rang out simultaneously.

Both balls hit home, and each man fell. The challenger, Cap- tain James Barron, would survive the day and live to an old age. The man who had reluctantly accepted the challenge, Commo- dore Stephen Decatur, was mortally wounded and would die in excrutiating pain within a few hours.

It was a senseless and unworthy duel, and the tawdry out- come shocked the nation. At a single blow, America was de- prived of one of its most attractive leaders, and all for nothing. The navy issued a General Order directing every American offi- cer around the world "to wear crepe upon the left arm for a period of thirty days as a testimony of respect for the late Com- modore," and from the day of his funeral everything connected with the late hero took on hagiographic importance. His elegant town house on Lafayette Square became a center for mourners. Worshipful citizens rechristened towns, counties, lakes, and rivers in his honor, and the name Decatur began to appear on maps of almost every state. The very pistol ball that killed him was solemnly placed on exhibition (it remains on display at the Naval Academy in Annapolis to this day). The cult of Decatur, founded on the deep romantic feelings of the American people, and stirred up and given direction by the commodore's beautiful widow Susan and others in Washington, emerged as a tangible force in naval circles.

The single most prominent memorial to the fallen hero was, of course, the British frigate he had so daringly captured and brought home in 1812. Decatur's death only enhanced her status, and as of March 22, 1820, the *Macedonian* became, in certain respects, the most important ship in the U.S. Navy.

VOMITO NEGRO

~~~~~~~~~~~~~~~

T HE BLUE-GREEN WATERS OF THE CARIBBEAN, ALONG WITH THE
archipelago of lush green islands that define its extent, have
been so heavily promoted by the tourist industry as havens
for honeymooners and other pleasure seekers that it sometimes
comes as a surprise to recall that throughout the nineteenth
century the same area was generally recognized to be just about
the most pestilential, dangerous quarter on the face of the globe,
a place of of misery and disease—a true hell on earth, with a
climate to match.

The pirates who roamed the Spanish Main, far from being
the amiable clowns trivialized by Walt Disney, were degenerate
sociopaths who delighted in torture and the most sickening vil-
lainy. The brightly dressed "natives" singing colorful work
songs on the sugar cane plantations were in fact African slaves
living in abject squalor. And the balmy trade winds that wafted
the fragrances of frangipani and jacaranda also carried some
of the most terrible and mysterious forms of death known to
humankind.

The ordeal of the *Macedonian*, which was overwhelmed by a
virulent yellow fever epidemic while on station in the Caribbean,
provides some glimmering of the kind of Gothic horror that was
once common in that awful place.

IN JANUARY 1822, New England maritime insurers were suffering huge losses from pirate attacks in the West Indies, and in
response to their repeated appeals for help, the Secretary of the
Navy agreed to establish a permanent station there to protect

the nation's trade. With an eye toward her symbolic value, he assigned the *Macedonian* to the new station, and sent orders to Isaac Hull, commandant of the Charlestown Navy Yard in Boston, to fit her out for a tropical cruise.

Frigates were invariably commanded by captains—the highest rank in the American Navy—but because the officer selected to command the *Macedonian*, Captain James Biddle, would also be in charge of subordinate vessels, he was allowed to adopt the honorific title of "Commodore" and to fly a special pendant. "Commodore" was a title, not a rank, and while it conferred no additional power or money, everyone wanted it.

Biddle was from Philadelphia, and was an energetic, well-connected, and supremely self-confident officer, with a reputation for the kind of diplomatic finesse expected to come in handy in the Caribbean, where virtually all the islands except Haiti were still in the hands of various European powers.

The *Macedonian* had been laid up in ordinary since her return from the Pacific the previous June, and Hull spent the months of February and March supervising her refitting and provisioning for her new assignment. The diligence of his supervision, and the quality of the work of the men under him, would later become the subject of bitter controversy between Hull and Biddle, and would eventually lead to a permanent break between the two captains.

On April 2, 1822, the *Macedonian* sailed from Boston in company with the four smaller vessels that made up the rest of her squadron, and headed south. In addition to the ships' crews, Biddle had two hundred marines with him so that he might chase down his quarry on land as well as sea. They left behind them a Boston winter that had been long and damp. On the day of departure, Biddle counted fifty-five men on the *Macedonian*'s sick list, most of them suffering from colds. As the frigate pushed into southern latitudes and encountered milder weather, he was pleased to note that the men recovered quickly, and by the time they reached Havana at the end of April, the sick list was down to twenty men, all of them convalescent.

Biddle planned only a brief stopover in Cuba. Havana was

notorious as the hemisphere's most pestilential port, and he was well aware that his arrival coincided with the start of the sickly season. He would remain only long enough to get the approval of the Spanish authorities for his campaign against the pirates—a simple formality, he believed—before returning as quickly as possible to the more benign environment of the open sea.

While the ship remained in port, the captain took steps to protect his men from the invidious influences of the sickness and fevers—particularly yellow fever—that were known to infest Havana. He insisted that the *Macedonian* be kept spotless, and gave orders that the spar and gun decks be scrubbed down daily, and the berth deck almost as often. It was generally believed that stagnant air and congestion encouraged the spread of disease, and to improve air circulation several staterooms and bulkheads were removed from the berth deck, and half the crew was rebilleted to the gun deck, in a move designed to relieve overcrowding. An awning was spread over the forecastle to protect the men, as far as practicable, from both the sun and the waters of the harbor, both of which were believed to be highly impure. To avoid fatigue, work was limited and the men were excused from standing watch at night.

Despite every attempt to make living conditions as comfortable as possible, the fierce heat and humidity of the tropics took its toll. The men's energy levels diminished, as did their appetites. Even the ship herself suffered. The sun beat down with such ferocity that the pitch soon melted out of the seams between her planking, and the oakum wedged into the gaps dried up and fell away. The men were set to work recaulking, but in the intense heat and humidity, the job went slowly. Adding to the discomfort was the stink from the bilge. It was bad enough in normal times, and it became increasingly noisome under the intense Cuban sun.

Biddle himself appeared impervious to the heat—he was, after all, one of *the* Biddles of Philadelphia—and set out briskly each morning for the city in full-dress uniform complete with a stout wool jacket. In his dealings with the Cuban authorities, he soon discovered to his dismay that the Spanish colonial government did not share his own nation's concern with pirates. To his immense irritation, they denied him the right to land marines in his pursuit of them, for fear that such an act would compromise Spanish sovereignty. Biddle argued that without permission to put his marines on shore, his entire operation was in jeopardy, but the captain general of Cuba was unmoved. Biddle, who had a profound belief in his own diplomatic skills, postponed his departure date in hopes of changing the Spaniards' minds. The *Macedonian*, days after her scheduled departure date, remained at anchor.

Biddle continued to worry about air circulation. In an effort to increase the amount of fresh air below decks, he ordered the gun ports opened and the ship warped with kedging anchors until it lay broadside to the wind. He ordered wind sails erected over the hatches. For all his efforts, the hold grew so warm the men could not enter it, even at night, and the air arising from it became unfit to breathe. To flush out the stinking bilge, Biddle flooded the hold with fresh water brought out from shore, and then pumped the vile-smelling residue into the harbor.

Biddle's principal fear concerned the possibility of yellow fever, or "yellow jack," as the sailors called it. He knew the horrors of the disease at first hand. It had decimated his native Philadelphia on several occasions during his childhood, wreaking havoc and forcing thousands to flee the city.

Health officials had no idea what brought on yellow fever, and could only guess at its possible causes. Biddle's orders for improved hygiene in the *Macedonian* represented the most advanced medical recommendations for dealing with the silent killer, but all his efforts to protect the ship from disease were bound to prove futile, since yellow fever is propagated neither by filth nor fetid air, but by the female of the *Aedes aegypti* mosquito, which passes the virus on from one human to another. The people in the *Macedonian* were relatively safe as long as they remained covered and on board the ship, which was anchored far enough from shore to escape all but the most ambitious and far-ranging of the *Aedes aegypti* females. The greatest danger arose when the men left the ship and came on shore. Ironically, it was Biddle, with his daily trips to the colonial office, who was exposing himself to greater risk than his men.

On May 8, a little more than a week after their arrival in Havana, an ordinary seamen who had been sent into town a day or so earlier complained of headache and back pains. The following day he was down with a fever, alternating with chills. Dr. Cadle, the ship's surgeon, noted his condition but did not diagnose it as yellow fever, perhaps because not all symptoms were present. Three days later, the sailor was dead.

"Died of the fever," the doctor's report stated matter-of-factly. It was a common enough diagnosis of the day, not in itself alarming. Biddle asked the doctor if he thought the cause of death might be yellow fever, but on receiving a noncommittal answer, gave orders for the burial and turned his mind to other matters.

The Spanish authorities remained adamant in their refusal to cooperate with his proposed campaign against the pirates, and Biddle was eventually forced to to shelve his land-or-sea strategy and try a different tack. If he could not stop the pirates, he could at least establish a means of guarding American ships from their depredations. He would set up a permanent convoy system covering the entire West Indies. It was a simple but effective plan. He laid out a roughly circular route covering the entire rim of the Caribbean, starting and ending at Havana, and touching at most of the important ports. Each armed vessel in his squadron was to sail from point to point on a regular schedule, moving in a clockwise direction from Havana to Key West, along the Bahamas to Puerto Rico, through the Mona Passage by Hispaniola (Haiti), south to Venezuela on the South American landmass, westward to Panama, up along the Mexican coast, east to New Orleans, and thence back to Havana. With the plan in operation, any American merchant captain wishing protection from pirates had only to wait in one of the ports along the circuit for a few days until one of Biddle's vessels arrived, at which point he could join the convoy to the next port he wished to visit along the route. It was a good scheme, but setting it up involved preparing separate schedules for each ship and coordinating the comings and goings from each port along the route, details that once again forced Biddle to postpone his departure.

On May 19, another seaman died.

Everyone dealt as best they could with the heat and the bad smells and the repeated sailing cancelations, and tried to make the time pass as agreeably as possible. On May 23, by which time the frigate had been anchored in the harbor for almost a month, a party of sprightly young women from the American colony in Havana visited the *Macedonian*. The youngest, aged about sixteen and described as "a beautiful girl, full of health and spirit," was escorted by Marine Lieutenant James Clements. Three days later the lieutenant was dead of the fever, and two days after that, so was the girl.

On May 28, exactly a month after their arrival, a marine private died, and by now there was no mistaking the nature of the disease. It was yellow fever, without question. On the morning of his death, the patient's face and eyes clearly exhibited the bilious yellow caste that gave the disease its English name, and during his last agonies he spat up mouthfuls of dark blood and the telltale black "coffee grounds" sputum that gave the disease its Spanish name: *vómito negro*.

Thoroughly alarmed, Captain Biddle ordered his squadron to sea as soon as possible, but it was June before they were finally able to get away from Havana, by which time Biddle had lost a total of seven men. More ominous was the fact that he now had fifty-one on the sick list, and he knew that not all would survive. The passage to Port-au-Prince was uneventful, and some of the sick men did in fact seem to improve, but Haiti turned out to be as fever-ridden as Cuba, and the number of sick began to rise again. Biddle departed as soon as possible, and the *Macedonian* continued its halting way around the convoy circuit, stopping at each port just long enough to arrange for agents and warehousing, and moving on as quickly as possible.

It was at this point that Captain Biddle became convinced that the malignancy attacking the *Macedonian* arose not from their tropical surroundings, but from the very ship he commanded—that the foul stink emanating from the bilge was generating "miasmic effluvias" that in some mysterious manner brought on the deadly yellow jack that was killing his men. He ordered sulphur fires set in the hold, in an attempt to fumigate the apparently poisonous stench.

By July, after they had completed their full circuit and returned to Havana, a total of thirty men were dead, and more were falling ill each day. By now there was no question that they were dealing with a particularly virulent strain of yellow fever. Biddle had refined his theory and was convinced that the harrowing conditions on board his flagship could all be blamed on the sloppy and insanitary work of the Charlestown Navy Yard, which, he was sure, had never properly broken out the hold of the *Macedonian* and cleaned the ship on her return from the Pacific. Oppressed by the dreadful scene about him, and livid at the imagined iniquities of Isaac Hull and his people in Boston, Biddle began collecting evidence for a court of inquiry.

One of the ship's midshipmen, a Mr. Turner, had spent the previous winter at the navy yard, and described to the captain how he had burned some of the firewood that the *Macedonian* had brought back from the Pacific and found the smell so offensive he was forced to leave the room. Thomas Pewmont, a seaman who had also worked at the navy yard, testified that on the frigate's return from the Pacific, her hold contained several casks of salt provisions in a rotten and putrid condition, and that despite the dreadful stench, the hold was not pumped out for upward of two months. Another midshipman, named Gerry, described the black mud and filth that coated the iron ingots of ballast in the newly returned *Macedonian*, and stated that workmen removed two cartloads of the evil-smelling ooze but neglected to take up the remainder.

The evidence of these three witnesses convinced Biddle of Isaac Hull's guilt, and he angrily—and publicly—informed the crew of his conviction that their misery and horror was directly attributable to slovenly work practices at Boston.

By July 15, Dr. Cadle, the ship's surgeon, was so sick he could no longer continue his duties, and five days later he too was dead. His assistant, Dr. Chase, fell ill as well, and Biddle was forced to bring in a local Havana physician to minister to the sick.

The captain was growing increasingly anxious to leave Havana, and was on the verge of giving the word to depart when secret orders arrived from Washington that made it impossible to get away. A letter to Biddle from Secretary of State John Quincy Adams described a crisis in Cuban-American relations that called for immediate attention. Spain was growing increasingly weaker internationally, and Washington was now worried that it might be persuaded to transfer its Cuban colony to France or Britain. The likely loser in such a transfer would be the United States. Adams wanted Biddle to visit several powerful plantation owners named in the letter who were eager to explore the possibility of bringing Cuba into the Union as a full-fledged state. Biddle had no choice but to postpone his departure and become a player in the great game of international intrigue. Negotiations were necessarily complex and secret, and therefore time-consuming, and meanwhile the *Macedonian* remained in Havana. The delay caused by Adams's letter cost the lives of at least another thirty men.

By July 24, Biddle felt he could no longer put off his departure, regardless of diplomatic imperatives. By now the *Macedonian* was little more than a floating charnelhouse. The death toll stood at forty-nine men, with eighty-four more on the sick list. If he were to delay any further, he might not have enough men left to put to sea. In desperation, he gave the orders to head for home. The voyage north must have been a scene out of Coleridge's *Rime of the Ancient Mariner*:

> *I looked upon the rotting sea,*
> *And drew my eyes away;*
> *I looked upon the rotting deck,*
> *And there the dead men lay.*

With no doctor on board, the unskilled seamen were administering calomel and jalap to their stricken messmates, and the sufferers were crawling about the decks with swollen faces and painful extremities. Every new appearance of the black vomit brought fresh despair. The stricken waited for death and release from their agony, while those still healthy tried to cope with a secret enemy that responded neither to purgatives nor prayers.

With the sick and dying everywhere about, the crew were allowed to sleep where they chose, and most chose to remove themselves as far from the others as possible. Some tried to sleep in the chains, some high overhead in the tops, some in the boats, and some on the booms.

In the ten days it took to reach the mouth of the Chesapeake another twenty-seven died, and a weary and distraught Captain Biddle, forced over and over again to recite the service for the dead, sometimes as often as two and three times a day, grew more and more depressed, his heart hardening by degrees against Isaac Hull and the Charlestown Navy Yard.

On August 4 the *Macedonian* crept into Hampton Roads, and Biddle transferred the fever-stricken to quarantine at nearby Craney Island, where they would either recover or die. In the end, a total of 101 men from the *Macedonian* died of the yellow jack that summer, a full third of her crew, and twice as many as the number of English sailors killed in the battle with Decatur.

IN DECEMBER, a court of inquiry sitting in Boston concluded that Isaac Hull and his staff had in every circumstance acted properly relative to the refitting of the *Macedonian*, and that the Charlestown Navy Yard should be held entirely free from blame for the unfortunate suffering and loss of life attendant to the late, tragic cruise of that ship to the Caribbean.

RIO AND ROT

~~~~~~~~~~~~~~~~~~~~~~

SILENTLY BUT RELENTLESSLY, AND DESPITE THE CONTINUOUS efforts of worried officials to stave off the inevitable, the *Macedonian* was falling apart. Only twelve years after her launching at Woolwich, her great timbers were metastasizing into white powdery dry rot, her knees were splitting, and her wales were pulling loose from their settings.

Even more insidious than the dry rot was the wet. Like all wooden ships, she was never truly watertight, and seawater seeped in through the sides and collected in dank pools amidships, near the step of the mainmast. In her humid, unventilated confines, putrid, corroding matter formed and spread throughout the ship, often invisibly, spreading along the grain of the wood. Rot ensued because "the sap juices of timber possess certain asescent, fermantative qualities destructive to their nature and tendency," according to one authority of the day. Whatever it was, it was taking a secret but significant toll.

Wooden ships were routinely subjected to fearsome natural forces—the wrenching effects of wind and wave, the shock of bombardment, prolonged periods of exposure and extremes of temperature, the ravages of sea worms—and their eventual demise was inevitable, but in the case of the *Macedonian*, that demise was taking place sooner than expected.

In part, her premature infirmity could be blamed on her Danzig Oak construction, but in large measure she was falling apart simply due to her history. She still showed scars on her hull from the battering of 24-pounder cannonballs she received in her battle with the *United States*, and the hasty manner in which she had been refitted after her capture undoubtedly contributed to her condition. The frightful storm she weathered off Bermuda in 1818 had loosened treenails, weakened joints, and exhausted the elasticity of her timbers, and her recent three-year cruise in the Pacific without an overhaul or any serious attempt at maintenance was still another contributing factor.

Soon after the *Macedonian*'s return from Havana with her gruesome cargo of yellow fever victims, the commandant of Gosport Navy Yard ordered a routine structural inspection. In due course the yard's constructor—the American equivalent of the English master shipwright—submitted a report indicating only that she was "in need of some repairs," a vague assessment that explained nothing, but provided James Biddle with all the excuse he needed to abandon his flagship and transfer his commodore's pendant to the *Congress* before returning to the Caribbean.

His officers and men followed their captain out of the *Macedonian*, and she was placed in ordinary, awaiting further orders. Her sails were unbent, her yards sent down, her topmasts and topgallant spars housed and the gun ports sealed. In an effort to discourage further rotting of timbers below decks, she was rigged with windsails over the hatchways to help maintain the circulation of air in the lower parts of the hold. The dreadful smell from the bilge subsided with the return of cooler weather, but it was impossible to thoroughly dry out the hold, so the stink of mold and wet rot lingered. Her crew, reduced to a carpenter's mate, four able seamen, and nine ordinary seamen, lived on board, carrying out routine maintenance and pumping out the bilge when necessary.

A YEAR LATER she was still in ordinary. In the Secretary of the Navy's annual report to the President, she was again briefly mentioned as requiring "some repairs," the nature of which remained unspecified. By 1824, her condition had grown more serious, and the Secretary now warned that she required "extensive repairs, which it is recommended to make during the next year." But it would not be for another year after that, not until 1826, that even minimal efforts were made to put the *Macedonian* back into fighting trim, and then only because Washington decided she was the best ship to represent the United States in the latest Latin American crisis.

The newly independent nations of Brazil and Buenos Aires had gone to war over Uruguay, and once again American merchants operating in the region found themselves caught in the middle, victimized by paper blockades and piratical privateers. The navy decided to establish still another permanent overseas station—the Brazil Squadron—and because the Royal Navy was already on station guarding the interests of British interests, the Americans felt constrained to once again call upon the *Macedonian* to serve as their flagship.

In the two years prior to her departure for Rio, the total money spent on the *Macedonian*'s maintenance and upkeep amounted to only $78,187.28. After subtracting for provisioning, new sails, and the replacement of normally expendable materials such as rigging and hawsers, the total came to less than $6,000, and amounted to little more than a lick and a promise.

ONCE AGAIN THE Secretary selected James Biddle to command the new squadron, knowing that his diplomatic skills were likely to prove essential, but Biddle was understandably loathe to return to a ship that still held so many anguished memories for him. To overcome his reluctance, the Secretary specifically promised in writing that the commodore would be allowed to carry specie in the war zone, at a suitable commission for himself. Biddle's command would include two smaller vessels, the 22-gun *Cyane*—another prize taken from the British in the War of 1812—and the brig *Boston*. He set sail from Norfolk in June 1826 and arrived in Rio two months later, on August 11.

The two years the *Macedonian* spent in the South Atlantic off the coast of South America were virtually a repeat of her previous cruise in the Pacific, except that Biddle's fees for carrying naval freight were something of a disappointment. John Downes held a monopoly during his tour of duty, and as a result had amassed a fortune because he could charge merchants pretty much whatever he wanted to. But Biddle had to contend with a large Royal

Navy squadron already on hand, and the additional competition cut heavily into profit margins. Not only did he have a smaller client list than Downes, but the 5–6 percent carrying fees that Downes could command were reduced to 2.5 percent and less.

By August 1828, Brazil and Buenos Aires had grown tired with their war and were ready to call it quits, and with the Treaty of Rio, peace returned. Biddle hurried home with the news, but the pleasure of his return was leavened by a grim irony that echoed his previous homecoming in the *Macedonian*. Dr. Benjamin Tichnor, the frigate's surgeon, reported that ten crewmen were down with smallpox. Resignedly, Biddle wrote the Secretary of the Navy, "As the good people of Norfolk, like the people of some other sickly places, are timid upon the subject of imported-diseases, I shall be careful to let them know that we have the small-pox aboard; and unless they consent to it, I will not discharge any of our men there."

Sicker still was the *Macedonian*. There was rot in her floors and futtucks, shrinkage in her seams, and her pumps were working around the clock.

She was very, very tired.

DEATH AND RESURRECTION

W HEN THE *MACEDONIAN* LIMPED INTO GOSPORT ON OCTOber 30, 1828, she was not just sick but terminally ill. Her two years in the South Atlantic had taken a heavy toll. A routine survey carried out soon after her return provided a grim litany of rotted timbers, weakened spars, and general decay. The navy yard constructor's inspection of her scantlings told the basic story—she needed "a thorough and extensive repair" before she could be sent back to sea.

In Washington, Captain John Rodgers, president of the Board of Naval Commissioners, read through the report in his office in the Navy Department. Rodgers was a bluff, stiff-necked veteran famous for his passionate defense of the navy and his equally passionate determination to get what he wanted. What he wanted now was to save the *Macedonian* and keep her on the navy list. It turned out to be a monumental job that took him nine years to accomplish, and before she again cleared the Virginia capes she would undergo a sea-change, becoming a stronger and more important vessel than ever.

RODGERS'S INTEREST IN the *Macedonian* was more than sentimental. He was an important figure on the Washington scene, and his political power base was an informal but influential clique known as the "Decatur party," a group that sought to maintain the navy's prestige and political strength by perpetuating the memory of its most popular hero. The group was led by Decatur's fiery widow, Susan, but it was Rodgers who recognized, perhaps more clearly than anyone else, the central role

the *Macedonian* played in the group's efforts. The frigate was
Decatur's most glamorous memorial, and Rodgers made sure
she was kept in the public eye as much as possible, and assigned
to prominent missions—always as flagship—to remind Americans, and their congressmen, of the navy's significant contribution to the national weal.

The U.S. Navy had grown mightily since the War of 1812.
Rodgers had seen the American fleet quintuple in size, and he
could take personal credit for much of this growth. But by the
autumn of 1828 his star was no longer in the ascendent, and
history and the pressure of events were conspiring against him
and his beloved navy.

On the first Tuesday in November, just a week after the *Macedonian*'s return from Brazil, American voters went to the polls
and elected a new President, General Andrew Jackson of Ten-
nessee. Jackson was an army man, the hero of the Battle of New
Orleans, and had no ties, political or sentimental, to the navy.
Significantly, he was also the first President from a non-salt-
water state. Jackson and the people who elected him saw America's future across the plains and mountains, rather than over
the seas, and John Rodgers, who could read the new political
signals as well as anybody, recognized that his efforts to promote
the interests of the navy would face new difficulties in light of
the dramatic shift in public sentiment. He would need all the
help he could get, which meant, among other things, keeping
the *Macedonian* on the active list, a goal which he was beginning
to think was not going to be easy.

Rodgers needed a more detailed report on the condition of
the ship, and called for a full-scale survey to find out what it
would take to save her. He ordered her "opened up," which
was the navy's equivalent of exploratory surgery, and because
Gosport had no dry dock, that meant she had to be hove down,
landed, and careened over on her side, so that the inspectors
could more accurately judge her condition.

The chief constructor at Gosport, a man named Francis Grice,
was reluctant to haul down vessels as large as the *Macedonian*,

and with good reason. The process placed enormous strain on the hull and its timbers, often causing internal damage that might not become apparent until it was too late to make repairs. But on this occasion Grice was not overly concerned. He already knew there was little to save, and was confident that the new survey would simply confirm his previous assessment.

In preparation for the survey, everything that was not physically attached to the *Macedonian* was taken out of her—every gun, every hogshead, every ingot of ballast—and her yards, topmasts, and topgallant masts sent down. On February 11, 1829, she was towed to shore on the high tide and left stranded on dry sand as the tide receded. There she rested, like a huge beached whale, a naked and improbable-looking giant with every inch of her exposed to view for the first time in years. A penumbra of shrieking gulls gathered overhead, searching for breakfast on her exposed underside.

A team of laborers clambered onto her upper deck, and after attaching holdfasts to her chains and stubby masts, sent down lines to a group of teamsters standing below with yoked oxen. With shouts and prodding, the beasts were made to pull mightily on the lines, and slowly and laboriously they rolled the huge vessel over on her side, while her great timbers popped and crackled and groaned in protest.

Mr. Grice and his men began their survey by examining her entire bottom for loss of coppering, incipient rot, or other damage. Then they climbed inside to inspect at close range her bulkheads, deck beams, knees, and other parts normally inaccessible or difficult to reach. The men pried up ceiling planks to examine the timbers underneath. They drilled holes into suspicious corners to search for hidden decay. Rapidly but methodically, with little wasted motion, they made their way from one end of the ship to the other.

The smell of corruption was everywhere. Even before Grice completed his inspection, he knew what his report would find. The *Macedonian* was dying before her time, the result of hard use and inferior building materials gone bad. "Stout English oak," scoffed the Americans, pointing to the telltale signs of decay, and unaware that the stuff of which she was made came not from Sussex or Hampshire but the forests of Central Europe.

Before the next tide returned, the men packed up their tools and left the ship before the incoming seas lifted her off and floated her out to her moorings, and Mr. Grice retired to his office to write up his findings. His report to the Board was uniformly glum in almost every detail. All of the *Macedonian*'s boats, water casks, rigging, appurtenances, and tackle were condemned. The entire hull was suffering from advanced decay, from her decking down through her timbers, strakes, and wales, even to the keel itself. Of all the tons of wood that made up the frigate, the only salvageable timbers were the floors and lower futtucks, which is to say, the short transverse timbers that fitted directly across the keel and formed the lowest sections of the great framing ribs.

Back in his office, John Rodgers read Grice's report slowly and carefully. He was neither surprised nor particularly distressed by its import. It was inevitable that wooden ships would deteriorate. The *Macedonian* was indeed in parlous shape, but that did not mean that her usefulness to the Decatur party, and to the navy, was lost. If her floors and lower futtucks could be salvaged, it would not be too difficult a task to make up the rest of the framing from stock timbers and rebuild the ship around those few of her original parts that remained.

Rodgers discussed the matter with Samuel Humphreys, the chief constructor of the navy, who pointed out that the floors and lower futtucks were of particular significance in the design and construction of a ship. They were the timbers that determined the turn of the bilge, and therefore governed the overall lines of the frigate herself. By retaining these elements, the navy could ensure that the repaired *Macedonian* would precisely duplicate the shape of the original.

Humphreys immediately set about drawing up detailed plans that would incorporate the salvageable old timbers. His object was not to improve upon the *Macedonian* but to replicate her, and his draft deliberately aped the British original in virtually every detail. His drawing of the forward half of the ship was as close to the original as he could make it, and the stern differed only in the curving of the aft transom, which increased the overall length of the ship slightly—by about six feet nine inches—and required him to fractionally reposition two of the masts and rework the angle of the stern post. These changes would allow greater flexibility for the ship's aft cannon, and give the ship additional speed when sailing before the wind, while only marginally altering the *Macedonian*'s lines. Only someone intimately familiar with the Woolwich original was likely to notice any difference. To the casual observer, she would look exactly as before.

A MAJOR RECONSTRUCTION such as the one contemplated for the *Macedonian* was bound to be expensive, but Rodgers and the other commissioners were not overly concerned. The money would come out of funds appropriated by Congress under the headings of Repairs of Vessels and Wear and Tear of Vessels in Commission. Since all such funds had already been allocated for the year 1829, no work on the *Macedonian* could begin for at least another year. In the meantime, Rodgers pigeon-holed Samuel Humphreys's plans for the ship and turned his attention to his new superior, the Honorable John Branch of North Carolina, Andrew Jackson's new Secretary of the Navy.

JOHN BRANCH WAS a party hack, who knew virtually nothing about the navy. He was selected for a cabinet position primarily because he and his wife gave good dinner parties, which it was hoped would promote the social prestige of Jackson's new Democratic Party. His almost total ignorance of naval matters did not deter Branch's enthusiasm for his new job. He was convinced he knew exactly what was wrong with the service, and how to fix it. It was his opinion that the navy was a sinkhole of cronyism and corruption, and he planned to throw out the money changers and bring the department's huge $3,500,000 annual budget to heal. To demonstrate his resolve he announced a halt to any further growth in the size of the fleet, and ordered work suspended on those new vessels already on the stocks.

Rodgers watched the activities of the Secretary of the Navy with interest. As far as he could see, John Branch's economy moves did not affect his plans for the *Macedonian*, which did not involve new construction, but simply rebuilding. With the arrival of the new year, Rodgers judged it was time to begin the work on her, and gave the order to start selecting the wooden timbers for the *Macedonian*'s frame. Virtually all the timbers for the *Macedonian* were to be of live oak—an extremely durable, fine-grained wood native to the southern states. The only parts of the frame that would not be of live oak were those elements that were to come out of the old ship, namely, the floors and lower futtucks, and the keel, which was by specification built of white oak. The individual pieces of live oak were already on hand at Gosport, standing in immense piles of sided timber that had been cut years previously, then slowly cured and roughly shaped to their final dimensions before being placed in protective sheds.

But if John Rodgers was not concerned about the Secretary of the Navy, he was acutely aware of a potential problem at the Gosport Navy Yard which related directly to the *Macedonian*, and which demanded caution. Unfortunately, in his anxiety to sidestep potential trouble, he committed a colossal mistake that came close to scuttling the rebuilding project before it began.

THE NAME OF the problem was Captain James Barron, commandant of the Gosport Navy Yard. By a bizarre accident of fate, Barron, the officer with the most direct supervisory responsibility over the *Macedonian*, was the one man in the entire world who hated the ship with a passion and wished her ill. If it had been in his power, he would have ordered the *Macedonian* broken up forthwith, her every trace destroyed, her memory wiped from the national conscience. James Barron despised her because she was Stephen Decatur's prize, and it was James Barron who had shot and killed Decatur on the Bladensburg dueling grounds. That doleful encounter had changed Barron's life, very much for the worse. Decatur's widow had extracted a pledge from President Monroe that Barron would never again be offered the command of a ship, and in the years following the duel he had become a pariah, shunned by his fellow officers and shuttled from one desk to another. The navy had no way of dismissing him from the service, since dueling was not specifically a crime, so in spite of his notoriety he remained on active duty, a sullen, embittered old man, deliberately kept from the centers of power.

Now, like a morose figure out of some Hawthorne novel, Barron found himself custodian of his enemy's most sacred totem. The *Macedonian*, swinging at anchor only yards offshore, haunted his every working hour. Although he was restrained by regulations and his own common sense from physically sabotaging the ship, there was no question of his antipathy toward her, or his determination, if given the chance, to destroy her.

In anticipation of Barron's hostility, Rodgers deliberately routed his orders for rebuilding the *Macedonian* outside of normal channels. Ordinarily such orders were forwarded directly to the commandant of the navy yard, but because Rodgers was anxious to keep Barron out of the picture as long as possible, he sent them across the hall to his own chief constructor in Washington, Samuel Humphreys, who then relayed them to his counterpart at Gosport, Francis Grice, thus bypassing the yard commandant. It was a clumsy maneuver, not least because it failed to take into account Mr. Grice's likely reaction. As a veteran government employee mindful of the realities of his job, Grice recognized that his loyalty had to lie with his immediate superior, and so he went directly to Barron and showed him the Board's orders. The commandant instantly grasped the reason for the unorthodox routing, and fired off an angry note to John Rodgers reflecting his fury.

Sir: I herewith enclose your requisition presented by Mr. Grice for the keel pieces of the *Macedonian* for my approval. Will you be pleased to inform me upon this subject?

Rodgers was momentarily embarrassed, but that was hardly the worst of it. What mattered was that Barron was now alerted to the Board's timetable, and could be expected to create problems at every turn.

Barely a month after the Board's abortive attempt to bypass Barron, Secretary Branch, in an unrelated move, made a routine visit to the Gosport yard. As a result of his order to suspend the construction of all new warships, navy yards up and down the coast had dismissed their building crews and erected wooden housing over any unfinished vessels still on the stocks. The purpose of the Secretary's visit was to see at first hand how his mandate was being carried out, and to learn whether the wooden housings were sufficient to keep the unfinished vessels free of rot so that they might remain securely on the stocks until some later time when it was decided to complete them. James Barron was able to assure the Secretary that the two vessels under housing at Gosport were in a state of excellent preservation.

During the course of Branch's brief stay at Gosport, the Secretary and the commandant found reason to discuss a wide range of subjects, including staffing, budgetary matters, and such future projects as the planned construction of a drydock at Gosport, and in the process they discovered a natural affinity. Both men were outsiders, working within the confines of a hostile navy establishment, each frustrated in his own way by what he saw as the high-handed maneuverings of the Board of Naval Commissioners. A level of trust grew up between the two, and when their talks touched on the proposed rebuilding of the *Macedonian*, it became quickly apparent to Barron that the Secretary, for all his zealous desire to cut budgets, had little understanding of the navy's broad interpretation of the word "rebuilding" and was assuming that because the money for the *Macedonian* was to come out of a fund for repairs, the work involved was in the nature of a patching up, when in fact it was going to be much closer to the kind of new construction that John Branch had forbidden.

Barron decided to enlighten the Secretary. It so happened

that there was at that time a vessel on the stocks at Gosport that provided a dramatic example of just how far the navy was prepared to go in stretching the meaning of "rebuilding." The sloop-of-war *John Adams*, originally launched in 1799, was in the final stages of being rebuilt, and was scheduled to be relaunched in a matter of weeks. Barron took the Secretary through the ship in detail, and showed him the manifests that listed all the materials used in her construction, which proved the *John Adams* had been built new from the keel upward.

Barron made a further point of informing Branch that in the case of the *Macedonian*, which was about to be rebuilt, the original floors and lower futtucks, which the Board planned to retain, amounted to perhaps 5 percent of her total materials.

John Branch was livid. The revelation came as a shock and simultaneously as proof of John Rodgers's perfidy. Here were the Secretary's darkest suspicions made manifest, incontestable proof of reckless fiscal knavery on the part of the Board. He returned to Washington in a towering rage, and ordered an immediate and complete halt to all work on both the *John Adams* and the *Macedonian*. He demanded to know by what feat of fiscal chicanery the Board, acting on its own, and directly in opposition to the expressed wishes of the office of the Secretary of the Navy, had authorized the construction of two brand new vessels, in the face of his explicit policy against any new construction.

Rodgers vehemently denied any wrongdoing, pointing out that the original plans for rebuilding the *John Adams* called for the replacement of only 40 percent of her materials, and that it was not until workmen opened her up and exposed rampant rot throughout her timbers that the decision was made to increase the new materials in her. As to the *Macedonian*, he protested that the navy "had always considered repairing and rebuilding synonymous." Branch replied loftily that he would leave it to the President of the United States to answer that question, and sent a request to the White House for guidance.

THE AMERICAN NAVY'S use of the word "rebuilding" to describe what was on occasion a wholesale recreation was a tradition imported wholesale from the Royal Navy. Doubtless, the somewhat liberal interpretation of the word began centuries earlier as a bookkeeping convenience, but in time it came to serve important symbolic and sentimental purposes as well. By identifying a construction project as "rebuilding," there was a clear inference that when the work was completed, the resulting ship would still be the original vessel, with her history, spirit, and provenance intact.

Navies, for good and sufficient reasons, will go to great lengths to maintain their most cherished traditions, and it was useful for a great ship, once she had passed the point of patching up or simple repair, to be reconstituted in such a way as to retain her original identity, so that a sense of continuity could be seen to connect the earlier version to the "rebuilt" version. Nelson's last flagship, HMS *Victory*, still in commission today on the south coast of England at Portsmouth, has been redesigned several times over the centuries, and in all likelihood contains not a stick of her original 1756 oak. Yet she is universally recognized as the original vessel because the Royal Navy has gone to great lengths to support such a claim.

John Rodgers was not interested in building a new ship, a copy of Decatur's prize. He was determined that the *Macedonian* from Samuel Humphrey's drawings would carry within her all the pride and glory of the *Macedonian* slowly crumbling to pieces at Gosport Navy Yard.

WHILE THE BOARD waited for Andrew Jackson to decide the meaning of "rebuilding," James Barron launched still another offensive against the detested *Macedonian*. On September 28, 1830, he forwarded a closely worded, detailed three-page estimate, prepared and signed by Francis Grice, covering the estimated costs to repair the *Macedonian*.

> . . . Your letter of this day [directing] an estimate of the cost of repairing the U. States Frigate *Macedonian*, 'conformably with the survey held on her the 11th of February 1829,' is

received, in answer to which I would remark, that the survey alluded to virtually amounts to a condemnation. . . . The whole of the Ship with the exception of the lower Futtucks and floors are in a state of decay. Should this Ship undergo a repair, *it would be bad policy to let those timbers remain, as they are only of White Oak, which would not remain durable as long as the other parts of the frame, which would be of Live Oak.* I would, therefore, estimate her cost at One hundred and twenty five thousand dollars—that is, for the hull, complete for sea. [italics in the original]

Grice's new estimate threw Rodgers's carefully formulated plans into disarray. Without her original floors and futtucks, every cubic foot of timber in the refurbished *Macedonian* would be new, and no matter what Andrew Jackson finally decreed the meaning of "rebuilding" to be, there was now no way that the work on the *Macedonian* could be charged to repairs.

IN NOVEMBER, ANDREW Jackson finally sent down his decision. He agreed with Branch that "rebuilding" was not the same as "repair," but he did not go so far as to support the Secretary's claim that the navy's traditional interpretation of "rebuilding" was tantamount to "new construction." In short, the President decided it was all right to complete and launch the *John Adams*, but the *Macedonian* could only be rebuilt on the specific authorization of Congress.

John Rodgers's instinct was to protest. He was not used to being told how to run the navy, even when the President of the United States was doing the telling. His fellow commissioners persuaded him to bow to the inevitable, and in due course, when the Board submitted estimates for the coming year to the Secretary of the Navy, they included a line item to rebuild the *Macedonian*. But Branch was not going to make things easy for his Board. He deliberately dropped the item from the budget which he then submitted to Congress for 1831. As far as the Secretary of the Navy was concerned, the *Macedonian* was a dead issue.

* * *

BUT STILL THE feeble, rotting ship survived. On February 21, 1831, Barron warned the commissioners of "recent indications of great weakness in the *Macedonian*," adding dryly, "she cannot long be kept afloat without an expense much beyond any object that I am aware of." Was Barron exaggerating her decrepitude? A penciled note from Rodgers in the margin of the letter assured his fellow commissioners, "I had this carpenters report." In other words, Barron was reporting the truth.

By early spring, the *Macedonian*'s hull was so porous that the tide ebbed and flowed in and out of her bilge. On April 6, 1831, Barron ordered her dragged out of the water and into the mudflats at the edge of the dockyards, there to rest, grotesquely canted to one side, a useless and ugly hulk. The strain of hauling her into the mud undoubtedly exacerbated her inherent weakness. A letter to John Rodgers confirmed his action and suggested what Barron saw as the logical next step.

> Sir: The United States Ship *Macedonian* has been hauled up on the bank, and is now in a Situation favourable for cutting up. The advantages of the season induce me to enquire if that operation shall now commence?

Of all the surviving letters Barron wrote to the Board concerning the *Macedonian*, this is the most telling. Along with the open suggestion to destroy the frigate, it is the only letter in which he refers to the ship by her complete, formal title: the United States Ship *Macedonian*. It is as if he wants to give his message a tone of great seriousness, like a judge passing sentence or a priest performing last rites.

Commissioner Rodgers was not amused. In a firm hand he penciled across the bottom of Barron's letter, "No. It is not intended to cut her up until it becomes necessary to use her materials in the construction of another vessel." Rodgers was in a state of total frustration. For almost three years now, he had pushed for a rebuilt *Macedonian*, and had been checked at every step, either by Barron or Branch, sometimes by both. The chances for the frigate's survival were growing increasingly dim. And then finally, out of the blue, the fates took a hand.

John Branch, who was originally nominated to the cabinet on the strength of his ability to give good dinner parties, came a cropper in the spring of 1831. A scandal arose when Branch's snobbish wife and daughters refused to invite Peggy Eaton, the wife of the Secretary of War, to one of their parties. The imbroglio became known as "The Mrs. Eaton affair," and threatened to tear apart President Jackson's coalition. It was an irreparable gaffe, and the Secretary of the Navy was forced to resign.

Suddenly, John Rodgers's principal stumbling block was gone. He swiftly solved the rest of the equation by shipping James Barron off to the Philadelphia Navy Yard, and replacing him at Gosport with Lewis Warrington, an old comrade he could trust implicitly. Suddenly and almost miraculously, the future of the *Macedonian* was assured.

IT WAS NOT until July 1832 that Congress finally passed "an Act to finish the rebuilding of the frigate *Macedonian*." Levi Woodbury, Andrew Jackson's new and obliging Secretary of the Navy, noted in his annual report of 1832 that the rebuilding "has already commenced," but in fact it was not until February 28, 1833, that the new keel for the *Macedonian* was finally laid. After such a long wait, the actual construction proceeded rapidly, and by the end of the year Warrington could report that she "is all timbered, one streak of Gun deck clamps in and bolted, wale on, Gun deck beams ready to go on board, knees sided, Gun deck port sills in." He estimated she could be completed in four months.

But now that the *Macedonian* was all but finished, the commissioners discovered they had no idea what to do with her. Work was abruptly brought to a halt until someone could find an assignment commensurate with her revived status.

The Board found itself faced with still another quandary: how were they to deal with the fact that there were now at Gosport two distinctly different *Macedonian*s, a brand new one awaiting completion, and a seastained old hulk rotting away on the Virginia mudflats? The old hulk was still the "official" *Macedonian*, and would remain on the register until she was ordered broken up; but the newer one could not properly take her place until she was launched, and no one could predict when that might be. The continued presence of both versions at the same location threatened to become an embarrassment. Newspaper reporters might get wind of it, with unforeseen results. It was obvious that something had to be done—the navy could only have one *Macedonian*—but it was important to the spirit of the surviving ship, and to the memory of the fallen Decatur, that the Woolwich *Macedonian* and the Gosport *Macedonian* be seen to be, if not the same vessel, at least the same entity. The Board's original plan—the scheme to incorporate the floors and futtucks of the old ship into the new one—would have solved the problem, but without that easily understood bridging device, the task of establishing a seamless unity between the two ships became more complicated. Frozen in time, the two versions sat out the winter of 1833–34 like Jekyll and Hyde, one shining and fresh, the other scarred and rotten.

Finally, in the summer of 1834, it was decided to break up the Woolwich *Macedonian*, but no official order was ever to be issued to that effect. The only direct evidence that proves she was broken up are records of two packages dispatched from Warrington's Gosport office.

The first one, sent to the Navy Board on August 2, 1834, contained a piece of tar-daubed cloth. It was accompanied by a letter which clearly shows that by that date the entire ship—right down to her keel—had been carefully picked apart and examined, doubtless to study British shipbuilding practices.

> Sir, I forward for the examination of the Commissioners, a piece of coarse, dark coloured cloth (serge I believe) which was in the scarph of the stern and keel of the *Macedonian*. The scarph is perpendicular, and I presume the cloth to have been inserted to prevent leakage. The keel is of elm, as is also the garboard streak.

And here Warrington adds a detail that shows that Britain's shortage of oak had reached acute proportions by the time the Royal Navy built the *Macedonian* at Woolwich:

> The streak above it is of oak, and the rest of the bottom of yellow pine. Her floors appear to have been made of any curved timber, that might offer, and the deficiency to allow of their mortising in the keel, is supplied by chocks (two on each) treenailed on the underside. A single bolt of copper confines each floor, and generally about one third smaller than either of the bolts put in the floors of our ships. Her treenails are oak and pine.

Warrington's second parcel, sent a few months later, in February 1835, was considerably larger. It was addressed to his friend Captain James Biddle, the last captain of the old *Macedonian*, and enclosed a distinctive souvenir: a section of the frigate's planking scarred by one of Decatur's cannonballs in the long-ago battle off the Cape Verde Islands.

WHAT PARTS, IF any, of the old ship were incorporated into the new? There seems little question that a great deal of the metal from the Woolwich version found its way into the Gosport version. There was the copper sheeting used to line the magazine as well as to cover her bottom below the waterline; there was the tin sheeting used to line the bread room; there was wrought iron that could be transferred intact; there was lead and castings, kentledge and anchors, hammock hooks, belaying pins and stoves, and of course the figurehead. Artisans were able to patch up the weatherbeaten bust of Alexander the Great and transfer it to the newer ship. By the 1830s, figureheads and similar fanciful adornments were losing favor among designers, and there may have been some objections to retaining the bust, but Rodgers would have insisted on its incorporation.

In 1836, by which time the old Woolwich hulk had long since disappeared, the Navy Department finally came up with a mission worthy of the resurrected *Macedonian*'s august provenance. She would serve as flagship for an ambitious three-year scientific and exploratory cruise to the Pacific and South Seas. Since she would be expected to contend with ice-choked Antarctic seas during at least part of the expedition, structural bracing was added to her hull at an additional cost of $13,475 while she was still on the stocks, and then, sometime between October and the new year, she was quietly launched with a minimum of fuss. It was still another year before she emerged phoenixlike from the Chesapeake on October 11, 1837, with sparkling new sails bent to every yard, bound for New York.

She had been away from the sea for almost ten years. Much had changed, including the national flag. Two new stars, representing Arkansas and Michigan, now adorned the colors at her mizzenpeak, attesting to the robust growth of the country she served. She sailed sluggishly, due to the excess weight of Antarctic stiffening in her hull, but answered smoothly enough to her helm.

Was she the same ship as the one Biddle brought back from Rio a decade before? Certainly the men who designed and built her, and the commissioners who wangled and fought for her existence through years of compromise and haggling, believed so. She looked the same. The distinctive lines defined by Samuel Humphreys's offset tables coalesce almost precisely with those first set down by Sir William Rule, except for the minimal variation in the treatment of the stern. The navy never would have built her if she was merely to be a new ship. The navy wanted—desperately wanted—the same ship that Stephen Decatur took as prize on October 25, 1812. The *Macedonian* that made her way into the Chesapeake in 1837 was, as far as men could make her, that very ship. She was the same in size, in design, and in spirit, insofar as the guile and determination of John Rodgers and the Board of Naval Commissioners could make her.

UNITED STATES

~~~~~~~~~~~~

FRIGATE

~~~~~~~~~~~~

MACEDONIAN,

~~~~~~~~~~~~

36 guns

(Rebuilt)

A VETERAN RETURNS

~~~~~~~~~~~~~~~~~~~~~~~~~~~

A S IT HAPPENED, THE *MACEDONIAN* NEVER GOT TO LEAD THE American surveying and exploring expedition to the South Seas and Antarctica. The Panic of 1837 got in the way, and when the navy sought to trim the budget for the ambitious venture, the expedition leader, Commodore Thomas ap Catesby Jones, resigned in a huff. Eventually a whittled-down version of the expedition was cobbled together and given to Lieutenant Charles Wilkes, but the Board of Naval Commissioners was not about to turn over command of the *Macedonian* to a mere lieutenant, and she was instead assigned to Commodore William B. Shubrick as flagship of the West Indies Squadron, operating out of Pensacola.

Her cruise was uneventful—happily, there was no recurrence of the devastating yellow fever epidemic that had killed a third of her crew in 1823—and in August 1840 she was directed to proceed north with the rest of the squadron to avoid the hurricane season. Commodore Shubrick used the opportunity to make brief stops at various navy yards along the coast, including New York. It was while she was tied up at Brooklyn that a prosperous-looking gentleman in his early forties approached the *Macedonian* and asked leave to come on board.

The gentleman was Samuel Leech, who thirty years before, as a thirteen-year-old English youth living with his mother at Blenheim Palace, had been recruited into the *Macedonian* by her first captain, Lord William FitzRoy. Much had happened to him in the years since he slipped off the *Macedonian* in 1813 and lost himself in the crowds of New York, rather than be returned to the Royal Navy. He had served a spell in the American Navy, then come ashore, tried his hand at a number of jobs, got religion and joined the Methodist Church, and after carefully hoarding his wages for a number of years, saved up a few hundred dollars and gone into trade. He was now a respectable merchant in Wilbraham, Massachusetts, with a wife and three children, and during a business trip to New York, had learned of the arrival of the *Macedonian*.

The sailors on board watched idly as the stranger wandered about on deck, poking his head into corners and pausing now and then to get his bearings, until he found the spot where he remembered standing during the battle with the *United States*. Leech described the scene later in his memoirs:

> The sailors, on witnessing the care with which I examined every thing, and supposing me to be a landsman, eyed me rather closely. Seeing their curiosity, I said, "Shipmates, I have seen this vessel before to-day; probably before any of you ever did."

(A pretty safe assumption, since Leech had first seen the *Macedonian* on July 12, 1810, while she still stood in the Thames, before she ever reached the ocean.)

> The old tars gathered round me, eagerly listening to my tale of the battle, and they bore patiently, and with becoming gravity, the exhortation to lead a religious life, with which I closed my address.

Whether Samuel Leech saved any souls that day is problematical, but the little scene dramatizes how well the American naval architect, Samuel Humphreys, had mimicked the original *Macedonian*. Although Leech complains in his narrative of the many alterations he found in his old ship, it apparently never occurred to him that she might not be the same *Macedonian* in which he first went to sea.

ECHOES

~~~~~~~~~~~~~~~~~~~~~~~~

O N AUGUST 17, 1843, ON THE BEACH AT HONOLULU, A DESTI-
tute young American sailor found himself stranded half
a world away from home. His name was Herman Melville, and
he had recently undergone a series of adventures in the Pacific
that would in a few years' time become known around the world;
but at present, he simply wanted to get back to his native New
York.

Just offshore Melville could see the American frigate *United
States* lying at anchor, while on the beach, a recruiting officer
from the ship was looking for a few extra hands to help take
her eastward to South America and eventually around the Horn
to Boston. After two weeks of deliberation, Melville signed on
as an ordinary seaman.

Years later the young man would write a book about his cruise
in the venerable frigate. He called it *White-Jacket*, and in it he
described listening to the ship's band, a group of musicians
that still included several of the foreign-speaking bandsmen that
Captain John Carden had hired all those years before in Lisbon,
and which Decatur had taken out of the *Macedonian* and installed
in the *United States* after the battle between the two ships in
1812.

INCIDENT AT LITTLE BEREBEE

~~~~~~~~~~~~~~~~~~~~~~~~~~~~~~~~~~~~~

THE SLAVE COAST OF WEST AFRICA LIES BETWEEN THE SENEGAL River, just north of Cape Verde, and the Congo River, six degrees south of the equator. From this grim and pestilential shore, over a period of four centuries, twelve and a half million black men, women, and children were forcibly removed from their homelands and transported, often under conditions of sickening cruelty and brutality, to work and die in the fields and mines of the New World.

It is a flat, low-lying coast, 3,000 miles in length, with long, sandy beaches punctuated by poisonous swamps, through which meander the uncounted channels of small rivers that penetrate the country. There are few harbors, and ships must lie off the coast at a safe distance, to avoid the long rollers that perpetually sweep in from the sea and pound ceaselessly upon the shore.

Early on the morning of December 13, 1843, with the sun still hanging sullenly on the eastern horizon like some mordant Eye of God, the US frigate *Macedonian*, flagship of the newly created African Squadron, lay hove to in company with the sloops-of-war *Saratoga* and *Decatur* and the brig *Porpoise*, off a place on the Guinea coast called Little Berebee. In the lee of the American warships a number of smaller vessels milled about—launches, cutters, and barges—filled with some two hundred sailors and marines preparing to land on the distant beach. Amid the general confusion, the leaders in each boat called out to one another to confirm signals, define positions, and complete the last-minute preparations required for even the simplest amphibious operation.

Overhead on the quarterdeck of the *Macedonian*, removed from the noise and bustle below, the commanding officer of the expedition, Commodore Matthew Calbraith Perry, stood stiff and alone, serenely oblivious to the noise, the oppressive heat, and the discomfort of his heavy full-dress uniform. Perry was a man in his late forties, a stolid, portly figure, who moved deliberately but with great assurety, and whose every gesture spoke to the essential seriousness of his character. Fortune and his own profound sense of self marked him as a man of gravitas, or in the more informal ward-room term, a man with "bottom."

The commodore, telescope in hand, was studying the distant shore with single-minded concentration. To the naked eye there was little to distinguish the particular stretch of beach from any other along that coast, but with his glass he was able to pick out a number of human forms gathered beneath the trees at the edge of the beach, and behind them he could just make out the hint of a village. Even at the distance that separated him from the shore, Perry could discern that the humans gave every indication of intense interest in his ships.

He lowered his telescope as his flag captain, Commander Isaac Mayo, approached to report that the boats were ready to proceed, and that the expedition only awaited the dignitaries who would lead the formation. The commodore nodded and asked Mayo about the Paixhans guns. Perry was an enthusiastic proponent of advanced technology, and it was on his orders that the new, longer-range and more accurate cannon had been installed in the *Macedonian*. He wanted to confirm that their gun crews would remain in the ship, and Mayo assured him they would, along with a sufficient number of men to repel any boarding parties, should such an unlikely event occur. The commodore nodded his approval.

There was a sound of footsteps at the companionway behind them, and Perry and Mayo turned to acknowledge the arrival of two civilians on deck. The newcomers, in mufti, were dressed to the same severe standards of formality as the naval officers, and wore swallowtail coats and beaver hats. In their mode of dress, general demeanor, accents, and manner of speech, they were typical of American men of affairs of the period, with the exception of one notable detail—they were black men, whose dark skin defined their African origins. If there was anything unusual about the sight of such men standing in attitudes of apparent equality on the quarterdeck of a United States warship at a time when a million and a half of their fellow blacks were held in abject bondage in America, neither they nor the white officers appeared to notice. Perry greeted the civilians warmly, then the group walked to the sally port to board the boats waiting for them below.

COMMODORE PERRY'S PUNITIVE expedition against Little Berebee rates little more than a footnote in the history of a decade crowded with significant developments—the electric telegraph, the Communist *Manifesto*, the annexation of California, and the founding of Samuel Cunard's transatlantic steamship line all date from the 1840s—but Matthew Perry's foray against the Guinea Coast has a resonance all its own, and speaks to issues as relevant today as they were a hundred and fifty years ago. It is an incident shaped by the deep ironies that help define a uniquely American heart of darkness.

Perhaps the most pointed irony associated with the raid concerned the very presence of the *Macedonian* and her squadron off the African coast. They were not there as an expression of American policy but of British policy, and Matthew Perry, a man who held a lifelong distrust of the English, undoubtedly resented the fact that his orders were more a reflection of the wishes of Parliament than of Congress.

After the defeat of Napoleon at Waterloo, Great Britain had looked about for something to do with its enormous navy, and decided to dedicate it to a noble cause: abolishing the slave trade. The Royal Navy established a virtual blockade of the west coast of Africa, and began to stop and inspect all vessels suspected of carrying slaves. Any slaves found on board were returned to Africa, and the ship's crews, branded as pirates, were sent in for trial.

The United States openly applauded the British move, and

promised to aid the Royal Navy wherever possible. America, of course, was one of the world's principal slave-owning nations, but leaders in Washington were quick to point out that while the *ownership* of slaves was protected by law, the importation of new slaves into the United States was illegal, and therefore there was no inconsistency in the promise to cooperate with the English. In practice, alas, that cooperation failed to evolve. Congress appropriated $100,000 for the suppression of the slave trade in 1819, but by 1823 the figure was reduced to $50,000, and by 1839 it had dwindled to just $7,433.37.

Strictly speaking, the Royal Navy could only stop ships sailing under British colors, but because of the Empire's dominance in international trade, the Foreign Office was able to coerce other maritime nations to go along with the campaign against the slave trade, and to allow the Royal Navy to board their ships. Only one major trading nation refused such permission, and that was the United States.

America had gone to war in 1812 to stop the Royal Navy from boarding its ships, and remained particularly sensitive on the issue. As a result of American intransigence, the Royal Navy was forced to ignore even the most obvious slaver if she was sailing under the Stars and Stripes. The predictable outcome of the American policy was to give ships wearing American colors a virtual monopoly in the trade in "black ivory," and Yankee vessels, usually variations on the swift Baltimore clippers, crowded the slave ports of Rio and Havana.

The American minister in Rio wrote to the Secretary of State: "I regret to say this, but it is a fact not to be disguised or denied, that the slave trade is almost entirely carried on under our flag, in American-built vessels, sold to slave traders here, chartered for the coast of Africa, and there sold, or sold here—delivered on the coast. And indeed, the scandalous traffic could not be carried on to any great extent, were it not for the use made of our flag, and the facilities given for the chartering of American vessels, to carry to the coast of Africa the outfit for the trade and the material for purchasing slaves."

For years, the British tried to pressure the United States either to renounce its ban on searches or to send some of its own ships out to investigate suspected slavers flying American colors, but to little avail. Then, in 1837, an opportunity arose in a totally unrelated quarter that finally gave Britain the leverage to induce the American government to give more than lip service to the suppression of the slave trade.

A small shooting war broke out betwen the state of Maine and the province of New Brunswick concerning the border between Canada and the United States. When Daniel Webster and Lord Ashburton sat down to sort matters out, Britain used the dispute as a means of forcing the United States to live up to its unfulfilled promises. In exchange for clear title to 7,000 square miles of forest along the disputed border, and as a condition of Article VIII of the Webster-Ashburton Treaty, the American government agreed to send a squadron of navy vessels to Africa, expressly for the purpose of interdicting slave traders sailing under American colors. The presence of the *Macedonian* and her companion vessels off Little Berebee was a direct result of that treaty.

THE COMMODORE SAT stiffly in the stern sheets of his launch, wedged uncomfortably between the two black dignitaries who had accompanied him into the boat. Sweating oarsmen at the thwarts leaned on the sweeps, pulling the boat toward shore. Directly ahead, and to either side of the commodore's launch, the accompanying boats of the squadron carried the armed guard of marines who would secure the beach moments prior to the arrival of Perry and his party.

The commodore and his two black companions kept their eyes on the beach and exchanged comments about the approaching meeting, or "palaver," as it was called in the local pidgin. The taller of two civilians was John J. Roberts, appointed by the President of the United States as governor of the infant state of Liberia. His companion was John B. Russwurm, governor of the Maryland Colonization Society settlement at Cape Palmas. Each man was in charge of a different colony for freed slaves from America. Each had dedicated his life to the struggle to establish a foothold on the African continent, and it was due to Perry's enthusiastic support of their efforts that they were with him in the launch, heading into Little Berebee. Today, it was hoped, they would bring to the Slave Coast something new and previously unknown—the concept of justice, and with it, a new level of security for the embattled freedmen from America.

COMMODORE PERRY HAD few illusions about slavery. He detested the institution, and like Henry Clay of Kentucky, considered it "the deepest stain upon the character of the country." But for all his fervor, he was not ready to align himself with the abolitionists. Perry felt strongly that the African Negro would never be able to find a place within a predominantly white society except on the basis of permanent inferiority, and that blacks could only realize their potential in a society completely divorced from whites. Left on their own, he was convinced they would produce leaders of the first rank, such as the fiery Toussaint L'Ouverture, the black liberator of Haiti. The only sensible way to end slavery in America, as Perry saw it, was to establish a homeland for freed blacks in Africa. With such a homeland in place, Congress could then simply outlaw slavery, pay off the slaveowners for their loss of chattel, and ship the newly manumitted blacks back to the continent form which their ancestors had been forcibly removed. America, freed of the blot of slavery, could finally begin to fulfill its promise.

Many in Washington shared Perry's views, and as early as 1817, as a first step toward resolving the problem of America's "peculiar institution," a group of concerned national leaders, with the active encouragement of such august figures as President James Monroe and Chief Justice John Marshall, founded the American Colonization Society, dedicated to emancipating blacks and establishing a colony for them in Africa. In a related move, in 1819 Congress outlawed the African slave trade, declaring it a form of piracy and authorizing the navy to capture slave ships wherever found.

As a young officer, Perry sailed to Africa on three different occasions to help establish such a colony, and to supervise the transport of the first colonists. On his second cruise, in 1822, he personally selected the harbor at Cape Mesurado as the site for the permanent settlement. The town that arose on the cape was subsequently named Monrovia, in honor of James Monroe, and remains today the capital of Liberia, the country founded by the American Colonization Society.

The difficulties involved in founding a colony on the African coast were monumental, and the story of the efforts of both blacks and whites to establish a permanent homeland for freed slaves is one of the forgotten epics of history. Disease was rampant. The colonists, who as slaves had been denied any education, were barely able to organize themselves. Most serious of all, the indigenous Africans already in possession of the land intended for the new immigrants from America were hostile in the extreme. The tribes living in the area adjacent to Cape Mesurado repeatedly attacked the new settlers, and their bloody raids made life both difficult and perilous for the newcomers.

IT WAS TYPICAL of Commodore Perry's compartmentalized mind that he perceived—or at least claimed to perceive—the confrontation at Little Berebee as a step toward abolishing the slave trade, when in reality it had nothing to do with the issue of slavery one way or another. The main goal of the raid was to publicly identify and punish the tribesmen who a year before had captured and plundered the American trading schooner *Mary Carver*, and murdered her crew after they had been tortured by the village women. If Perry managed to accomplish this first goal, he could claim with some justification that he was making the area safe for American commerce, but nothing more.

His second goal at Little Berebee was to obtain $12,000 in reparations for the burned sloop and her cargo, which he knew was an impossibility, since the tribesmen had virtually no money or means of raising any. When Governor Russwurm suggested that the Berebee people might work off the expense by providing labor for various construction and agricultural projects at Cape Palmas, Perry enthusiastically endorsed the idea. Here again, the commodore claimed that such a step would help put down the slave trade, when in fact it would help support a colony of former slaves, which was a different matter entirely.

Matthew Perry was not stupid. If he claimed that something was so when it was not, it was not due to ignorance so much as to an understanding that it was often profitable to remain unclear. Years spent dealing with the frustrations and confusions of African colonization had given Perry a thorough understanding of the complexities of the slave question. His basic aims were simple: He wanted to get rid of slavery in America, and he wanted to get the former slaves out of the country. Any activity that advanced either of these goals, even in the most peripheral way, received his unwavering support.

Conversation in the launch ceased as the boat reached the line of breakers, plunged through, and came to rest on the low, sloping beach. The sweeps at the forward thwarts scrambled out to haul in the launch, and Perry, Roberts, and Russworm, barely damp from their ride, stepped ashore just as the band struck up a patriotic air. All along the water's edge to either side, the marines stood at post, their muskets at the ready.

The panoply and ceremony served a purpose. If there was a moment of danger, Perry knew, it was now, before the tribesmen could be made to understand how powerful were the forces ranged against them. From where he stood, he could see, half hidden among the trees, any number of large, powerfully built warriors poised to run or to attack. The Berebees could undoubtedly muster a fighting force equal in number or larger than the two hundred sailors and marines under Perry's command, but he knew they did not have the muskets or other firearms his men carried, and they certainly would have nothing equal to the Paixhans shell guns aimed at them from the *Macedonian*.

These were not docile men, Perry knew, not the kind who made good slaves. These were the men who *sold* slaves, he reminded himself. Slaves came from the weaker tribes, who lived in the interior. Only the strong, the ambitious, the brave and crafty lived on the more dangerous coast.

With a wave of his hand, the commodore indicated where he wanted the palaver tent pitched, and then sent word by messenger to summon King Ben Krako, chief of the Berebees.

COMMODORE PERRY'S SAILING orders left no doubt as to what was expected of him. He was specifically directed to search out all slavers sailing under American colors, to return to Africa any slaves discovered on board, and to send back the masters and crews for trial. The orders, which included enthusiastic suggestions on how best to detect and intercept the offending vessels, were written by Secretary of the Navy Clarence Upshur, a Virginian who was both a slaveowner and a vocal advocate of the advantages of slavery. The fact that an official could simultaneously support slave ownership while abhorring the trade in slaves was an apparent inconsistency common throughout the antebellum period, when thoughtful Americans, north and south, found it increasingly difficult to justify the colossal hypocrisy of a nation that could champion the idea that "all men are created equal" while simultaneously condoning the ownership of slaves, and in the process of attempting such justification, stumbled into equal absurdities.

Nowhere was the apparent inconsistency more evident than in the rigorous moral philosophy of Matthew Calbraith Perry, whose views of slavery were every bit as multifaceted as those of Secretary Upshur, although exactly the reverse. While the Virginian championed slavery and hated the trade in slaves, Perry detested slavery, but was noticeably ambivalent concerning the trade in human cargo, an ambivalence that arose out of his Rhode Island heritage.

THE PERRYS CAME from Newport, and the commodore's roots in that city ran deep. He shared with the people of Newport the New England faith in hard work and self-reliance, and adhered to a tradition of personal freedom that made slavery abhorrent philosophically. At the same time, Newport was a leader in maritime commerce, including the traffic in slaves, and while that trade might be condemned each Sunday from the pulpits of Newport, the best of families gave it their tacit approval. Matthew Perry's brother Raymond, for example, was married to a daughter of George deWolf, a notorious slaver and highly respected citizen of Bristol, Rhode Island.

Slave trading was simply too important for the merchants of Newport to disparage it. They knew it was the most profitable of all cargoes, and that it would remain so as long as slavers could buy a healthy black in Africa for twenty dollars and sell him in Rio or Havana for three or four hundred. Anyone with money to invest understood it was prudent to lay off a small amount on a slaver, as a form of insurance, in case disaster struck one of your more respectable ventures. The doleful fact was that slave trading was such an ingrained part of the Rhode Island maritime economy, and such an important bulwark of the social order, that it was perceived as a necessity by everyone connected with the sea. Matthew Perry had good reason to be reluctant in his search for slave traders. If he were successful, he ran the risk of running up against a friend or even a relative. Even at best, his capture of a slaver was likely to hurt somebody's pocketbook in Newport.

THE PALAVER tent formed a large square canopy on the beach, firmly anchored in the sand with all four sides tightly furled so as to leave it open in all directions. A portable table stood under the tent, and a clerk busied himself arranging boxes and files on it.

Perry was anxious to show the Berebees that the negotiations were to be public, and that there would be no opportunity for either party to practice ambush or deceit. The Berebee warriors appeared to understand the message, for they now stood in full view, shoulder to shoulder, no longer wary of a surprise attack, quietly watching the Americans and alert to every move they made.

There was a momentary break in the wall of onlookers, and King Ben Krako emerged from the forest, surrounded by five or six of his men. They were all dressed in boldly patterned calico robes, and strode in a dignified manner across the open ground to the canopy, to take their places opposite the Americans. Krako was a tall, proud bull of a man, Perry noted. His massive shoulders gave evidence of great strength, and his quick, darting eyes took in everything and hinted at great cunning. If he was in the least apprehensive about the meeting about to begin, he did not show it.

Perry studied the chieftain somberly, pondering the possibilities. He knew that Ben Krako was one of the men guilty of the murders of the *Mary Carver*'s crew. Perry planned to accuse him of the crime, and call upon the villagers to execute him and his fellow murderers. How would Krako react? How would the villagers? In all likelihood this confrontation was going to lead to some dangerous, possibly harebrained reactions and certainly some bloodshed.

Perry opened the meeting by ordering Krako to state his case, which the ruler did through an interpreter. The interpreter, who was also one of the murderers, proceeded to place blame on the *Mary Carver*'s master, John Farwell, claiming the Africans only killed him in self-defense. Perry made a great show of anger at this claim. Moving toward the interpreter and wagging a finger in his face, he warned the African that his story was a pack of lies, and ordered him to "utter no more falsehoods."

At this moment, a gun went off, and total confusion ensued. The interpreter, who was growing increasingly nervous at the way the palaver was progressing, bolted for the trees, but was killed by a rifle ball before he could reach safety. Ben Krako tried to run as well, and Perry seized him by his long calico robe, which fell away, at which Perry grabbed at the king's loincloth, and holding on for dear life was dragged through the sand for fifteen or twenty yards before some sailors, wielding rifle butts, managed to knock the king down. Krako pretended to be unconscious, but seeing a musket on the ground, made a leap for it just as Isaac Mayo, flag officer of the *Macedonian*, tried to pick it up. The two men grappled, and Mayo stabbed him with a pistol bayonet. The king fell, mortally wounded.

There was much shooting, and when the natives fled into the rain forest, Perry told his men to burn the village. It was the dry season. As soon as the huts were fired with torches, they burst into flame with a roar. The furious and frustrated natives, hiding in the forest and seeing their houses and possessions disappear in flames, beat their drums and rattled war bells in an attempt to scare the Americans away.

Perry ordered one of the boats back to the *Macedonian* with the body of the failing Krako, and then ordered the destruction of the other villages that made up the Little Berebee community. The troops fell in and marched down the beach to the next village. In short order they destroyed three of the four towns before stopping for lunch. "We had done work enough to insure an appetite," one of them would later write in his journal, "and history does not make mention of such destruction of cities so expeditiously effected." Later, they found and destroyed the fourth and last village.

"Few of us had ever spent a day of higher enjoyment than this," the diarist wrote, "when we roamed about with a musket in one hand and a torch in the other, devastating what had hitherto been the houses of people."

On board the *Macedonian*, the surgeons worked throughout the remainder of the day and into the night to save Krako's life, but he did not respond to their ministrations and died the following morning.

So ENDED THE attempt to bring justice to Little Berebee. How many times had precisely such a confrontation occurred in the centuries since Europeans began to force their way into every dark corner of the globe? Beginning with Columbus, a parade of conquistadores, Jesuits, Puritans, fur trappers and miners, sea captains and land agents of every stripe had moved inexorably against their more primitive neighbors, insisting everywhere on new priorities, establishing new values, demanding new methods of accounting, in a grand but largely uncharted scheme for the occidentalization of the world. From Mexico to Australia to Canada and the Philippines and the Sudan and a thousand other venues, the white men came, sometimes with guns, sometimes with words, but always they conquered. Little Berebee was simply one more setting for a drama that had already been enacted so many times its outcome was monotonously predictable.

HISTORY HAS BEEN kind to Matthew Calbraith Perry. He achieved much in a long career, and in death has been honored by the greatest distinction open to an American naval officer—a full-scale biography by the country's foremost marine authority, Samuel Eliot Morison. Partly as a result of that worshipful account, he is widely regarded as a man of outstanding vision, granitelike integrity, and towering moral authority. Quite possibly he was all those things, but Perry was also a creature of his times. He saw what he wished to see, and overlooked those things he found disagreeable. He wanted to make the west coast of Africa a haven for America's freed slaves, and insofar as it was within his power to do so, he was successful. He did not want to admit that Americans were active in the slave trade, and here, too, he succeeded.

The action at Little Berebee occurred within Perry's first month on the African coast, and was virtually the last activity of note for his entire tour of duty, which lasted another two years. News of the carnage and the death of King Krako spread quickly, and within days Perry obtained agreements from the chastened leaders of Rockboukah, Grand Tabou, Bassa, and Grand Berebee, binding them to befriend American merchants. This, he firmly believed, would ultimately benefit the colonies at Liberia and Cape Palmas.

As to the principal mission of his African cruise, to suppress trade carried on by American slavers, Perry simply denied that such a trade even existed. In the face of reports from the Secretary of the Navy, the American minister to Brazil, and eyewitness accounts of Royal Navy commanders on the scene, Perry refused to even admit that any Americans, or ships wearing American colors, were involved in the slave trade. With overwhelming evidence to contradict him on every side, he could complacently report to the Secretary of the Navy: "I cannot hear of any American vessels being engaged in the transportation of slaves; nor do I believe there has been one so engaged for several years prior to 1841."

"ANOTHER CURIOUS INCIDENT"

MATTHEW CALBRAITH PERRY PRIDED HIMSELF ON HIS DEEP sense of history and naval tradition. An example of his understanding, particularly relevant to the *Macedonian*, is found in one of his official letters from the African coast to Secretary Upshur:

> Another curious incident may be appropriately mentioned in this communication: on the 16th of March last [1844], this ship being on her passage to the North, crossed at 2 PM the very point of her capture, which according to the official despatch of Commodore Decatur was in Latitude 29°00′ N Long. 29°30′w—the position of the ship at noon, two hours previous, was ascertained by meridian observation and by three good chronometers to be in Lat 28°48′N and Long 29°27′w so there could be no possible error as to her position at 2 PM.
>
> This frigate . . . during her present cruize has passed over the very spot upon the ocean where she struck her flag to an American frigate 32 years ago.

Relevant here is that both Commodore Perry and Secretary Upshur were fully aware that the *Macedonian* was rebuilt from the keel up ten years prior to the time she crossed the site of the battle. Yet for all that, she was still the same vessel, in their eyes, as the one captured by Decatur, which of course was precisely what John Rodgers and Samuel Humphreys had intended.

A New Word Enters
the Navy's Lexicon

~~~~~~~~~~~~~~~~~~~~~

STEAMPOWER WAS MOVING IN, MAKING SHIPS LIKE THE *MACE-donian* ever more obsolete and irrelevant with each passing year. Steam meant speed, and with it the need for ever quicker decisions. And steam meant noisier ships, with a greater potential for confusion and misunderstood orders. The need for greater clarity and precision reached right into the language of the sea:

<div align="right">February 18, 1846</div>

GENERAL ORDER
It having been repeatedly represented to the Department that confusion arises from the use of the words "Larboard" and "Starboard" in consequence of their similarity of sound, the word "Port" is hereafter to be substituted for "Larboard."

<div align="right">

(signed)
G. Bancroft
Secretary of the Navy

</div>

MISSION TO IRELAND

I N THE LATE WINTER OF 1847 AMERICA WAS ONCE AGAIN AT WAR, this time with Mexico, and far away in the Pacific and the Gulf, the navy was storming beaches and bombarding fortifications in a hugely popular adventure directed against a weak and poorly organized enemy. President James Polk, who had arranged the patently unfair fight, was already making plans to annex everything from the Rockies westward as soon as the smoke cleared, and while thoughtful Americans like Henry David Thoreau and Abraham Lincoln argued against the war as immoral, the country at large was delighted at the prospect of gaining California and the remainder of the Far West at such trifling risk.

The fact that the *Macedonian* lay at anchor in the peaceful backwaters of the Brooklyn Navy Yard while the navy was busily waging war says much about the increasing importance of steampower in naval warfare, and the consequently decreasing significance of sailing vessels, particularly large, deep-drafted sailing vessels such as frigates and line-of-battle ships. Warships such as the *Macedonian*, while not yet obsolescent, were already regarded as artifacts of another time, vessels of distinctly limited usefulness.

If the navy could find no immediate use for the *Macedonian*, it turned out there were others who could. That late winter of 1847, she was enlisted in a unique humanitarian effort which would not only reflect widespread credit on the nation but would also provide, in the words of one disgruntled private citizen, "a comforting relief, as far as it goes, to the disgrace and inhumanity of the Mexican war."

The man who would find a new use for the *Macedonian* was an otherwise unremarkable New Yorker, a friend of poets and a frequenter of artists' studios and salons. His name was George Colman De Kay, an amiable and well-to-do former sea captain, who lived in semi-retirement at "Slongha," his estate on the Hudson, where he and his wife raised their family of six children in the wilds of New Jersey across the river from Manhattan. Each morning, weather permitting, De Kay would sail over to the city in his launch *Janet*, and spend the first part of the day looking in on his various business ventures before enjoying a leisurely lunch in the company of his friends, the leaders of New York's artistic community. Although he was not an artist himself, De Kay was connected, both through marriage and his own inclinations, with the leading writers and painters of the day. His wife Janet was the daughter of the lyric poet Joseph Rodman Drake, celebrated as the American Keats, and his closest friend was the equally renowned poet and critic Fitz-Greene Halleck. De Kay would occupy himself in this pleasant company through the early afternoon, then repair to the western edge of Manhattan opposite his house and fire a gun in the air to summon his manservant, who would sail over in the *Janet* to bring him home.

This leisurely lifestyle obviously suited the former sea captain, who at heart was a uxorious type. But there was another, more dynamic side to De Kay as well. As a sailor and sea captain in his younger days he had known his full measure of adventure and derring-do, and he still fancied himself as something of a romantic figure, in the style of a Decatur or a Byron.

He had been a dreamy youth. His father, also a sea captain, died when young George was an infant, and the boy was brought up by his Irish-born mother, who he adored. In childish fancies young George pictured himself following in the footsteps of the father he never knew, and when it was time to enter Yale, he chose instead to make those dreams come true, and ran away to sea. He took well to the maritime life, and while still in his early twenties rose to a position of command.

The course of his career took him several times to South

America, where he became a personal friend of Simon Bolívar, and in 1826, when he found himself in Buenos Aires, he decided to try his hand at combat and volunteered his services to the Argentinians in their war against the Brazilian Empire. The young man was given command of an 18-gun blockade runner, and quickly proved his mettle. In a number of daring engagements he captured several Brazilian prizes, and for his exploits, the Argentine Navy, which was still in a rather informal state, promoted him to the rank of *teniente-coronel*, or lieutent colonel. As if to make up for this rather unsalty rank, they also named a Buenos Aires street in his honor. When the war with Brazil finally ground to a halt, De Kay, who by now had developed a taste for naval warfare, set off to the Mediterranean to join the fight for Greek independence, before finally returning to New York to live off the proceeds of his many prizes.

Upon his return, he married and settled into the comfortable life already described. It was also at this point that he began using the title "Commodore," a rank which he decided was the equivalent of his Argentine lieutenant colonelcy. It was, admittedly, a liberal translation, but New York society accepted it without question. After all, the Wall Street financier Cornelius Vanderbilt had awarded himself the same rank on the basis of once piloting the Staten Island ferry. To go with his glamorous self-commissioned rank, De Kay also designed an elegant uniform, resplendent with gold braid and epaulets, which he was pleased to wear on formal occasions.

Life for the De Kay family might have continued undisturbed in its agreeable course, had it not been for the dreadful news that reached New York in January 1847, with the first reports of the devastating potato famine in Ireland. Heartrending newspaper accounts described entire villages dying of hunger and disease, of rotting corpses left unburied beside the road because there were none strong enough to dig graves, of misery of a most appalling nature that had overtaken the entire country of Ireland as well as the western parts of Scotland.

De Kay, reading the reports, was profoundly moved. His adored mother had filled his childhood head with memories of her own girlhood in Ireland, and although he had never been to that country, he felt it his duty to do everything in his power to alleviate the dreadful circumstances described in the press stories. But how could he help? His mind turned to thoughts of raising some sort of rescue mission, and when he discussed his ideas with his poet and artist friends, they were enthusiastic in their support. De Kay made some preliminary enquiries at the shipping lines, but learned to his distress that the chartering costs for a large enough ship to make a difference were prohibitive, and money aside, all the available merchant bottoms were already on lease or had been commandeered for use in the war. There simply were no ships to be had for such an errand of mercy.

As he made his way between the various shipping offices in downtown New York, De Kay could not fail to notice the frigate *Macedonian*, lying at anchor in plain sight, directly across from the South Street docks, but it is unlikely that at that early stage it occurred to him that perhaps she might answer his purpose. Would a civilian today think to ask the Pentagon for the loan of a spare B-52 or perhaps an aircraft carrier? But circumstances and the pressing need for immediate action soon forced the issue. When he was at last convinced that there were no ships to be had in New York, De Kay remembered the *Macedonian* and began thinking of her as a possible solution to his problem. But would the navy cooperate?

A few letters to some well-placed friends in Washington soon brought a surprisingly encouraging response. President Polk, it appeared, was immediately intrigued with the scheme, and put his weight behind it. The President was eager to make some sort of national response to the tragedy in Ireland, but thought it inadvisable to send a public vessel as a relief ship, given the fact that the navy was supposed to be fighting a war. De Kay's proposition altered the formula significantly: the *Macedonian*, manned by a civilian crew and hurrying eastward for the relief of the unfortunate, could be seen as a charitable gesture on the part of the United States, while at the same time it took nothing from the war effort. Acting with a speed and will only rarely seen in Washington, the White House sent a bill to Congress to give De Kay his ship.

While the House leadership started moving the bill toward a vote, De Kay and his poet friends in New York began to organize the appeal for funds to purchase the needed relief items. The Quakers, as might be expected, were the first to respond, and were generous with both their gifts and offers of help. The commodore announced that he would provide his own services as captain without charge, and the rest of the crewing of the *Macedonian* would as far as possible be volunteers as well, although it was anticipated that it might be necessary to pay at least some of the officers and crewmen if volunteers could not be found.

Other cities around the country, roused by the effort in New York, began making plans either to contribute goods and cash to the *Macedonian* project, or to initiate their own charitable missions. In Boston, a group of businessmen inspired by De Kay's idea decided to petition the government for a similar loan of the sloop-of-war *Jamestown*, then lying at the Charlestown Navy Yard, but when their appeal reached Washington it was already too late to initiate a new act, and they hurridly arranged to tack their request onto De Kay's bill. The commodore wired his enthusiastic support.

Early in March, only weeks after the idea was first broached, Congress passed the bill authorizing the Secretary of the Navy "to place at the disposal of Captain George C. De Kay of New Jersey the United States Ship *Macedonian* for the purpose of transporting to the famished poor of Ireland and Scotland such contributions as may be made for their relief, and that the said Secretary be also authorized to place at the disposal of Captain Robert P. Forbes of Boston, the United States sloop of war *Jamestown* for the like purpose." To this day, the act remains unique in the history of Congress. It authorized the navy to lend warships to individuals, on their own recognizance—not to corporations or municipalities or any other political or legal entity, but to individual citizens—with full responsibility for the care, maintenance, and safe return of the vessels lying on their shoulders alone. Few documents so strikingly illustrate with what unquestioning faith and high esteem the public once held sea captains.

In Boston, work proceeded smoothly. Captain Forbes, collaborating with his cadre of local merchants, was able to start loading the *Jamestown* within a fortnight—on St. Patrick's Day, by happy coincidence—and he left for Ireland before the end of the month with some eight hundred tons of relief provisions. Just fifteen days later, after a notably swift crossing, the *Jamestown* anchored off Cork. After delivering her cargo and receiving the overwhelming thanks of officials and private citizens, Captain Forbes turned around and sailed for home on April 22, arriving back in Boston on May 16, exactly forty-nine days from the date of sailing.

On his return, the captain was shocked to learn that the *Macedonian* still lay in New York, her holds half empty, with no date set for her departure. Forbes had seen the famine at first hand and understood the desperate need for more and greater relief efforts. He had promised the officials in Cork that De Kay's ship, much larger than the *Jamestown*, and carrying three times the cargo, could be expected momentarily. Pressed by the need for speed, he hurried to New York to see if he could help sort out the matter.

He found the *Macedonian* lying off the Battery with only two thousand barrels of supplies on board, and Commodore De Kay, sitting in the captain's quarters, almost beside himself with anger and frustration. What had gone wrong? Practically everything. To begin with, on receiving the orders from Washington to turn the *Macedonian* over to De Kay, the commandant at the navy yard ordered extensive refitting to improve her carrying capacity. The work, of dubious value at best, required weeks of effort, and meant that De Kay was not able to take delivery of the frigate until three days before the *Jamestown* sailed from Boston. But that was only the start of De Kay's troubles.

Unlike the Boston effort, which from beginning to end was run by the city's business leaders, who were men familiar with solving problems and skilled at getting things done, the fund raising in New York was being handled for the most part by artists and intellectuals, contemplative men given to endless discussion and dithering, and who for all their good intentions had already managed to alienate the entire business community and the newspapers to boot.

The New York press, more interested in creating news than helping De Kay feed the Irish, had been ferocious in its attacks. Editorialists lampooned the commodore as a windbag and parvenu for insisting on his grandiose self-styled fancy title. What, wondered the papers, was De Kay's game? In a city known for its colorful montebanks, it required only the slightest suggestion to blacken a man's name, and from there it was an easy step to insinuating that De Kay was probably involved in this little adventure for his own advantage.

The object of their derision was sensitive to matters dealing with his honor, but was willing to put up with the jibes in order to get the work done; but inevitably the newspapers' hatchet job cooled the public's ardor and made it almost impossible to raise funds. When the donations began drying up, De Kay assured the public that all funds collected would go solely for food for the starving Irish, but his assurance was not enough for the critics. If all the money was going for relief supplies, the papers wanted to know, who would pay for the cost of getting the food to Ireland? The frigate itself might be on cost-free loan from the government, but what of pilotage, of stevedores' labor, of crew's wages and provisioning? De Kay pointed out that the British government had volunteered to meet the cost of all such incidental expenses. But this answer, instead of quieting the protesters, only increased their anger. The critics argued that to accept payment from the British under the circumstances was simply against the sentiment of the voyage.

To add to his list of woes, the beleaguered De Kay was now receiving only lukewarm support from the Quakers, the group that was so central to the success of the mission. He could sympathize with their position. It was difficult enough for them to funnel their donations through a naval officer and to cooperate in a project that would involve a warship. They could not then be expected to lend their moral support as well.

The initial flurry of antagonistic stories died down in time, and the fund raising and purchase of relief goods began to pick up again, when an entirely new question arose out of thin air to bedevil the commodore. Wasn't the *Macedonian* a prize ship taken from the British, demanded the critics, and would not Britain take it as an insult to have her sail into an Irish port? De Kay responded angrily that "she was built at Gosport by American architects and out of American materials. There is not a plank of the old *Macedonian* in her." All of which might well have been true, but it hardly answered the question. In maritime circles she was still recognized as the same ship as the one captured by Decatur. A far more pertinent response would have been that there was no other ship to send.

Hounded by carping critics, De Kay found his attempt at simple charity thwarted at every turn. By the time of Forbes's visit he had been forced to put almost his entire personal fortune—some $30,000 in gold—into the kitty to cover costs.

Captain Forbes listened sympathetically to the commodore's litany of sorrows and frustrations. He saw a proud man humbled by a coterie of noisy citizens, motivated in all likelihood more by resentment of his grand airs than suspicion of his motives. A noble idea was being subverted by petty squabbling. But Forbes had been at the scene of disaster, and knew there was no time to spare.

He went back to Boston, and after consulting at length with his partners, returned for another meeting with Commodore De Kay. Gently but firmly he presented an offer to the beleaguered New Yorker. The Boston committee would agree to provide enough foodstuffs to fill the *Macedonian*'s remaining cargo space, Forbes told him, providing that De Kay would abide by certain restrictions demanded by the committee. First off, he must promise not to accept payment from the British government for freight charges. Second, the Boston committee would designate an agent of their choosing to sail in the *Macedonian*, who would have ultimate control over the distribution of the cargo furnished by them. Third, the entire enterprise was to be carried out as a private, civilian matter, which meant that De Kay must agree not to fly a commodore's pendant or wear his elegant uniform. Forbes knew the terms were stringent, even humiliating, and had pleaded with his partners not to make such demands. To insist that their own man would oversee the distribution of the Boston foodstuffs went directly to De Kay's honor, and must have been particularly hard to accept.

For De Kay to put his name to such a paper meant that in all likelihood he would never see his $30,000 again, unless he could somehow convince Congress to refund it to him. His noble humanitarian gesture was coming apart at the seams, and taking his good name and personal fortune with it. But Ireland suffered still. There could be no further delay. Without so much as a murmur of protest, he signed.

The Boston merchants were as good as their word, and the moment Forbes delivered De Kay's capitulation, relief supplies that had been sitting in Charlestown warehouses began to arrive in New York, assigned to the *Macedonian*. Some five thousand fresh barrels of grain, meal, and clothing was loaded into her capacious hold.

In the latter part of May, the New York relief committee discovered a new means of raising funds. A notice appeared in the press offering passage in the *Macedonian* for one hundred dollars, of which seventy-five dollars would go for the purchase of additional relief supplies, and the remainder for cabin provisions for the passengers. The offer was immediately oversubscribed, indicating that at least some citizens of the city had put aside their skepticism for the opportunity to take part in the historic voyage. The enthusiasm of the ticket purchasers signaled a shift in sentiment as New Yorkers finally began to appreciate the true worth of the enterprise.

To increase the *Macedonian*'s carrying capacity, and at the same time lessen her presence as a warship, the navy had removed all her guns with the exception of four carronades on the upper deck, which had increased her buoyancy significantly. But under the weight of the supplies that continued to pour in— barrels of corn meal, Indian meal, rice, beans, and clothing—the frigate sank deeper and deeper in the water, and De Kay was forced to move her from her East River berth to one in the Hudson that could accommodate her greater draft.

At last, on June 19, more than three months after the act of Congress made the voyage possible, and almost a month after the return of the *Jamestown*, the heavily laden *Macedonian* lay wallowing in the choppy seas off Sandy Point, with twelve thousand barrels in her hold, some one thousand eight hundred tons in all, valued at an estimated $80,000, and with six feet less freeboard than normal, answering ponderously to her helm as her captain set her eastward course.

From the top of the mainmast, where a commodore's pendant might have flown but for the insistence of the Boston merchants, a newly devised white flag emblazoned with a wreath of shamrocks snapped briskly in the breeze.

On deck, the *Macedonian* was as densely packed as a refugee ship, with almost five hundred ticket-paying passengers augmenting the hundred-man volunteer crew. Everyone was cheerfully putting up with the overcrowding for a chance to be part of such a grand enterprise. A beaming and delighted Commodore De Kay, the humiliations and frustrations of the past months forgotten, squeezed cheerfully into the great cabin along with his wife, their two eldest children, and the family servants, and watched through the gallery windows as the coast of America slipped slowly below the horizon.

Twenty-seven days later, on July 16, the mercy vessel arrived in triumph at Cork, the deepest and safest harbor in Europe, to the tumultuous cheers of the local populace. A delirious welcoming party, which immediately set out to greet the new arrivals in the mayor's brightly beribboned barge, must have been momentarily stunned when they were in turn greeted by Commodore De Kay manning the braces and leading six hundred Yankees in three thundering cheers.

* * *

THE HORROR OF the Great Irish Famine of 1846–49 is generally recognized as one of the worst natural disasters in recorded history. It destroyed, in one devastating sweep, the basic food source of the Irish poor, and led to the death of hundreds of thousands of men, women, and children. A full quarter of the population—two million people—either perished or emigrated as a direct result of the famine, and the festering trauma of those terrible years continues to be a major factor in the politics of Ireland to this day.

The most horrifying aspect of the tragedy was that virtually all the deaths could have been prevented. In the whole of Ireland, potatoes were the only crop to fail. Wheat, barley, beans, peas, carrots—which grew in profusion throughout the island—continued to produce bumper crops throughout the years of the Great Hunger, but through a combination of shortsightedness and just plain stupidity, these bountiful harvests never reached the starving. They were cash crops, grown on the extensive farms of absentee landlords—most of whom were English—and they were routinely harvested and shipped to markets in England, where they fetched better prices than in Ireland. The Parliament in London could have solved the emergency simply by halting the export of these crops from Ireland, therefore forcing the landowners to distribute them among the starving victims of the potato blight. Instead, Parliament did nothing. The leaders of the British government simply turned a blind eye to the harrowing descriptions appearing regularly in the London papers, and behaved as if the whole matter was irrelevant. As a result of this curious and horrific apathy, which was in fact out of character with the generally enlightened manner with which Britain governed its Empire in the nineteenth century, the famine affected only the poorest in Ireland, the country people, while the shopkeepers and city dwellers survived more or less unscathed. It was the Irish peasantry, who had over centuries come to rely almost exclusively on the potato for nourishment, who died by the thousands, surrounded by plenty.

The arrival of the *Macedonian* in the midst of this overwhelming misery represents one of the few bright spots in an otherwise dark and tragic tapestry. Parliament aside, her arrival was hailed as an important event throughout the United Kingdom, and she received generous praise from the press. The *Illustrated London News* featured a large picture of the ship, with an excited report on her arrival at Cork, and singled out "the brave and noble De Kay, [who] with a liberality which entitles him to the gratitude of Ireland and the admiration of the world, has carried out this magnificent undertaking at his own expense."

A Dublin firebrand named Charles Gavan Duffy took the opportunity to twist the lion's tail by pointing out the *Macedonian*'s status as a prize captured from the British, but *Punch* brushed the charge aside, and effectively disarmed a potentially bothersome issue by making fun of his speech.

Now followed a seemingly endless series of parties and festivities to celebrate the arrival of the *Macedonian*, each gala replete with its own stemwinding orations and generous speechifying, each orator apostrophizing the undying love and loyalty shared by both givers and receivers. The commodore, no slouch at speechifying himself, gave as good as he got, having made a brief (and probably unnecessary) side trip upcountry to kiss the Blarney Stone.

An organization called The Citizens of Cork sponsored a sightseeing trip in Cove Harbor aboard the pleasure steamer *Royal Alice*, which included a sit-down dinner at which the ship's band played "Rule Britannia" and "Yankee Doodle" for the assembled guests. The menu lends grim proof to the assertion that only a portion of the population had been subjected to the cruel horrors of the famine. According to one account of the festivities, it featured "substantial and delicate viands," including "Turbot, Salmon, Spiced Beef, Rump of Beef, Hares, Tonges, Pigeon Pies, Lamb, Chickens, Ducklins, turkeys, Lobster Salads, Veal, Haunch of Mutton, Sponge Cakes, Jellies, Creams, Ices, Blancmanges, Pies, Tarts, Cheese Cakes, Tartlets, etc., Grapes, Apples, Plumbs, Cherries, Strawberries etc., etc." The wines included Champagne, Claret, Port, and Sherry.

The report described further aspects of the celebration: "HMS

Crocodile fired a royal salute of 21 heavy guns, which was responded to by the *Macedonian*, from which a royal salute of the same number was also fired." The American gun crews must have shown considerable alacrity to manage such a large salute with only four carronades.

A Mr. H. B. Oliffe entertained the ensemble with a song specially composed for the occasion, to the tune of "Fill the Bumpers Fair," which included the stanza:

> *Brave De Kay has come*
> *As did Forbes and others*
> *From his starlit home*
> *To his clouded Brothers . . .*

and finished up with still another song—this one to the tune of "My Eye and Betty Martin O!"—which offered felicitations to virtually everyone connected with the glorious event, including a last stanza addressed to the commodore's thirteen-year-old daughter, Kate De Kay.

On August 11, the *Macedonian* departed for Scotland to deliver the remainder of her cargo, and as soon as they were back at sea the commodore discovered that the ship, after having landed a great amount of cargo at Cork, was now dangerously under-ballasted. With such a shallow draft, even a moderate storm could have made her unmanageable, and the Americans were fortunate to experience fair weather in their four-day journey across the Irish Sea.

At Greenock, the port of Glasgow, they were received with the same warm enthusiasm they had met in Ireland, and as at Cork, the festivities were laid on with a generous hand. The arrival of the *Macedonian* coincided with a royal visit by Queen Victoria and her consort, Albert, and one of the Scottish hosts noted in his address that Commodore De Kay "has at last turned a ship of war into a ship of charity, and taught American guns, instead of breathing forth death against the British nation, to peal forth loud and hearty welcome to Britain's Queen. [Cheers]" The next speaker proclaimed that De Kay had managed to exchange "bombs for buns. [Cheers and laughter]"

With her remaining cargo offloaded at Greenock, the *Macedonian* was now seriously unseaworthy. De Kay and his officers determined that she would require a great deal of additional ballast, amounting to six hundred tons of pig iron, to ensure proper trim for her return to New York. De Kay arranged for the purchase and stowage of the requisite ballast at Greenock, and as usual, paid the costs out of his own pocket. The incident, clearly innocent of suspicious intent, would, like so many other things connected with his mission of charity, come back to haunt him.

No sooner had the commodore completed the uneventful return voyage to New York, and bade farewell to his five hundred passengers, or at least those who had remained on board for the round trip, than the trouble began. Before returning the *Macedonian* to the navy yard, De Kay arranged to land the ballast and sell it, receiving in payment enough to cover his outlay for the original purchase in Scotland. Technically, the pig iron ingots were of foreign manufacture, and therefore the sale was subject to the payment of duty, but both the customs officials in New York and their superiors in the Treasury Department agreed that since the *Macedonian* was a naval vessel, she was not obliged to pay such duty.

All was straightforward and aboveboard until newspapermen got wind of the matter, at which point it quickly blew up into a flurry of accusations. Had there been a profit on the sale? Where had the money gone? How could it be claimed that the *Macedonian* was a naval vessel when, in this particular case, she was not under the command of the navy? The stories tried to create a scandal, and while they ultimately failed to do so, the uproar lasted long enough to give De Kay still another lesson in just how dangerous and fickle public sentiment could be. Far from being hailed as a hero, he found himself once again under suspicion as a profiteer and swindler. The incident did not bode well for his plans to petition Congress to recoup his personal losses.

All told, De Kay had spent thousands on the venture—for relief goods, for salaries and wages, for cordage and extra spars and every kind of equipment—and without reembursement he faced penury. For a man with a wife and six children, and another child on the way, the financial question was of utmost importance. He knew he would have to move quickly and decisively. While friends and allies began working on his behalf in Washington, De Kay remained in New York throughout the autumn of 1847 fending off creditors; but in January 1848, when matters in Washington failed to progress, he moved his family south, rented a town house not far from the White House, and gave himself over to what quickly turned into an endless series of meetings and personal petitionings on behalf of his cause. The constant pleading and negotiating occupied the entire winter and spring, of 1848, and can be said to have cost him not only his self-respect, but his health as well.

One can sense the underlying pain in a memorial this once proud man addressed to one of the congressmen who was looking into his case:

> "[I] fully intended, on applying for the ship, that it should not cost the country one dollar to send her out, [but] subsequent events, not under my control, rendered it necessary that I should expend and risk a considerable sum, or make the country a laughing stock to the whole world. The money having been honestly and economically expended in the most honorable service of the country—the country having had the full credit and benefit of the same, at home and abroad . . . the question for Congress to decide is, whether one citizen shall suffer a ruinous fine for faithfully executing its orders, or assume payment of the same.

Congress, which had acted with unusual speed to grant De Kay the use of the *Macedonian* the year before, now deliberated with exquisite slowness. What started out as a simple and reasonably straightforward issue grew ever more ambiguous with the passage of time, while new matters, which demanded more immediate attention, inevitably arose before the Congress and eclipsed such minor details as a personal "debt of honor."

In April 1848, a report from Mr. Cabell from the Committee on Naval Affairs was filed, and later, in August, Senator Dix of New York "moved an item of $16,000 for money paid out on account of the trip of the U.S. ship *Macedonian* with food for the people of Ireland." In time, Congress voted to cover part of De Kay's debt, but nowhere near the amount he had put out. By late spring, the House had moved on to other matters and most representatives considered the matter closed. The commodore, weakened by illness and anxiety, found it necessary to redouble his efforts. Doggedly, he continued to plead his cause to indifferent and even hostile strangers, as his wife and friends grew increasingly concerned for his mental stability as well as his physical health. In time, the humiliation was more than he could bear, and he died on the last day of January 1849.

TWENTY YEARS AFTER the events described, Captain Forbes revisited Cork for the first time, and found the memory of the American rescue mission still fresh in the public mind, and the people's gratitude still very much alive. He was introduced to young men and women born in 1847 who had been christened Jamestown and Macedonian in honor of the ships, and when shopkeepers learned his identity, they refused to accept payment, because Captain Forbes had saved them from death as small children.

Later, in his memoirs, Forbes pondered the vastly different experiences he and De Kay had encountered in pursuing the same humanitarian goal. "I made no sacrifice," he noted, "all was smooth and pleasant from beginning to end," while in New York, De Kay's efforts were bedeviled from the beginning, and led inexorably to his ruin. "Commodore De Kay," wrote the thoughtful but unsentimental Forbes, "may be said to have sacrificed his life to the voyage of the *Macedonian*."

United States
~~~~~~~~~~~~~~~~
Sloop-of-War
~~~~~~~~~~~~~~~~
Macedonian,
~~~~~~~~~~~~~~~~

20 guns

(Razeed)

MEMORIES

~~~~~~~~~~~~~~~~~~

J OHN SURMAN CARDEN, THE MAN WHO LOST THE *MACEDONIAN*
to Decatur on that bloody Sunday in 1812, was still alive and
on active duty at the time of Commodore De Kay's visit to Ireland
in 1847. He was by now a rear admiral, seventy-seven years old
and nearing retirement. The reemergence of the *Macedonian*'s
name in the public press awakened painful memories in the old
veteran, and touched a raw nerve. Carden had been cleared in
a court-martial convoked to investigate his handling of the battle,
but the preeminent chronicler of the Royal Navy, William James,
had been harsher in his judgment of the same action in his five-
volume history of the Napoleonic Wars, and Carden had learned
to his sorrow that it was the public record that people remembered, rather than the judgment of his peers.

A year after De Kay's visit, Carden, who by now was retired
and living outside London in Egham, determined to tell his side
of the story. He sat down to write his memoirs, covering his
more than sixty years of service to the crown, which, as readers
may remember, stretched all the way back to duty in the American War of Independence. The task took him two years, and
the result is a most singular document. After covering in considerable detail his career, first as an officer in the army in the
Carolinas, and later as a naval officer in Egypt, India, Ireland,
and off the coast of France, he arrives at his command of the
Macedonian. His eighteen months duty in the frigate fills almost
20 percent of the book, at which point his chronicle simply stops.
The last *thirty-six years* of his service are shrugged off in a couple

of pages, as if his career had come to an end on October 25, 1812. In many ways it did.

Carden died in 1858, having risen by that date to the rank of full admiral.

JAPAN

~~~~~~~~~~~~~~~~~~~~

SAILING VESSELS, BECAUSE THEY ARE DEPENDENT UPON THE winds for their propulsion, must zigzag across the sea, tacking and clewing, always in search of a breeze to get them where they want to go. Steamers, on the other hand, carry their own means of propulsion within them, and can move in any direction they choose, maintaining a course regardless of the vagaries of the weather. It was this simple distinction that made it inevitable that steampower would in time take over from sail, and there is no more striking illustration of the growing ascendency of the new technology than the fact that in 1848 the U.S. Navy found it necessary to educate Congress on the subject of great circles.

In that year Lieutenant Matthew Maury went up to Capitol Hill to explain the advantages of establishing a steamship line linking Oriental markets with the ports of the newly annexed California. In support of his proposal he presented charts of the Pacific Ocean with curiously arched lines drawn on them indicating the proposed sealanes. When questioned about the curved lines, Maury explained that they were in fact straight lines *as drawn on the surface of a sphere*, and as such they defined the shortest distance between two points on the earth. To illustrate, he produced a globe, and placing one end of a piece of string on the city of Shanghai, he stretched the other end eastward to the Monterey–San Francisco area of California. The congressmen were quick to grasp the three-dimensional demonstration. They could see that the string was indeed straight, and they also noted that it did in fact arch in a northerly direction for the first part of the way, before dipping southward again as it neared the American coast.

Maury pointed out that the proposed 5,400-mile trans-Pacific link to China indicated by the piece of string offered dramatic advantages to the United States. In 1848, a traveler in New York wishing to go to Shanghai had to sail south across the Atlantic, around the Cape of Good Hope, and north again over the Indian Ocean, an 18,000- to 20,000-mile journey, to reach his destination. With the establishment of Lieutenant Maury's steamship line, that same New York traveler could cut his journey in half by sailing to Panama, crossing the isthmus, running up to California, and thence across the Pacific to Shanghai, a total distance of about 10,900 miles.

Maury promised an even more dramatic savings in time and distance that could be brought about as soon as the country built a transcontinental railroad system, at which point the New York–Shanghai passage would shrink to little more than 8,000 miles.

The congressmen were greatly impressed by Maury's geography lesson as well as his arguments for commercial development. They also took note of a seemingly trivial detail which in fact represented a major drawback to the scheme. When Lieutenant Maury stretched his bit of string from Shanghai to California, it traced a route that passed precisely through an opening in the Japanese archipelago known as the Tsugaru Strait that ran between the islands of Honshu and Ezo. Tsugaru Strait, it quickly became apparent, was strategically vital to Maury's vision. It was not only a potential gateway, but its principal city, the port of Hakodate, was seen as a very convenient coaling station.

There was, however, a hitch, well known to everyone in the hearing room. Any effort to enact Maury's suggestions would necessitate the close cooperation of the Japanese government, and in all likelihood that was going to be impossible to obtain. For over two hundred years the Empire of Japan had closed itself off from the world, holding itself aloof, neither exchanging embassies with other nations nor accepting their overtures, living in splendid isolation and maintaining a medieval society totally divorced from outsiders. Foreign sailors unlucky enough to be shipwrecked on Japan's coast were likely to be executed, lest they contaminate the home islands with their alien presence. Japanese mariners who had suffered similar misfortunes at sea and been rescued by foreigners were not allowed to reenter their homeland. The only Japanese entry point open to foreigners was the southernmost port of Nagasaki, and even there the restrictions were severe. The Dutch were the sole nation allowed to maintain a tiny trading station there, and they were limited to bringing in one small merchant ship a year.

Despite the formidable negatives involved with dealing with the Japanese, Washington refused to be discouraged. Inspired by Maury's scenario and driven by the expansionist credo that saw American hegemony as the nation's "manifest destiny," Congress began immediately drawing up plans to "open up" Japan. It would prove a daunting assignment, and would bring about a most curious cultural confrontation that is still a long way from resolution.

WHEN THE NAVY Department first began planning the epochal mission to Japan, a great deal of thought went into the ships that would make the journey. For obvious reasons, the navy wanted a squadron made up entirely of steamships, since such a powerful representation would go far to express America's dynamic might and its determination to have its way. Unfortunately, the steamers available to the navy were all highly inefficient paddlewheelers, steamships which used so much coal that even if the squadron were based in China, it could not possibly carry enough fuel for the round trip to Japan. Sailing ships would have to be a necessary component of the squadron, if only to carry fuel for the steamers.

At the time, the *Macedonian* was lying in ordinary at the Brooklyn Navy Yard, where she had been since her return from Ireland in 1847. The navy had a number of other unassigned vessels that would appear to have equal or superior qualifications for inclusion in the squadron bound for Japan, but three distinct factors would shortly affect the status of the *Macedonian* and make it inevitable that she would not only be selected for the adventure, but would play a significant part.

The first factor was the appointment of Matthew Calbraith Perry to command the expedition. Perry, who of course had served in the *Macedonian* on the African Station, was a traditionalist who could appreciate her historical value to the expedition. The second factor, closely allied to the first, was Perry's awareness of the deep anxiety that the Japanese felt concerning the growing British presence in Southeast Asia. For the Americans to include a trophy ship captured from the British as part of their flotilla would send a clear signal that the Japanese would be sure to appreciate.

But for all her symbolic value, Perry would not have selected the *Macedonian* had it not been for the third factor, which was the almost magical metamorphosis the ship had undergone in the Brooklyn drydock in 1851 and 1852, when in the process of a routine rebuilding she was dramatically transformed from a quite ordinary frigate into one of the swiftest and, for her size, most powerful warships in the fleet.

In technical terms, she had been razeed. The word is an English corruption of the French verb *raser*, "to shave," and describes a form of rebuilding in which the entire top deck of a ship is shaved off and her upper tier of guns removed. The ship thus modified was almost always faster, since her weight would be reduced, and more responsive, since her lowered sides would make it possible to sail closer to the wind.

In the case of the *Macedonian*, her poop deck (added at the time of her African service) was removed and her profile thereby reduced; her masts, yards, and sails were increased in size; and she was given about eighteen inches more keel. Her foremast was stepped slightly further aft, giving her a more rakish look, and significantly, she was entirely rearmed. All of her 18-pounder long guns and large-bore carronades were removed and replaced with sixteen powerful new 8-inch shell guns, which had been cast specifically for her at the West Point foundry, along with two even larger 10-inch shell guns and four 32-pounder long guns that fired solid shot.

But by far the most important change in her was not visible from the outside. Much of the heavy additional timbering that had been built into her in 1836, when it was anticipated that she would lead an expedition to Antarctica, was removed or modified. Her interior strengthening had made her so heavy and unwieldy that she had earned an unenviable reputation as a slow and dull sailer. Now at last she was divested of her excess weight, and the results were immediately apparent. She not only had an enhanced appearance—many now considered her the most beautiful ship in the navy—but on a shakedown cruise to Madeira and back, she proved admirably swift and maneuverable. In recognition of her dramatic change in size and her improvement in sailing quality and firepower, the navy decided she was no longer a frigate, second class, but a sloop-of-war, first class.

As evidence of her importance to the upcoming expedition, Perry assigned the *Macedonian* to Captain Joel Abbot, his favorite captain, a veteran officer as old and grizzled as himself, and the only man in the squadron who he addressed by name, prefixing his surname with "My dear." Perry had once said that "when he wanted anything done and well done in the shortest possible time under difficult and trying circumstances, he always sent Abbot."

In April 1853, the *Macedonian* departed New York to join Perry's command in the Far East, and immediately displayed her new seaworthiness. A letter from Madeira written by one of her officers appeared in the Portsmouth, Virginia, *Daily Transcript*, reporting: "Here we are at anchor, having made the passage from New York in seventeen and a half days. The good old ship, which many thought would not sail, has made a shorter passage than either the steamer *Mississippi* or the *Powhatan* [also a steamer]. It seems that the alterations effected previous to her leaving New York make her one of the fastest ships now in the navy." After doubling the Cape of Good Hope in leisurely style, she eventually dropped anchor at Cum Singh Moon, off Hong Kong, in August.

"You will be pleased to learn," Abbot reported to the commodore, "that the *Macedonian* now sails remarkably well, and is one of the most formidable and powerful ships in the navy, when efficiently officered and manned." On her trip out she had consistently logged up to fourteen knots, almost twice her previous speed. To his wife, Abbot wrote that she "attracts great attention . . . the Commodore seems to be very proud of her. He says she is the most splendid ship he ever saw. . . . The English Admiral . . . on his arrival at Canton a few days since, remarked to numbers there that the *Macedonian* was the Most Magnificent Ship that had ever been in these seas." Perry designated Abbot his vice-commodore, which allowed him to fly a red pendant.

By the time of the *Macedonian*'s arrival at Cum Singh Moon, Perry had already completed his first visit to Japan, where he had left behind the American proposals for a pact of amity and trade. He had promised the Japanese he would come back the following spring for further negotiations, but when he learned in November that the French admiral in the Far East had left port suddenly under sealed orders, and that the Russian Admiral Pontiatine had just returned from Nagasaki, where he had attempted to open negotiations with the emperor, Perry feared they might be engaged in a diplomatic flanking maneuver, and decided on a midwinter return to Japan in order to forestall them, notwithstanding the fact that navigation of the China Sea at that time of year was considered exceedingly hazardous.

THE *MACEDONIAN*'S FIRST contact with Japan was hardly a propitious augury for an enterprise of such conceptual grandeur. She led the advance party of sailing ships, which left before the steamers, and first raised the south coast of Japan on February 5, 1854, in company with the sloop *Vandalia* and the store ship *Supply*. She proceeded slowly northward along the Pacific side of the islands, battling headwinds and high seas, searching for the entrance to Edo (Tokyo) Bay. The weather turned progressively nastier throughout the week, and what with rain, hail, and wind, they managed to cover only ten miles a day. Early on the afternoon of Saturday, February 11, the trouble started.

Vice-Commodore Abbot mistook a cove on the Sagami Peninsula for the entrance to the bay, and promptly ran his ship hard and fast onto a reef. Abbot, who was notorious for his short temper, had no one to blame but himself, since the other two ships, using identical charts, did not make the same error. "O God," Abbot scrawled in his diary, "grant this favour I beseech thee for Christ sake and worthiness in his name. O God I ask it beseechingly!" Abbot's distress was made all the more painful by the arrival of several Japanese boats on the scene, full of curious onlookers, and was compounded by the onset of a fresh gale, which swiftly broke over their heads, churning up the seas and making it dangerous to remain on deck.

Fortunately for Abbot and his crew, the coast stood in the way of the worst of the wind and provided some shelter; but with each passing hour the combined effect of wind and tides was wedging the *Macedonian* ever more firmly into the reef, and the situation quickly reached a crisis, at which point Abbot was forced to order the ship lightened, in hopes that they might kedge her off the reef before the combined grinding of wind and rocks tore open her bottom. The crew began frantically throwing overboard tons of shot, sand, coal, provisions, and spare spars. The captain of the *Vandalia* brought his ship as close to the stranded *Macedonian* as he dared, and her boats assisted through the night and the following day. By noon on Sunday they were still stuck, and Abbot was preparing to jettison the *Macedonian*'s proud new battery of guns, but held off such drastic action until he had no other choice. Finally, around three o'clock in the afternoon, after almost twenty-four hours of exertion in the rain and cold, the crew was able to heave the ship off the reef and into deeper waters, where she floated at anchor, apparently none the worse for wear.

Soon afterwards, Commodore Perry hove in sight with the three steamers and anchored nearby. Seeing the *Macedonian*'s distress, he sent the *Mississippi* to assist, and she towed the stricken vessel to a safer anchorage near the commodore. It was an inauspicious beginning to the great enterprise, and given the Japanese penchant for auguries and omens, potentially disastrous.

Surprisingly, the near loss of the *Macedonian* seems to have attracted little attention beyond the curious onlookers at the scene of the accident, and it had no adverse effect on the negotiations; but a postscript to the incident illustrates the kind of misunderstandings that inevitably characterized so much of the epochal meeting of two such alien cultures. Soon after the *Macedonian* and the other American ships took up anchorage off Yokohama, and Perry's diplomatic efforts got under way, a delegation of villagers who had witnessed the ship's tribulations on the reef arrived at her gangway carrying a cargo of jettisoned coal that the crew had thrown overboard. The tide had eventually carried it in to the beaches, where the puzzled villagers, who had no idea of the purpose of the little black rocks, collected them and after carefully washing off any encrusted salt left by the sea, journeyed overland to the anchorage to return them to the foreign ships.

FOR ALL THEIR centuries of isolation, the Japanese retained a pretty good idea of the sort of things that sailors—even round-eyed foreign sailors—might enjoy. One cold morning in March, the second officer in the *Macedonian*, Lieutenant George Henry Preble, was riding into Yokohama in a ship's launch when he noticed a group of Japanese standing on shore frantically waving and trying to catch the eye of the Americans. When they had at last succeeded, one of the men in the group, smiling and gesturing in the most lascivious manner, let it be known through graphic sign language that the women with them were available for recreational purposes. As evidence, the ladies, at a signal from him, threw open their kimonos to reveal all. Preble, who was mindful of Commodore Perry's strict orders forbidding any shore leave prior to the signing of a treaty, ordered his men to pull away smartly.

In his journal, the lieutenant professed to be disgusted by

such an "exhibition of lewdness." How his men might have felt about the incident is not recorded.

PERRY WAS FULLY in charge of every detail of the negotiations. Each day's conference was carried on with great ceremony and ritual, and included a formal exchange of gifts. Because Perry assumed the Japanese would be mainly interested in machinery, he had arranged to bring with him a selection of farming implements, clocks, stoves, a daguerreotype camera, a working telegraph, and grandest of all, a miniature railroad train, one-quarter size and accurate in every detail, complete with tender, coach, and a narrow little 18-inch gauge track.

Joel Abbot was given the honor of making the formal presentation of the railroad train, which was an immediate sensation. It was set up to run in a little circle 350 feet across, and in size was somewhat smaller than the miniature train that visitors can ride nowadays at Disneyland. It was so tiny the engineer had to sit in the tender to operate the locomotive, and the coach could hardly hold a small boy, but the Japanese officials were so delighted with it that they threw decorum to the wind, and insisted on riding the wonderful machine regardless of dignity or the proprieties. It soon became a familiar sight to see a grinning samurai in full dress riding on top of the coach, his robes flapping in the winds, holding on for dear life and shouting gleefully to his friends, while the little engine huffed, puffed, and whistled around the track at twenty miles per hour. The Japanese immediately insisted on taking over the train and running it themselves, and made something of a nuisance of themselves with their constant requests for fresh supplies of coal.

The telegraph line, which represented a far more advanced technology than the steam locomotive, simply baffled the Japanese. A line was set up between Yokohama and Kanagawa, and the Americans demonstrated how a message could be sent instantaneously from one end to the other. The shogun's men had no trouble grasping the value the telegraph held for them, but since they had no inkling of electricity, they simply could not imagine the nature of what was shown to them.

Perry was determined to demonstrate that Americans were not the uncultured barbarians the Japanese suspected them to be, and brought along an entire case of books, which included George Bancroft's *History of the United States*, four volumes of *Annals of Congress*, sixteen volumes of *The Natural History of the State of New York*, New York Laws, Documents and Assembly Journals, reports of the U.S. Lighthouse Board, a two-volume *Farmers' Guide*, Morris's *Treatise on Engineering*, two book-length accounts of the Mexican War, and to top off the selection, copies of Audubon's two magnificent elephant folios, *Birds of America* and *Quadrupeds of America*, purchased at a cost of a thousand dollars each.

The Japanese reciprocated with an equally magnificent folio of exquisitely detailed full-color pornographic prints.

THE NEGOTIATIONS CONTINUED throughout the month of March, with the two parties communicating haltingly in Japanese-to-Dutch-to-English translations and back again. The reluctant hosts, suspicious of American intentions, questioned every element of the proposed treaty, suggesting fresh changes and demanding new options, and when Perry dug in his heels and refused to compromise, they retired to the capital at Edo for further instructions. The commodore, as sensitive on matters of protocol and dignity as the Japanese, never threatened or cajoled, and retained an air of benign serenity at all times. His ships, with their Dahlgren shell guns, only twenty miles from the Imperial Palace, were intimidation enough.

Finally, toward the end of the month, Perry and his staff sensed for the first time that matters were moving their way, and the commodore ordered a gala to help alleviate any remaining Japanese anxieties. On the blustering morning of March 27, a Monday, the three Japanese commissioners in charge of the shogun's side of the negotiations were piped on board the *Macedonian*, while the steamship *Mississippi*, anchored directly ahead, boomed out a 17-gun salute in their honor. After a ceremonial inspection, during which a Japanese quick sketch artist, who was part of the official entourage, managed to make a visual record of virtually every aspect of the ship, the guests were escorted into their boats by Lieutenant Preble and ferried across to the steamer *Powhatan*, the commodore's flagship, while the *Macedonian*'s 8-inch cannon boomed out another 17-gun salute.

In spite of the inclement weather, a grand feast was laid out on the quarterdeck. Perry gave instructions that the guests should be shown the warmest possible hospitality, which in practical terms meant plying them with as many intoxicants as they could be persuaded to ingest. Preble soon had them knocking back an enormous range of alcoholic refreshments, including Champagne, Madeira, cherry cordial, punch, and corn whiskey, with the predictable result that the Japanese, who were used to the comparatively mild effects of sake, were soon hooting and hollering and dancing up and down and having a glorious time. One of the shogun's emissaries, well into his cups, threw his arms around Perry's neck and embraced him in a great bear hug, quite out of keeping with his usual Oriental reserve. The American officers standing nearby, who were all familiar with the commodore's dignified, even stuffy character, looked on in shocked amazement. "Oh," said Perry happily, "if he will only sign the treaty he may kiss me."

After an uproarious and doubtless very confusing performance by the *Powhatan*'s minstrel band, in which crewmen in blackface performed sentimental and farcical musical numbers, the Japanese returned in their boats to Yokohama, to the roar of still another 17-gun salute, this one from the sloop-of-war *Saratoga*.

Those members of the official party who were still sober undoubtedly recognized that the multitude of salutes, each from a different ship, had less to do with honoring the commissioners than it did with reminding them of the significant power Perry had at his command.

THE TREATY OF Kanagawa was concluded on the last day of March, 1854, which was also of Kayei the seventh year, third month, and third day. It called for "perfect, permanent and universal peace, and a sincere and cordial amity" between the

Empire of Japan and the United States of America, "without exceptions of persons or places," and was signed with great ceremony at Yokohama.

Perry had hoped to establish trade between the two nations, but the Japanese refused even to discuss his overtures on the subject. Instead, he had to settle for agreements relating to the protection of shipwrecked American sailors, and a concession on the part of the Japanese that allowed American ships to stop at two specific ports for water, coal, firewood, and other provisions that might be available. The first port was Shimoda, on the main island of Honshu; and the second was Hakodate on the northern island of Ezo (Hokkaido). The shogun's commissioners may have been puzzled by Perry's repeated insistence on the second location as a stopping place for American vessels. They were extremely sensitive to their own national privacy, and no doubt must have been relieved that the Americans were interested in such a remote spot, so far from the vital center of the Empire. They might have been surprised to learn that Perry's interest in that particular location stemmed from the day, six years earlier, when Lieutenant Maury stretched a piece of string from Shanghai to Monterey, and his congressional audience noted that it passed directly over Hakodate.

WITH THE TREATY secured, Perry finally permitted the sailors shore leave, and for the first time, liberty parties were allowed to stroll around Yokohama under the watchful eye of Japanese officals who made sure they did not stray beyond prescribed limits.

One group, wandering high on Hachinji Hill, could not resist the opportunity to mark their passage, and in traditional American style, they boldly spelled out their names in white paint on a prominent rock. The Japanese were fascinated by this amiable vandalism, which was something totally beyond their experience. They were unfamiliar with Roman lettering, and puzzled over what the strange scribbles might indicate. A local artist copied the graffiti as carefully as he could, and it has come down to us in a subtly orientalized form:

One learned expert, Seki Hakuryu, physician to the Lord of Awa, finally solved the mystery by translating it as "In the year of the First Tiger [1854], since it was his birthday, he could not but stop; King Hatan therefore gave up commencing war that day." This interesting interpretation is considerably more colorful than the probable truth, which is that a certain William Ash, able-bodied seaman of the *Mississippi*, simply wanted the world to know he had been there.

THROUGHOUT THE SPRING and summer of 1854, the *Macedonian* meandered in leisurely fashion across the western Pacific, stopping off to survey potential coal mines and to establish coaling stations in the Bonin Islands, Formosa, and the Philippines, before returning to Hong Kong in September. Commodore Perry was waiting for her. He was eager to return home to report to the President and Congress on his negotiations, and had remained in Hong Kong only long enough to turn the command of the squadron over to Joel Abbot.

Abbot, like every captain in the navy, hungered for the honorific of "Commodore," which carried with it no emoluments but considerable prestige, and he was more than a little put out when Perry, always a stickler for the proprieties, insisted he continue to fly the red pendant of vice-commodore until Washington confirmed his appointment. That confirmation finally arrived on January 6, 1855, four months after Perry's departure, and Abbot immediately ordered his blue pendant hoist to the top of the main.

Once again, the *Macedonian* was the flagship.

IDENTITY CRISIS

~~~~~~~~~~~~~~~~~~~~

W HAT KIND OF SHIP WAS THE *MACEDONIAN*? EVERYONE could agree that she had been a frigate prior to 1852, but after her upper deck was sliced off and her innards rearranged, what was her new rating? Was she a "razee sloop," as some authorities described her, or a "sloop-of-war," as others called her, or a "covette," as still others insisted? It depended entirely on who was doing the defining, and for a time all three terms were used more or less interchangeably. Such inconsistencies in nomenclature were common enough in navies, and no one took the matter too seriously, with the exception of one man, a warrant officer on board the *Macedonian* named Richard T. Allison, to whom the precise rating was a far from academic question.

Allison was the *Macedonian*'s purser throughout her long Asian cruise, and he was acutely aware that pursers of frigates received higher pay than pursers in lesser vessels. In his case, the differential amounted to a lot of money—$1,000 a year. During his long months and years in Japan and the East Indies, Allison had time to ruminate on the fact that his relatively meager salary was a direct result of an arbitrary redefinition made by faceless minions in Washington, and to reflect on the plain injustice of it all. Eventually he came to see himself as the innocent victim of a massive bureaucratic confusion, and he became convinced that the *Macedonian*, for all her reconstruction and rerating, was still a frigate, had never been anything else but a frigate, and that therefore he was entitled to a small fortune in back pay.

His reasoning was simple, and not without merit. What was

a sloop-of-war? It was a three-masted vessel with all her guns on one deck. And what was a frigate? Any dictionary would confirm that a frigate was a three-masted warship with two decks of guns. When the *Macedonian* was rebuilt in 1852, her old battery of forty-six guns had been replaced by a lesser number of shell guns, the majority of which were positioned on her gun deck. But two of her new cannon, the 10-inch shell guns, were located on the spar deck, which meant, pure and simple, that she still had two decks of guns, and therefore remained a frigate.

Over the length of the cruise Allison had plenty of time to put together a bill of particulars, and soon after the ship returned to Boston in August 1856, he submitted his claims to the authorities. The navy, finding it difficult to refute his arguments out of hand, turned the matter over to the U.S. Attorney General, Caleb Cushing, and in effect asked a civilian lawyer to decide the very nautical question: What kind of vessel was the *Macedonian*?

Cushing issued his opinion in 1857. His first line of argument focused on the broad question of authority. Did the navy have the right to designate—or in the case of the *Macedonian*, redesignate—the rating of a warship? His answer, surprisingly, was in the negative. The navy had been reorganized most recently under an Act of Congress of August 31, 1842, and since that act did not specifically grant the power to establish classes of vessels to the navy, it was the Attorney General's opinion that such authority rested solely with the Congress itself.

He then traced the history of the ship, noting that her designation had been, in congressional terms, unambiguously that of a frigate. After her capture in 1812, she was "immediately repaired, and placed in commission as a frigate," and in 1832, Congress passed an act "to finish the rebuilding of the frigate *Macedonian*." Under a general appropriation of 1852, "she was repaired, and her armament was then materially changed," but did such a repair and rearmament constitute enough of a change to alter her identity as a frigate? The navy believed it did, and reclassified her as a "razee sloop." But Cushing pointed out that such a designation was totally without sanction of law, since, in a legal sense, no such class of vessel existed.

But if she could not be a razee sloop, could she be a sloop-of-war or corvette? (The latter term was a British usage, borrowed from the French, and was synonymous with the American sloop-of-war.) Here the Attorney General relied on the same line of reasoning advanced by Richard Allison. Even after her conversion, the *Macedonian* "still remained a two-decker, with guns on each deck, not being razeed in that respect; and although her bulwarks were lowered, yet her masts and spars were lengthened." Whatever she might be, the *Macedonian* could not be a sloop-of-war, since by definition such a vessel mounted all her guns on a single deck. Even if "the name frigate, as applied to the *Macedonian,* and to ships of her tonnage and armament, were wholly inappropriate,—and if there be reasons of foreign policy to suggest the inexpediency of the present designations,—still, for state purposes, they must remain so long as it is the pleasure of Congress," the Attorney General concluded. The "statute designation" of the *Macedonian* as a frigate, "if not mathematically exact, seems to be a nearer approximation to exactness than the substitute designation."

The *Macedonian,* at least legally, was still a frigate.

ALLISON GOT HIS money, and the Navy Department, which was not about to start calling the *Macedonian* a frigate again, began negotiating with Congress for the right to call its ships whatever it damn well wanted to call them.

CHUTZPAH

~~~~~~~~~~~~~~~~~~~~~~~~~~~~~

In the late spring of 1858, the *Macedonian*—which had been languishing at the Charlestown Navy Yard in Boston Harbor since her return from the Orient eighteen months earlier—was undergoing the last stages of a refitting prior to joining the Mediterranean Squadron. The newly enlisted crew members were going about their work in a state of heightened anticipation, focused not so much on their upcoming cruise as on the imminent arrival of their new captain, who was expected on board momentarily.

His name was Uriah Phillips Levy, and he was awaited with a mixture of curiosity and wonder. Few if any of the men in the *Macedonian* had ever laid eyes on Captain Levy, but everyone had heard of him. He was, in a very literal sense, a legend in his own time, and his reputation as an eccentric and unpredictable officer was known throughout the navy. Just how one perceived that legend depended in large part on one's rank. Common sailors worshipped him as a hero for his lifelong campaign against flogging and his fight for sailors' rights; but officers, mindful of Levy's six courts-martial and his innumerable and notorious battles with his superiors, held a more equivocal view of the man.

His supporters—and he had many in the officer corps—admired his keen intellect and eloquent sense of justice. His critics—and he had many of them, as well—complained publicly of his fiery temper and excessive pride, and deplored his unorthodoxy. Privately they loathed the man, in part because he had risen from the ranks and "was not a gentleman," but primarily because he was a Jew.

Just why the American Navy should have been such a hotbed of anti-Semitism at a time when there were only about 3,500 Jews in the entire country remains something of a mystery, but there is no question that throughout Levy's long career, his enemies, motivated by strong anti-Jewish sentiments, had waged a bitter campaign against him, using every means at their disposal to bring him down and force him out. Over a forty-six-year period they had repeatedly blackened his reputation with innuendo, denied him advancement, and by twisting the rules of evidence past all recognition, managed to put together not only six courts-martial, but three dismissals from the service as well. A number of officers who held no anti-Semitic bias found it easy to go along with the persecution of Levy, for he was a maverick and unpredictable, and to many these were equally dangerous qualities.

ON THE EVE of his arrival on board the *Macedonian*, Levy gave the ship's company a taste of the kind of surprises they might expect from him. A brief message addressed to the first officer advised him that the *Macedonian* would be carrying a passenger on the cruise to Europe, namely, Virginia Levy, the captain's wife. The ship hardly had time to absorb this astonishing and unprecedented intelligence when the man himself arrived in person from New York, and true to his word, he had his lady in tow.

Captain and Mrs. Levy made a striking couple as they alighted from their carriage in the navy yard. He was a very tall, somewhat stiff officer in his mid-sixties, with a round, stubborn face, and dark, intelligent eyes set off by a black, tightly curled handlebar mustache. His wife was every bit as distinctive as her spouse, although barely a third his age. She was in her early twenties, and was a dainty and vivacious beauty, with large, dark eyes and a creamy complexion. She was dressed in the height of fashion and carried herself with a confidence and aplomb she had undoubtedly learned from her distinguished husband.

It must have been an interesting scene, with the officers and men of the *Macedonian* standing to attention as the new captain helped his lady negotiate the narrow gangway with her hoop skirt and crinolines, the two of them finally emerging amidships to the ruffle of drums and the keening of the boatswain's whistle. The officers and crew studied them with more than ordinary curiosity. Most of the men had never seen a Jew before, let alone two Jews.

After the brief ceremonies involved in taking command, the Levys quickly settled into the great room of the *Macedonian*, where the privacy offered by Lord FitzRoy's bulkhead was now more than ever appreciated. As if to mark the uniqueness of the occasion, the ship's carpenter, under the direction of Virginia Levy, installed a mazzuzah on the frame of the cabin door.

URIAH PHILLIPS LEVY was born in 1792 in Philadelphia, when it was still the largest and busiest seaport in the country. He grew up in the shadows of Joshua Humphreys's shipyard, and a familiarity with things nautical was a part of his life from the beginning. The Levys were one of only a handful of Jewish families in Philadelphia; and while their religion caused them to be treated as outsiders, they experienced little hostility in a city that had been founded by Quakers, who practiced toleration of all beliefs.

Levy's roots in America ran deep. His maternal grandfather, Jonas Phillips, arrived in South Carolina from Rhenish Prussia as an indentured servant, and by the time he had worked off his terms of service and was ready to marry, he was firmly entrenched in the local establishment. No less a figure than Colonel George Washington of Virginia attended his wedding.

The young Uriah, who inherited his grandfather's energy and ambition, ran off to sea at the age of ten, and although he dutifully returned home two years later for his bar mitzvah, it was clear that the sea was in his blood, and he soon left again, this time for good. Years later, as an adult, he would proclaim, "I am an American, a sailor and a Jew," identifying his priorities in precise sequence.

By the time he was nineteen, in 1811, Levy was already a
seasoned mariner who had survived any number of perilous
adventures, including a shipwreck, a pitched battle with French
pirates, and impressment aboard a British man-of-war. He had
also prospered, and was now master and one-third owner of a
merchant schooner. But with the advent of the War of 1812,
Levy decided to join the U.S. Navy. He shipped out as sailing
master in the *Argus*, a heavily armed brig, and took part in a
celebrated cruise in the Irish Sea that seriously disrupted British
commerce, forced the marine insurance rates at Lloyds to sky-
rocket, and remains to this day a proud legend in the American Navy. Levy exhibited great energy and resourcefulness
while in the *Argus*, and in recognition of his clear thinking
and bravery under fire was appointed an acting lieutenant. Officially he remained a mere petty officer, but he now shared the
responsibilities and privileges of a commissioned officer, and
found them very much to his liking. His enjoyment of his new
status was brief. Within weeks of his promotion he was captured by a Royal Navy warship and spent the next year and a
half as a prisoner of war in Dartmoor. Characteristically, Levy
made good use of the time, taking language lessons from French
prisoners.

When he returned to Philadelphia after the peace treaty, Levy
surprised his friends by expressing an ambition to remain in the
navy. Although he had experienced more than a whiff of anti-
Semitism during his duty in the war, and had no illusions about
the vein of prejudice that ran through the naval officer corps,
he was confident that the problem, while disagreeable, could be
overcome. His old friend and partner John Coulter was not so
sure. He warned Levy that "nine out of ten of your superiors
may not care a fig that you are a Jew, but the tenth may make
your life a living hell." Levy was not to be dissuaded. His reply,
couched in the bombastic and vaguely messianic diction that
was to become his signature, spoke of a higher duty: "What will
be the future of our Navy if others such as I refuse to serve
because of the prejudices of a few? There will be other Hebrews,

in time to come, of whom America will have need. By serving myself, I will help give them a chance to serve."

For all of Levy's eloquence and high ideals, Coulter's warning proved prophetic. Within a year of his return to the navy, Levy was forced to fight a duel in which he killed a man who had publicly denounced him as "a damned Jew." A year after that he was banned from serving in the USS *United States*, which was known as a "gentleman's ship," for his religion and his humble origins. In succeeding years his enemies, determined to maintain the purity of their navy, tried every means short of manslaughter to get rid of him. They conspired against him in matters of promotions and appointments, brought him to trial on trumped-up charges and falsified evidence, and generally made his life a misery.

Uriah Levy fought back furiously, convinced of the rightness of his course, but in 1828, at a point when his enemies appeared to have brought his career to a dead halt, he opted to take temporary leave from the navy and try his hand on Wall Street. In short order he parlayed an investment in New York real estate into a fortune eventually valued at several hundred thousand dollars, and discovered the powers and pleasures of philanthropy. Levy was a worshipful admirer of Thomas Jefferson, and devoted much of his wealth to honoring his great hero. He personally commissioned and paid for the heroic statue of the third President by Pierre-Jean David d'Angers that stands today in the Capitol rotunda, and when he learned that Jefferson's beloved Monticello was falling apart from neglect and was due to go under the hammer for back taxes, he purchased the entire estate and spent years and many thousands restoring it to its former grandeur. A provision in his will called for it to be turned over to the American people as a gift upon his death.

For all his financial success, his first love remained the navy. Levy retained his commission and returned to active duty whenever possible, but his enemies were so pervasive that it was virtually impossible for him to remain in the service on a regular basis, so he kept a foot in each camp, military and civilian.

His career in business opened up a new world to Uriah Levy, introducing him to men of affairs and people of distinction he could not have expected to meet through the navy, and he was quick to cultivate their friendship.

So it was that when the Levys installed themselves on board the *Macedonian*, the ship quickly became a magnet for the more elevated and distinguished citizens of the Boston area. By early June 1858, when Henry Wadsworth Longfellow came down to the Charlestown Navy Yard to wish the couple a happy voyage, he was only the last in the parade of dignitaries, artists, and men of affairs who had made the same journey for the same reason in the fortnight following their arrival in town. Governors, college presidents, lawyers, and intellects of every stripe— the captain seemed to know everyone worth knowing in Boston, and the ward room was duly impressed.

The *Macedonian* departed Boston on June 6, and ran down to Key West for final provisioning before setting sail for Europe. The three-week journey, which included a brief stopover at Havana, gave the officers and men an opportunity to observe their captain's style of command at sea. He was generally solicitous to the crew, particularly to the new hands, and questioned them in a kindly manner to see if they understood the precise nature of their tasks, carefully explaining to them how their work fitted into the overall management of the ship. He was considerably less deferential to his officers, who he treated in a fair but distant manner, and who he held to a strict level of accountability. He insisted they study the ship's roster, and that they address the individual sailors by name, "but never 'you,' as it is degrading to so address a man."

Upon their arrival at Key West, the Levys' parade of distinguished visitors resumed. Senator William Henry Seward of New York dropped by to pay his respects, and the captain was delighted to run into his longtime friend Commander John Dahlgren, the ordnance engineer who was changing the navy with his fresh ideas on gunnery.

Key West offered ample opportunities for the crew to get

into trouble, and soon after their arrival it became necessary for Captain Levy to sit in judgment upon the offenders. Courts-martial were important affairs on any ship, but the interest aroused by a court-martial run by Uriah Phillips Levy was electric, and attracted the attention of the entire naval station. How would he decide the cases? What would be his judgments? Would he adopt the same quixotic forms of punishment he had pursued so long ago on the *Vandalia*?

Everyone knew the story of Levy and the *Vandalia*.

ON JULY 7, 1838, Uriah Levy was captain of the sloop-of-war *Vandalia*, cruising off the Gulf coast. A young sailor named John Thompson was brought up on charges for making fun of one of the midshipmen "by imitating his voice." It was a childish prank, and Levy considered it a trifling matter, but agreed that some sort of punishment was required. On any other ship the sentence for such an infraction would almost certainly have been the cat, but Levy detested flogging and sought to find a punishment more suitable to the crime.

He had the accused sailor brought before him. "Have you been mimicking Midshipman Ammen?" he asked solemnly.

Thompson admitted he had.

"Very well then," Levy said. "If you must be a mimic, I will show you the proper way—I will make a parrot out of you."

He ordered the ship's carpenter to fetch a pot of tar, and sent someone else to pluck a half dozen tail feathers from the parrot belonging to the chief gunner. Everyone on deck stood by, totally mystified, wondering what the captain might possibly have in mind.

When the materials Levy had requested were ready, the captain directed that Thompson be bent over a gun and his trousers let down. He then ordered the boatswain to touch a dab of tar—"as large as a silver dollar"—to the boy's buttocks, and stick the feathers in it.

The boatswain did as ordered, and stepped back. Thompson remained leaning over the gun, puzzled.

"There," explained Levy, in a voice loud enough for everyone to hear. "Now you are in a condition to mimic. You are a proper parrot, and you will remain so for five minutes."

It took a moment for the crew to grasp the captain's message, and then a great shout of glee went up, the men laughing and pounding one another on the back. Later Levy would report that young Thompson "was much mortified, breaking into tears."

After five minutes the miscreant was released. Sheepishly, he pulled off the feathers and the dab of tar, hitched up his britches, and fled below decks. Five minutes later he was laughing as loud as the others, agreeing that the punishment was infinitely better than the dozen lashes he would have received on another ship.

There the matter appeared to have ended. The "parrot incident" faded into memory, and over time was all but forgotten by those who had been present that day in the *Vandalia*. Then, five years after the affair, out of the blue, Commander Levy was ordered to Baltimore to stand court-martial for "cruel and scandalous conduct" in the matter of seaman John Thompson. The charge was brought not by the supposedly injured Thompson, but by a longtime enemy of Levy's who had not even been on board the *Vandalia* at the time of the incident, and it specified that such "cruel and unusual punishment" was "highly scandalous and unbecoming the dignity of an officer."

At the trial, a bemused and outraged Levy listened to testimony purporting that the crew had been appalled at the inhumanity of his treatment of Thompson, and had come close to mutiny. When his turn came to defend himself, he lashed back at such a totally distorted description of events. Thompson's punishment was unusual, he admitted, but hardly cruel. His defense was succinct, accurate, and reasonable, if a little wordy, but the judge advocate managed to give the court a highly colored and grossly inaccurate description of events. The dab of tar "the size of a silver dollar" became, in his description, a gruesome, full-fledged tar and feathering that sent the poor Thompson into a state of shock. Levy had "trampled on rules and regulations," and his "tyrannical punishment made good and wholesome discipline impossible."

The trial lasted six days. The case against him was such a travesty that Levy was confident he would be exonerated. "At the most, I anticipate no more than a reprimand," he wrote cheerfully, while he awaited the court's decision. Remarkably, this highly intelligent man, this worldly realist who had distinguished himself in combat and command, who had shown the cunning and calculation to prosper in the perilous waters of New York finance, and who had endured decades of attack from his fellow officers, was almost childishly unaware of what was happening to him, and totally blind to the true machinations of the court. He did not have the wit to see that the men sitting in judgment on him were not in the least interested in the validity of the charges, and that they were simply using whatever means they could find to rid themselves of this Jonah, this imaginative, unorthodox troublemaker, whose mere presence in the navy caused them such severe discomfort. Undoubtedly, anti-Semitism contributed to the court's animus, but so did the natural conservatism and blinkered outlook of the judges.

After six days of blatantly trumped-up testimony, they announced their decision: ". . . after mature deliberation the court does adjudge and sentence that Commander U.P. Levy be and is hereby dismissed form the Navy of the United States." The entire trial had been so biased and distorted that any verdict of guilty was by definition prepostrous. President Tyler wasted little time overruling the court, and only three months after the decision against him, Levy was back on the navy lists.

The *Macedonian* was Levy's first ship command in the twenty years since he had skippered the *Vandalia*. Had he learned any lessons from that previous time?

THE *MACEDONIAN*'S LOGS for the years of Captain Levy's command are preserved in the National Archives, and include the full text of each one of his disciplinary sentences. A typical judgment, from July 20, 1858, when the ship was still at Key

West, indicates that perhaps the irrepressible captain had indeed
learned something from the *Vandalia* experience. The entry for
the day, after tersely setting the scene, "12 M. called all hands
to muster where the following sentence of a court martial was
read," presents Levy's measured judgement of a fairly typical
breech of regulations:

> You, Carmichael, Purdy and Graham, have been guilty of a
> great crime, you have deserted your flag, and your life ac-
> cording to the strict letter of the law is forfeited to your coun-
> try. The 17th Article says, Shall any person desert or entice
> others to desert, he shall suffer death or such other punish-
> ment as a Court Martial shall adjudge.

Warming to the subject, the captain points out the evenhand-
edness with which the court has dealt with the miscreants:

> Nothing can be urged as an excuse for your offense, you are
> well treated and are only required to do your duty. If you
> have any wrongs to complain of, the means of redress are
> opened for you, and you must take no other way than that
> provided to right real or imaginary wrongs. The Court com-
> prised of three commissioned officers has treated you with
> great fairness, for although you confessed a guilt you could
> not deny, the Court heard patiently all you could urge to
> incline it to leniency.

Finally, he offers up the dreaded sentence of the court:

> The Court has sentenced each of you to suffer forfeiture of
> two months pay to be confined in the cage for twenty days,
> one half of the time on bread and water, to have no tobacco
> or grog during the time of confinement.

But then there is a pause for reflection, and perhaps a ray of
hope.

This is not an unmerited sentence, *it is even lenient*, & I would at once order you to undergo the full penalty adjudged, were it not that I am moved by your youth and inexperience and former good character, to remit, and I do remit that part of the sentence in each case which subjects you to confinement, restraint, and bread & water diet.

And now at last, the captain is ready to define the sentence as it will be carried out:

You are to be punished by the loss of two months pay, and are to be deprived of grog and tobacco for 20 days. Let your future good conduct, your alacrity in the performance of your duties and respectful obedience to your officers, justify the leniency shown to you. (Signed), U. P. Levy, Captain.

Levy's sentences given on board the *Macedonian* lack the imaginative creativity of the "parrot incident," but they reflect a continued determination to bring about a rehabilitation of the miscreants with a minimum of punishment.

THE FACT THAT there was a woman aboard the *Macedonian*— especially a young and pretty woman—added a novel quality to shipboard life, although as far as the woman in question was concerned, the novelty was not all of a positive nature. Virginia Levy, who very much enjoyed being cosseted by her indulgent husband, longed for a personal maid to deal with the endless housekeeping details attendant upon a lady of fashion; but Captain Levy, having bamboozled the Secretary of the Navy into permitting her presence on board, was not willing to go back and seek approval for a second female.

In an attempt to solve her problem, Virginia brought aboard a young boy named Jack in the hopes that he might be trained to take the maid's place, but her plan failed. "The sailors spoiled him so that he was of little use to me," she confided in her journal. "They put him up to all sorts of pranks on the officers."

Prospects brightened for Virginia when the ship finally arrived on station in the Mediterranean in the late summer. At Marseilles she and the captain were received "with open arms. There we met that wonderful man, Viscount de Ferdinand Marie Lesseps, the creator of the Suez Canal." Uriah Levy's personal parade of dignitaries was once more on the march.

There was little actual work for the Mediterranean Squadron, which was under the command of Commodore Eli Lavalette, a pompous and generally undistinguished officer who wore his pendant in the steam frigate *Wabash*. His orders to his captains called for them to do little more than cruise from port to port, showing the flag and putting on a display of good manners. Their duties included attending at an almost endless round of balls, receptions, and reviews, and when Virginia Levy rejoined the ship in Egypt, after a whirlwind shopping trip to Paris, she and her husband immediately entered into a hectic round of social activities, rubbing elbows with any number of distinguished folk, including Queen Victoria's second son, Prince Alfred, the future Duke of Edinburgh, who was in Alexandria that winter for his health.

Uriah Levy enjoyed parties immensely. He delighted in dressing up in in uniforms covered with gold braid, showing off his pretty young wife, and rubbing elbows with the movers and shakers of the world. He was an excellent dancer, and he and Virginia cut a swath through the ballroom, whirling to the mazurka, the gavotte, the polka, and the waltz. Such pleasures are not gained without effort, however, and it was during that winter in Alexandria that the crew learned their captain's darkest secret—he dyed his hair and mustache to maintain an aura of youth.

AT LEAST SOME of the junior officers in the *Macedonian* must have wondered, as they watched the Levys depart for still another soirée, why the captain, an independently wealthy man who could purchase any comfort in the world, chose to traipse about the Mediterranean at the beck and call of Commodore Eli Lavalette, a man who made no secret of his dislike for him, when he might well have been better off leaving such goings on to younger men while he remained at home among his rich cronies in New York.

Why, indeed. Certainly one answer was that Uriah Levy enjoyed parties. But to leave the answer at that would have entirely missed the essence of the man. The plain and simple fact is that Uriah Levy was head over heels in love with the United States, and with its navy. Passionately in love. Deliriously, rapturously in love. He adored America with a primitive, emotional simplicity so intense that it governed his every thought, and he loved the U.S. Navy with an equal ardor because it was the instrument and protector of his beloved country. Such a passionate, unreasoned, worshipful love of country is no longer acceptable in a century that has seen the horrors of nationalism run rampant, but in Levy's day many Americans shared his ardor. They were acutely aware that they were part of a noble experiment in a kind of self-government not seen on earth since the Age of Pericles, and they took inordinate pride in the fact.

Levy saw himself as the embodiment of the American dream. He, a Jew, a member of a despised and suspect group, was living proof that a man could rise above his humble origins and could succeed solely on the basis of his native wit and determination, protected by the radical and inspiring power of the Constitution. It was Uriah Levy's intense patriotism that had led to the great crisis in his life, and indirectly, to his command of the *Macedonian*.

THE CRISIS AROSE in 1855, at a time when Captain Levy was grudgingly coming to terms with the fact that his increasing age made it less and less likely that he could ever again hope for a sea command. His future in the navy, while secure as far as he could see, was in all likelihood limited now to deskwork in one of the many bureaucratic offices of the Navy Department, and while such a fate could hardly have appealed to a man of such vigorous romanticism, he could take comfort that he was not alone—any number of his contemporaries shared a similar fate.

But Levy was too optimistic. His future in the navy was nowhere near as secure as he believed, and his enemies, who had never stopped plotting against him, had finally come up with a way to rid themselves of the pushy, prideful, obstreporous Jew. One morning in September 1855, while at home in his residence on St. Mark's Place in New York, Uriah Levy received the most stunning and most shocking letter of his career.

Sir:

The Board of Naval Officers assembled under the "Act to Promote the Efficiency of the Navy," approved Feb. 28, 1855, having reported you as one of the officers who should, in their judgement, be stricken from the rolls of the Navy, and the finding of the Board having been approved by the President, it becomes my duty to inform you that accordingly, your name is stricken from the rolls of the Navy.

> *I am respectfully,*
> *Your obedient servant,*
> *J. C. Dobbin*
> *Secretary of the Navy*

The letter was addressed to "Mr. Uriah P. Levy, Late Captain, U.S. Navy."

"Stricken from the rolls." Levy was dumbfounded. "The traveler," he wrote, in his usual overblown style, "moving forward under a clear sky, with a light step and a gay heart, who is suddenly stricken down by a thunder ball, could not be more astounded than I by the contents of this letter."

It was worse than that. Secretary Dobbin's blunt message, so totally lacking in any grace or deference, had at a blow shattered Levy's whole system of belief, his faith in America. To accept such a decision would have required him to deny his entire career, to define his life as nothing more than a charade.

Here was a challenge indeed, far more difficult than any he had encountered in his more than forty years in the navy—a secret, star chamber court, with no records to devulge the nature of their findings, and offering no recourse. The "Late Captain, U.S. Navy" hurried to Washington to consult his friends in power. Influential senators, equally appalled by the secretive nature of the Board's findings and the draconian nature of its judgment, advised him to find a good attorney and draft a petition to Congress. And so at the age of sixty-three, when most men might simply have opted to get on with life, Uriah Levy returned to New York and began plotting what the Washington *Union* described as "one of the greatest fights for justice in the annals of the armed forces."

IT WAS A grand and glorious battle, and it took two years to decide the issue. The opening salvo was Levy's 9,000-word memorial addressed to Congress, which eventually caused that body to pass an act providing that upon written request made "by any officer who was dropped, furloughed or relieved . . . the Secretary of the Navy shall cause the fitness of such officer of the Naval Service to be investigated." A court of inquiry was set up, to which Levy immediately applied. His hearing was set for November 1857.

The navy presented its case first, weighing in with a recitation of Levy's six courts-martial. When Levy's lawyer pointed out that his client had been cleared of all the old charges, and had subsequently been promoted, the court overruled him.

Reading the old records took several days, after which the navy brought in an array of senior officers to testify personally against the defendant. They pronounced him "vain," "quarrelsome," "impulsive and eccentric in his manner, fond of speaking of himself and his accomplishments," and the owner of a "bad temper." There was no mention, of course, that he was a Jew, which was the principal reason for the antagonism toward him.

The most senior officer to testify against him had not seen Levy since they both served in the *United States* thirty-nine years before, but his memory of that time was not complimentary. He pronounced Levy "quarrelsome, insubordinate. His temper and disposition were not such as to promote discipline," he averred, and warned ominously, "as far as I know, he is that at this time."

With this somber possibility hanging in the air, the navy rested its case, and Uriah Levy's lawyer, Benjamin Butler of

New York, rose to present the defense. Now, for the first time, the court heard evidence of anti-Semitism. Witnesses testified to the extreme prejudice that had marked Levy's career. A Captain McDowell stated bluntly that "Levy was liked by all but the anti-Semites." Commodore Isaac Mayo, who had served with Levy in the *North Carolina*, testified that the defendant had been ostracized solely because he was a Jew. A deposition from Captain Francis Gregory declared flatly: "The prejudice against Levy originated in his being a Jew." George Bancroft, a former Secretary of the Navy, took the stand to state that "I perceived a strong prejudice in the service against Captain Levy, which seemed to me, in a considerable part, attributable to his being of the Jewish persuasion."

With the damning evidence of anti-Semitism now in the record so clearly defined and irrefutable as to be impossible to ignore or overlook, the judge advocate wearily enquired of Benjamin Butler whether his long list of witnesses was at an end. By no means, Butler replied. His client had been vilified, his character brought into question and his career destroyed by the infamous decision of the Board, and he intended to fight back with every means at his disposal.

There followed an amazing spectacle. Into the courtroom trooped a parade of distinguished witnesses to Uriah Levy's character: the governor of New Jersey, the president of the Bank of New York, the editor of the *New York Globe*, senators, businessmen, government officials, and even a poet. One by one they took the stand to testify on behalf of Uriah Phillips Levy. There were fifty-three of them in all, and it took the court another three days to hear them.

At last, after weeks of testimony, Uriah Levy himself stood up to present his final argument, a massive, hundred-page document, which he read aloud, page after page, a turgid, at times bombastic, often repetitious, but powerful plea for justice. It took almost four days to enter it into the record.

It went over the old ground in detail, at first coolly and with dispassion, but with increasing energy and emotion as the nature and enormity of the injustice unfolded. On the morning of the final day of the hearing, December 22, Levy reached his peroration. In the words of one account, "It was one of the most glorious, if not brilliant pleas ever made by an individual in the history of the United States Navy: a plea that 'right should be done!' This became the crowning triumph in Uriah Levy's career: it was a half century of experience speaking, experience as a seaman, but most of all, experience as an American Jew."

Reading from his text, Levy stood ramrod straight before the court and began, "My parents were Israelites, and I was nurtured in the faith of my ancestors. In deciding to adhere to it I have but exercised a right guaranteed to me by the Constitution . . ." He discoursed on the uniqueness of that guarantee, which in fact could not be found in the laws of any other country in the world at the time, and how it protected every citizen.

This is the case before you . . . are American Christians now to begin the persecution of the Jews? of the Jews who stand among them the representatives of the patriarchs and prophets,—the Jews, to whom were committed the oracles of God;—the Jews, from whom these oracles have been received, and who are the living witnesses of their truth;—the Jews, from whom came the founder of Christianity;—the Jews, to whom, as Christians themselves believe, have been made promises of greatness and glory, in whose fulfillment are bound up the hopes, not merely of the remnant of Israel, but of all the races of men?

Like an Old Testament prophet, he laid a warning before the groggy court. "What is my case today, if you yield to this injustice, may to-morrow be that of the Roman Catholic or the Unitarian; the Episcopalian or the Methodist, the Presbyterian or the Baptist." Returning at the very end to a consideration of the First Amendment, Levy gazed in turn at each sitting member of the court as he concluded: "I have the fullest confidence that you will faithfully adhere to this guarantee; and therefore, with like confidence, I leave my destiny in your hands."

There was a moment of silence as he collected his papers

and quietly sat down. Then spontaneously, from the gallery of onlookers, arose an outburst of applause and cheers. Many in the crowd were partisans, but the majority were simply curiosity seekers, and Levy had stirred them all.

The judge advocate, charged with presenting the navy's closing arguments, waited until the applause died down and then pointed out dryly that the several days of testimony by civilian witnesses was irrelevant, since it could not be applied to Levy's professional competence; but by then he knew he had lost his case.

The navy's argument had been shown to be baseless, and the officers of the court recognized that for the good of the service, they had to find for Levy, and do so emphatically. Unanimously, they found that "the said Levy is morally, mentally, physically and professionally fit for the Naval Service and does respectfully report that he ought to be restored to the active list of the Navy."

Before the exultant Levy returned to New York, he was invited to discuss his future with the Secretary of the Navy, Isaac Toucey, who made it very clear that the navy wanted to make amends. The service had suffered a serious loss of public esteem as a result of the court of inquiry, and it was important that the wound inflicted by the revelations not be allowed to fester. The Secretary gave vague but solemn assurances to the newly reinstated Captain Levy that he would soon receive the sea duty he had so long and fruitlessly sought.

Here was an unforeseen lagniappe, and a doubly pleased Levy entrained for New York, where three months later the orders arrived posting him to the *Macedonian*. If Secretary Toucey believed he had solved his public relations problem by that appointment, the return mail quickly taught him otherwise. Levy, while carefully making clear that he accepted the assignment, was equally clear in expressing his scorn and bitter disappointment. "I must, in candor, confess to you that it is not such a command as I expected," he noted sourly. "I fully expected, from my work and experience, to receive the command of a squadron."

The Secretary was so shamed by Levy's anger over the *Macedonian* that two weeks later, when Levy demanded the unprecedented right to bring his wife on the cruise, he caved in without a murmur.

VIRGINIA LEVY WAS enjoying her tour of the Mediterranean to the fullest. As the *Macedonian* followed a leisurely schedule from port to port, the captain's lady would at times leave the ship for a sightseeing and shopping trip to Paris or elsewhere, and return to meet her husband at a later stop. "My sojourn in Italy was as enjoyable as my stay in Egypt," she wrote in her journal. "Particularly so in Naples, where I occupied an apartment for some time. Captain Levy was compelled to leave, but everyone was very kind to me, including our Ambassador & his wife, Mrs. Chandler."

The following November she "spent Yom Kippur with Baron and Baroness Rothschild, who had a synagogue in their home. I have always admired the Rothschild family, and in whatever country I met them was impressed by their nobility of character. They understood perfectly *noblesse oblige*."

It now appeared that Isaac Toucey also understood something about *noblesse oblige*, for he had arranged one last surprise for Uriah Levy. Toward the end of 1859, Commodore Lavalette, almost seventy years old and in poor health, received orders at his anchorage at La Spezia to return home and turn over the squadron to Levy. Lavalette, who fully understood the ramifications of the order, reluctantly sent word to Levy, who was again in Alexandria, and then departed, leaving a brusque note for his successor, the new squadron commodore.

Commodore! The stunning news was brought to the *Macedonian* by the American minister in Alexandria. An exultant Levy immediately ordered the departure for Italy, and on February 21, 1860, in the harbor of Genoa, he watched his personal pendant hoisted to the top of the mizzenmast, to the accompaniment of a 13-gun salute from the rest of the squadron. "The Sardinian and Russian frigates also fired a salute of 13 guns," a proud Virginia Levy wrote. The *Macedonian* was now flagship of the

Mediterranean Squadron, as she had been previously flagship of the Pacific Squadron, of the West Indian Squadron, of the African Squadron, and of the Far Eastern Squadron. There was glory still in her creaking old timbers.

URIAH LEVY HELD the command of the Mediterranean Squadron for less than three months before he, too was ordered home, but that was long enough to establish him as a commodore for the rest of his life. In April 1860, his tour completed, and with Virginia's return passage booked on a commercial ship for a change, Levy took the *Macedonian* through the Pillars of Hercules and headed home.

In her hold she carried a wagonload of earth from Palestine, a gift to the Congregation Shearith Israel in New York, for use in the traditional Jewish burial service.

PARIS

~~~~~~~~~~~~~~~~~~~~~

W HEN THE CIVIL WAR FINALLY BROKE OUT IN THE SPRING
of 1861, the newly dis-United States found itself caught
up in a war so terrible and all-encompassing it would in time
redefine every institution in the country. Nothing would remain
as it had been—economics, politics, technology, the accepted
terms of the social order, all would change.

One of the first institutions permanently altered by the impact
of the war was the United States Navy. For decades the service
had dallied and experimented with new power sources and
weaponry, but for all the talk and paper shuffling, at the out-
break of hostilities the Union fleet was still made up largely of
wooden sailing vessels—ships like the *Macedonian*—which were
now seen to be totally unfit for modern marine warfare. Not only
had steam engines made sails obsolete, but the new ordnance—
exploding shells fired from highly accurate rifled cannon, rather
than solid balls fired from smooth-bore guns—now made fragile
wooden hulls equally irrelevant. Only ironclads could stand up
to the destructive power of the new shells, and the northern
states instituted a desperate construction campaign to turn out
enough such vessels—powered by steam—to meet the need.
As the new ships joined the fleet, the obsolete wooden sailers
they replaced were ordered home, where they were either consigned to ordinary or condemned to be broken up.

The *Macedonian*, which had been hurridly dispatched to Florida in January 1861 in one of the Federal government's last-
minute attempts to forestall hostilities, remained in southern

waters for a year or so after the war began, serving on picket duty in the Gulf. Then in 1862 she too was ordered north, but because of her special provenance and her historical significance, she was not to suffer the fate of her sisters. Instead, she was assigned to the Naval Academy as a training ship, where she would join a small squadron of other wooden sailers, including the storied USS *Constitution*.

The academy was operating at full capacity, cranking out record numbers of brand new naval officers as quickly as possible to fill the growing need and to replace the one quarter of the officer corps that had resigned their commissions and "gone South" to join the Confederacy. Because of the government's fear that Maryland, a slave state, might secede from the Union at any moment, the Annapolis campus was closed, and the entire school relocated to temporary quarters at Newport, Rhode Island. It was there, in the same port where she had made her first landfall after her capture exactly fifty years before, that the *Macedonian* took up her new assignment as a training ship and temporary barracks for the Union's midshipmen.

A YEAR LATER, in the summer of 1863, while the fate of the nation was being decided on the bloody fields of Gettysburg and along the riverbanks of Vicksburg, a large and noisy party of American midshipmen arrived at the Hôtel de Rivoli in Paris, opposite the Tuileries Gardens, eager for a few days of sightseeing. The young men had come by train from Cherbourg, where their ship, the *Macedonian*—now designated a corvette rather than a sloop-of-war—lay at anchor. The young men were on a practice cruise which had already taken them to Plymouth and Spithead in England, and would eventually include stops at Lisbon, Cadiz, and Madeira before returning home.

Paris had never been more beautiful. The court of Louis Napoleon was at its zenith, and Baron Haussmann's glorious renovations of the city were nearing completion. The broad new avenues and magnificent public buildings and monuments were already establishing new standards for urban beauty, and Paris was universally recognized as the brightest, most stylish, most elegant city in the world.

But for all the novelty and glamour that surrounded them on every side, the ebullient young Americans in the Hôtel de Rivoli were far more excited by a fresh rumor that the Confederate raider *Florida* was anchored at Brest. It was well known that southern men-of-war often used French ports to refit, and the midshipmen, who were eager to try out their fighting skills in actual combat, speculated excitedly on what might occur should they come across the rebel ship when they returned to sea. The *Florida* was a steamer, and therefore had a huge advantage over their ship, but the *Macedonian* was well armed for a practice ship. She had eight 64-pounders and four 32-pounders on her gun deck and two 100-pounder rifled pivot guns on her spar deck, and the consensus of these fledgling Decaturs was that should they encounter a rebel raider, they might reasonably expect to get in one or two effective broadsides at the start of any action, and that might carry the day. It was schoolboy bravado, and no one, least of all the midshipmen themselves, took it all that seriously.

One morning not long after their arrival, some of the midshipmen were navigating the Place de la Concorde when they spotted a group of Confederate naval officers studying a tourist map. As it turned out, the men were not from the *Florida*, which was not even in European waters at the time, but were probably on leave from some other cruiser or had crossed the ocean as blockade runners, and were now looking to join anything that might be fitting out. When the men from the *Macedonian* also recognized two or three of their former classmates among the group and tried to call out to them, both the commander in charge of the academy students and the senior Confederate officer reacted sternly, and refused to allow any fraternization. Moments later, the two parties moved away from each other without speaking, each disappearing into the crowd.

The eerie circumstances of coming across lost friends and colleagues—now enemies—thousands of miles from home,

struck a responsive chord in the minds of all. One of the midshipmen, Charles E. Clark, would write feelingly about the incident
in his memoirs half a century later, when he was a rear admiral
and the nationally revered hero of Santiago.

Another of Clark's memories from that trip to Paris had a
happier resolution. One afternoon the entire party of midshipmen descended on the Invalides to visit the Tomb of Napoleon.
The gatekeepers and the guards inside were all aged veterans
of the Grande Armée, and the Americans could not but notice
that from the moment of their arrival they were met with hostile
stares and scowls from every one of the guards, who made no
effort to hide their disdain. Their guide, who was also an elderly
veteran, was equally disagreeable, but since he spoke no English
and the midshipmen's French was of the schoolbook variety,
they were at a loss to understand the Frenchmen's puzzling
coolness. In due course it occurred to one bright fellow that their
regulation blue uniforms and brass buttons, along with the fact
that they spoke English, had undoubtedly convinced the old
Napoleonic veterans that they were British. The young men
quickly set about clearing up the confusion, and with the help
of sign language and gestures conveyed to the old veterans that
they were in fact Americans.

As soon as the message was made clear, the aloof Gallic hauteur melted, and all was warmth and hospitality, with much
hands-across-the-sea sentiment and general laughter. One of
the veterans insisted on taking the midshipmen to see the governor, who greeted them as honored guests as soon as he learned
of their nationality. With the help of an interpreter, there ensued
a lively exchange, with warm toasts to Washington and Lafayette
and to revolutionary fervor in general.

Eventually one of the midshipmen caused a minor sensation
by pointing out that their ship, the *Macedonian*, had in fact once
been British, but had been taken as a prize of war. The governor
was thrilled by this intelligence, and insisted on learning the
details of the glorious victory against the despised British, all of
which he carefully recorded in his journal. By now it was getting
late, and the young men were eager to get to Napoleon's tomb

before it closed, but the governor would not let them go, and insisted on pumping them for everything there was to know about the battle between the *Macedonian* and the *United States*. Finally satisfied, he arose and thanked the midshipmen for their heart-stirring story, and then personally led them down to the tomb, where, in the somber presence of the enormous sarcophagus, he gestured proudly to the British flag that hung among the captured trophies on display.

A WEEK LATER, the *Macedonian* was once again at sea, in the Bay of Biscay. Her captain, Commander Stephen B. Luce, was as anxious as any of the midshipmen to tangle with any rebel cruiser that might be in the area, and he shared their optimistic assessment of their chances should such an encounter materialize. He knew that the British were eager to help the Confederacy in any way possible short of joining in the war, and that any rebel raider would speak an English ship if they came across one. With that in mind, as soon as the *Macedonian* left Cherbourg, the captain did everything he could to give her the appearance of an English vessel. He ordered her royal poles cut off in the English manner, and then to strengthen the impression, ran up British colors, but all to no avail. No Confederate raider showed above the horizon, and eventually the *Macedonian*, after making her other scheduled stops, steered southwest out of Funchal until she struck the trades, then altering course due west, made for home.

The *Macedonian* would remain a part of the academy for eight more years. It would be her last naval assignment.

CITY ISLAND, THE BRONX

~~~~~~~~~~~~~~~~~

B Y THE YEAR 1871, MOST OF THE PEOPLE WHO HAD BEEN IN-
volved with the *Macedonian*'s rebuilding in 1836 were either
dead or had long since disappeared from the scene, and the old
sailing vessel, which was still on duty as a practice ship at the
Naval Academy, was universally believed to be the same En-
glish-built frigate that Decatur captured off Cape Verde. As such,
she was revered as a proud and irreplaceable relic from a golden
age of heroes—an age growing ever more golden with the continuing passage of time.

When a routine survey in 1871 showed that the *Macedonian*
was due for some basic repairs and a major refit, the authorities
ordered her to Norfolk Navy Yard, to be laid up in ordinary
until such time as the parties responsible for her could find the
money to effect the necessary repairs. There was no thought of
breaking her up or selling her out of the service. Everyone assumed she would soon return to Annapolis to provide her
unique sense of history and inspiration to still another genera-
tion of midshipmen.

But budgets, particularly military budgets in a time of peace,
can have a will-o'-the-wisp quality to them, and somehow the
money to repair the *Macedonian* never materialized. All too
quickly, the ship that had entered the navy yard in 1871 as a
priceless trophy gradually metamorphized into a leaky hulk taking up space that could otherwise be more profitably utilized.
Eventually, in the fullness of time, the navy chose the course of
sense over sensibility and decided that after sixty-three years, it
could get along without a *Macedonian*. On December 31, 1875—

the date suggests there was a fiscal imperative involved in the decision—the old ship was sold by Leigh Bros. & Phelps, auctioneers, for $14,071. The purchasers, a northern firm named Wiggin & Robinson, announced plans to put her into merchant service, but no record of such has survived, and it is highly unlikely that they ever did so.

The next definite citation we have of the *Macedonian* is a quarter century later, in 1900, when a footnote in a book written by Park Benjamin (Annapolis class of '67) makes reference to her being converted into a hotel on City Island in the Bronx. A contemporary account in a New York newspaper confirms that there was indeed a Hotel Macedonian on City Island at that time, standing at the eastern end of Ditmars Street overlooking Long Island Sound, and that it had in fact been built from the old timbers of the frigate *Macedonian*; but what had transpired between the time she was sold out of the navy and her reappearance as a hotel is only sketchily documented.

We can posit that early in 1876, soon after purchasing her on New Year's Eve, Wiggin & Robinson towed the hulk to New York, planning either to refit her and put her into merchant service or break her up for salvageable parts. Very likely on the trip north the new owners came to understand just how unseaworthy the *Macedonian* had become in her years in ordinary, and decided to beach her at Cow Bay, near Sands Point on the north shore of Long Island, and break her up for what they could get out of her. There the old ship caught the attention of a boat yard owner from City Island named Charles McClennan.

City Island was a yacht-building center on the other side of the Sound—many America's Cup challengers have come from there—and Charles McClennan would have been particularly interested in purchasing the *Macedonian* to get hold of her live oak timbers. Live oak, a comparatively rare American wood, was so tough it was reckoned to be five times more durable than the best European white oak, but because of its importance to national defense the navy held a monopoly on it, and civilians who wished to obtain this superb building material were forced to scavenge it second hand from condemned warships. City Islanders were fully conversant with the superiority of live oak, and not just for building ships. The bridge connecting their island to the Bronx proper was built entirely from live oak timbers pulled out of the ship-of-the-line *South Carolina*.

Charles McClennan bought the *Macedonian*, and floating her timbers on empty oil barrels across the Sound to City Island, hauled her into shore on the spring tide. For ten years or more the ship remained at the yard, a towering motherlode of spare parts and raw material for McClennan and other builders. Individual live oak timbers, as tough as iron, were carefully removed one at a time, reshaped, and installed in new vessels. The tin lining of the *Macedonian*'s bread room was used to rat-proof the yachts of millionaires. Copper sheathing found a hundred uses. Some of the great timbers of the hull were used as poppets to brace up the narrow bilges of thin-hulled yachts whose tons of leaded keel rested on the ground.

By 1887, even though much of the ship remained intact, Charles McClennan decided he had salvaged as much as he wanted out of the hulk. He sold the remainder to a Jake Smith for $25, provided Smith could somehow find a way to get the whole thing off his property. The new owner used much of the remaining mountain of timbers to build the Macedonian Hotel. The principal room downstairs was framed by the heaviest remaining timbers, and an old cupboard from the galley became a bar. The captain's cabin, complete with its gallery of ironbound windows, was preserved intact as a private dining room on the second floor. The only surviving photograph of the room does not indicate whether Lord FitzRoy's special bulkhead survived, but it might well have proved useful, even in its new venue. After completing the hotel, Smith still had enough timbers remaining to fence in a nearby cemetery.

The Macedonian Hotel, offering sea breezes and an unobstructed view of the Sound, quickly became a popular rendezvous for members of the New York Yacht Club, as well as Tammany officials and other sporting life, who met there regularly to swill beer and wash down the local oysters while they discussed the latest Cup challenge and arranged for the disposition of municipal contracts and other city business.

There is a story of an unidentified English visitor who, upon hearing the history of the hotel, was so distressed to learn that a Nelsonian warship should be reduced to such an uninspiring fate that he offered to pay Mr. Smith $50,000 to send her remains back to England. The offer was not accepted, but then they seldom are in stories of that nature.

Some time after 1912 the hotel, complete with the *Macedonian* captain's cabin, was sold to a syndicate that added a lot of bathhouses and changed the name to the City Island Casino, but kept the saloon unchanged.

And then, finally, came the fire.

SHORTLY AFTER MIDNIGHT on June 9, 1922, the manager of the casino was awakened by excited employees pounding on his door and shouting that a fire was raging on the top floor of the hotel. Fortunately, the casino had not yet fully opened for the summer, and the bleary-eyed manager, after quickly ascertaining that no one remained in the building, ran in his slippers and bathrobe to the firebox on the corner of South Ditmars Street and pulled the alarm.

By the time the trucks from the City Island Fire Company arrived, the fire was too far gone to be checked. Flames engulfed the third floor and threatened the rows of wooden bathhouses that led down to the beach. Soon the entire hotel was a huge torch, throwing so much light over the water it was possible to pick out landmarks on Harts Island, two miles away. By dawn the firemen managed to contain the blaze, but the casino was a total loss. A few sticks of framing timber were all that remained.

The fire had been large enough to attract some newspaper reporters, and a man from the *Herald* was poking around the still smoldering embers of the casino's annex, looking for a possible peg for his story, when he noticed that a single section of the wall remained standing, miraculously untouched, its white paint not even blistered. A large painted notice covered most of the wall. As the reporter stepped back to get a better look in the early morning light, he knew he had found his peg:

> This building is the remains of the British Frigate *Macedonian*, captured on Sunday, October 25, 1812, by the U.S. Frigate, *United States*, commanded by Captain Stephen Decatur, U.S.N. The action was fought in Lat. 24° N., Long. 29° 30'' W., that is about 600 miles NW of the Cape de Verde Islands off the west coast of Africa. Towed to Cow Bay in 1874.

The slightly garbled but generally accurate statement gave the reporter the sort of angle that might turn his routine news item into a possible front-page feature. He began interviewing the remaining spectators, seeking anyone who might shed some light on how an old British frigate had somehow been transformed into a rundown resort hotel in the Bronx.

The following day, the *New York Herald* ran the story prominently:

FRIGATE MACEDONIAN BURNS AT CITY ISLAND
Original Ship Captured by Stephen Decatur

One of City Island's oldest landmarks, the British frigate Macedonian, was destroyed by fire early yesterday. The ship had been an annex to a hotel on the beach. . . .

It had all the makings of a good yarn, a sort of Cinderella story in reverse: how a crown jewel of the Royal Navy ended her days as a blind pig in the Bronx. It was a story that begged for a follow-up, a longer piece that would provide details, answer questions, and put things in perspective. But there never was a follow-up, either in the *Herald* or in any other newspaper. The old ship that burned up in the City Island Casino fire was never heard of again.

Until now.

Appendix:

~~~~~~~~~~~~~~~~~~~~~~~

OPERATIONAL HISTORY

(* denotes flagship)
HMS MACEDONIAN

1810	Launched, Royal Naval Dock Yard, Woolwich	
1810	Lisbon Station	Capt. Lord William FitzRoy
1811	Lisbon Station	Capt. William Waldegrave
1811–12	Lisbon Station	Capt. John Surman Carden

USS MACEDONIAN

1812	Captured, Oct. 25, 1812	Lieut. William Henry Allen
1813	New London	Capt. Jacob Jones
1815	Mediterranean Station	Capt. Jacob Jones
1816	Caribbean Sea	Capt. Lewis Warrington
1818–21*	Pacific Station	Capt. John Downes
1822*	West India Station	Commo. James Biddle
1826–28*	Brazil Station	Commo. James Biddle
1829	Gosport Navy Yard Receiving Ship	Capt. Silas Duncan
1832–36	Gosport Navy Yard, Rebuilt	
1837–38*	Gosport and New York, Flag of	Master Comdt. James Armstrong

	Commo. Thomas ap C. Jones, Exploring Expedition	
1839*	West Indies, Flag of Commo. William B. Shubrick	Capt. Beverly Kennon
1840*	West Indies, Flag of Commo. William B. Shubrick	Capt. Lawrence Rousseau
1840	Hampton Roads	Lieut. S. B. Wilson
1840–41*	Boston and Norfolk, Flag of Commo. Jesse Wilkinson	Lieut. J. Rudd
1843–44*	African Station, Flag of Commo. Matthew C. Perry	Capt. Isaac Mayo
1844–45*	African Station, Flag of Commo. Matthew C. Perry	Comdr. Joel Abbot
1847	Ireland	George C. De Kay
1852	Brooklyn Navy Yard, Razeed and rearmed	
1853–55	Japan	Capt. Joel Abbot
1855*	Far Eastern Station	Commo. Joel Abbot
1855–56*	Far Eastern Station	Capt. John Pope
1858	Mediterranean Station	Capt. Uriah Phillips Levy
1859–60*	Mediterranean Station	Commo. Uriah Phillips Levy
1860–62	Gulf of Mexico	Capt. James Glynn
1863–66	Naval Academy Practice Ship	Lt. Cdr. S. B. Luce
1867–68	Naval Academy Practice Ship	Lt. Cdr. Thomas O. Selfridge
1868–69	Naval Academy Practice Ship	Lt. Cdr. George Dewey

1869–70   Naval Academy   Cdr. J. S. Skerrett
           Practice Ship
1875   Norfolk Navy Yard.
           Sold out of the U.S.
           Navy, Dec. 31

ACKNOWLEDGMENTS

When I set out to write the history of the *Macedonian* I had in mind a sort of nautical version of Viollet-le-Duc's *Annals of a Fortress*. In my innocence I hoped to come up with a manuscript that would not only tell a straightforward story, but would also support my romantic contention that wooden warships were somehow the Georgian equivalent of the cathedrals of the Middle Ages—glorious public monuments of great beauty and high technical achievement created by anonymous craftsmen to express the highest aspirations of their age. Years of immersion in the world of those seagoing cathedrals has disabused me of much of my romanticism—the ships were neither particularly beautiful nor particularly high tech—while at the same time greatly enhancing my respect and admiration for the tough, practical men who built and sailed them.

The world of sailing navies, with its gun-for-gun salutes and weather-gages, is full of strange and wonderful things, not always easily accessible to confirmed landlubbers such as myself. I have had to make many "groping attempts at learning the difference between a slab-line and a selvagee," and if, like Dr. Maturin, I can at times claim that "I am become tolerably amphibious," I owe an enormous debt to the many people who have helped me. Preeminent among them has been Bill Dunne, or W. M. P. Dunne, Ph.D., as his readers and students know him, a multi-talented naval historian cum naval architect cum professional racing driver who, as readers of the Notes and Comments section will quickly ascertain, was responsible for a significant number of the key elements in the story. Bill's extraordinary wealth of knowledge concerning every aspect of wooden ships has contributed to almost every page herein, and it is safe to say that without his high energy and insightful suggestions, this would have been a far more limited work. It would also have many more mistakes in it—although I am sure there are plenty as it is. (One of the comforts of spending months in libraries searching for minutiae is the discovery that even Samuel Eliot Morison can be guilty of the occasional howler.)

Others who have been particularly helpful to me in the creation of this book include Paul Wilderson, who pointed me in the right direction and gave me invaluable help on where to begin; William Dudley, who gave me the best advice on my project ("Forget it"), and then provided generous help, including introducing me to Bill Dunne; Richard A. von Doenhoff of the National Archives, who guided me through the awesome treasures under his supervision; Henry Silka, who sent me tidbits from his research, including important reports on the *Macedonian*'s performance under sail; my cousin Eckford de Kay, who shared his marvelous trove of data on our common ancestor, the "Commodore"; Steve Duffy, who alerted me to key aspects of the ship's vital statistics; Jim Cheevers, of the Naval Academy, who gave me the provenance of the *Macedonian*'s figurehead; the staff of the G. W. Blunt White Library at the Mystic Seaport Museum, and particularly to Paul O'Pecko, who kept finding things for me that I did not know I needed, and Norm Clarke, who showed me how to research the Royal Navy.

Closer to home, I owe much to my neighbors Charles Storrow, who on first hearing of my plans for this project forced me to face up to the questions posed by Howard I. Chapelle, and Victor Taliaferro Boatwright, whose awesome knowledge of the wooden navy was helpful any number of times.

In England, I owe much to Antonia Macarthur, who sent me one treasure after another from London's great record sources, and who corrected me on a number of misconceptions, including my confusion on the *Macedonian*'s lineage; and a special note of thanks to Graham Hunt, for providing me with one of the most unexpected phone calls of my life, and whose photographs of

Treddington Court provided a fresh insight into the character of John Surman Carden.

To my family, and particularly to my wife Belinda, whose wisdom is only matched by her patience, and her patience by her enthusiasm for an off-the-wall book idea that kept interupting our lives, I can only say thank you, and I will try to pick an easier subject next time.

And lastly, I would like to thank my great-grandfather, George Colman De Kay, who borrowed the *Macedonian* to feed the Irish, and thereby sparked my interest in that particular ship. I wish I had known him. I think I would have liked him. I am certainly very proud of him.

James Tertius de Kay
Stonington, Connecticut

NOTES AND COMMENTS

~~~~~~~~~~~~~~~~~~~~

Warships, like most large, complex, tax-supported undertak-
ings, tend to leave a paper trail in the form of ship's logs, audi-
tors' records, constructors' estimates, repair bills, manning
rosters, newspaper stories, and the like. What makes the *Macedonian* a little different is the remarkable number of personal accounts that have survived detailing life on board, beginning with
Samuel Leech's *Thirty Years from Home* (Boston, 1843), which
chronicles the *Macedonian* from her maiden voyage through her
capture by Decatur, all the way to Park Benjamin's *United States
Naval Academy* (New York, 1900), which includes an account of
her 1867 cruise up the Hudson to West Point. My guess is that
the sheer number of these personal accounts reflects the high
esteem in which the ship was once held, and the importance of
many of her assignments.

WOOLWICH

For details on the *Macedonian*'s construction, I am indebted to
those two invaluable London resources that house so many of
the records of the Royal Navy in the age of sail, the National
Maritime Museum (NMM) at Greenwich and the Public Records
Office (PRO).

Of the many publications consulted for details of Royal Navy
shipbuilding practices, the most important to me were *Building
the Wooden Fighting Ship*, by James Dodd and James Moore (New
York, 1984), an amazingly detailed work that includes the best

illustrations I have ever seen of wooden shipbuilding minutia, along with a thoroughly readable text; "The Timber Problem of the Royal Navy, 1652–1862," by Robert G. Albion (*Mariners Mirror*, 1952); *The Anatomy of Nelson's Ships*, by C. Nepean Longridge (Annapolis, 1989); *The Royal Dockyards During the Revolutionary and Napoleonic Wars*, by Roger Morriss (Leicester University, 1983); *Ships of the Royal Navy*, by J. J. Colledge (Annapolis, 1987); and *Building the Wooden Walls*, by Brian Lavery (Annapolis, 1991). I would also like to express my particular debt to Brian Lavery's *Nelson's Navy, The Ships, Men and Organisation 1793–1815* (Annapolis, 1989), an enormous, fact-crammed compendium which must be the single most comprehensive book ever published on the subject. I only wish I had it when I first encountered the Hornblower novels many years ago.

A very useful—if unorthodox—source was *Stephen Biesty's Cross-Sections Man-of-War*, with text by Richard Platt (Ontario, 1993), a visually stunning and witty overview of the structure and functioning of a wooden warship. I would like also to acknowledge a real but indefinable debt to a little book called *Ships and Boats: The Nature of Their Design*, by Douglas Phillips-Birt (London, 1966), which provided, for this landsman, an understanding of the aesthetics of naval architecture which I have endeavored to incorporate into the texture of this book where appropriate.

FITTING OUT

Lord FitzRoy's letter to the Admiralty is in the Public Records Office (PRO). Other background on FitzRoy is from *The Biographical Dictionary of Living Naval Officers*, Volume 1, also at the PRO, as well as Samuel Leech's *Thirty Years from Home*, and *The Royal Navy: A History*, by William Laird Clowes (Boston, 1897–1903).

FitzRoy

The account of the confrontation between Lord FitzRoy and G. D. Lewis is based on the transcript of Lewis's court-martial, March 7, 1811, which is in the Public Records Office. Significantly, Samuel Leech, in *Thirty Years from Home*, gives an account of the same confrontation which is almost identical, down to the smallest detail. Naval historians, both British and American, are all familiar with Leech, but have tended to cite him cautiously and to take his account of life in the *Macedonian* with a grain of salt, on the assumption that his gruesome tales of floggings and other distressing aspects of sailors' lives were highly exaggerated. A comparison of the official court-martial transcript of the FitzRoy-Lewis imbroglio and Leech's account of the same shows clearly that the latter—written from memory a quarter century after the fact and with no access to official records—precisely parallels the official record. Based on that discovery, I have assumed an equal degree of accuracy throughout Leech's narrative, and I have accepted his description of life in the *Macedonian* without reservation.

Interim Captain

Most of the details of this chapter are from Samuel Leech's *Thirty Years from Home*. Berkeley's letter appointing Waldegrave to the *Macedonian* is in the Public Records Office. Leech mentions a Captain Carson assuming the command briefly between FitzRoy and Waldegrave. It is quite possible that someone named Carson did indeed hold such an appointment temporarily, until the decision of the court-martial sitting on FitzRoy's case clarified the latter's future. Captain Carden, in his memoirs, makes no mention of either Carson or Waldegrave, but names a Captain George Seymour, one of Berkeley's sons-in-law, as FitzRoy's successor. This is probably simply a mistake on Carden's part.

CARDEN

C. S. Forester's assessment of Captain Carden is from *The Age of Fighting Sail* (Garden City, NY, 1957), and Theodore Roosevelt's is from *The Naval War of 1812* (Annapolis, 1987). The biographical material on Carden is from his autobiographical writings, published as *A Curtail'd Memoir* (Oxford, 1912), and in particular from the introduction by C. T. Atkinson. Samuel Leech's *Thirty Years from Home* is again a principal source for the actual life on board ship. The story of Carden's aborted effort to smuggle specie out of Norfolk is based on a long and detailed letter of February 27, 1812, from Littleton Waller Tazewell to Secretary of State James Monroe (Reel Two, James Monroe Papers, New York Public Library). Decatur biographer Dr. W. M. P. Dunne came across the letter in his search for confirmation to the often claimed but undocumented contention that Carden and Decatur became acquainted during Carden's visit to Norfolk. The letter is written by Decatur's prize agent and close friend, and provides ample proof that the two captains met on several different occasions during the Englishman's stay at Norfolk. Dunne was kind enough to send me a copy of the letter—just one of the innumerable ways he has contributed to the present history.

Carden's own description of the specie incident is muddled and almost impossible to understand, without Tazewell's letter as a guide. In his memoirs, the British captain describes how he ". . . was Order'd with Seald Dispatches to proceed to the Chesapeake, for our Minister at Washington, & I was expected to bring back a Heavy Freight of Money on Government & Merchants Account. I reach'd there early in 1812, & sent my Dispatches on through the British Consul at Norfolk in Virginia, Colonel Hamilton, of that Rank in the British Army. . . . I pressed the forwarding of my Dispatches, & made his House my Home until a return from our Minister at Washington.— After a long waiting for a reply, in what I call'd a long Period, it at last came to say, 'That as War was sure to be the result of the deliberations of the President of the United States, they had recourse to the unjust measure of arresting my Dispatches, & on opening them, finding my object was to obtain Money, had put a total stop to the possibility of its being attainable'.—Upon which Official Information, I left the American Port & proceeded back to Lisbon."

29°N × 29°30' W

There are any number of descriptions of the battle between the *United States* and the *Macedonian*, but the best is unquestionably the records of the court-martial of Captain Carden, held in Bermuda on May 27, 28, 29, and 31, 1813. This was my primary source. The court-martial—which exonerated Carden—contains the single largest collection of eyewitness accounts of the action, and due to the ill feeling between Carden and his first officer, David Hope, there was no possibility of collusion or whitewash in the testimony of the officers.

The New York Public Library has a microfilm of the copy of the court-martial records made in England in 1905 at the behest of A. T. Mahan. Other eyewitness sources cited include Samuel Leech's *Thirty Years from Home* and Captain Carden's memoirs. Ironically, Decatur never left an account of the action. There is an interesting sequel to the battle. In its findings, the Bermuda court-martial singled out Lieutenant David Hope for praise, commending his zeal and courage under fire from Decatur's guns. Fifteen months later, in January 1815, Hope's brother, Captain Henry Hope of HMS *Endymion*, managed to even the score by capturing Decatur in the *President*.

DECATUR

Carden's letter reporting the loss of the *Macedonian* is in the Public Records Office. Decatur's victory letter is in the National Archives, Washington, D.C., among Letters Received by the Secretary of the Navy from Captains ("Captains' Letters"). The quote from Oliver Hazard Perry is cited by Samuel Eliot Morison in *"Old Bruin": Matthew Calbraith Perry* (Boston, 1967). The account of the naval ball in Washington is from a description of the occasion written by one of the guests, a Mrs. B. H. Latrobe, in a letter now in the possession of Decatur House in Washington, D.C., and is also based in part on the particularly evocative description of the event in *The United States Navy: 200 Years* by Edward L. Beach (New York, 1986).

GALLATIN

Luke Wheeler's letters to Littleton Tazewell detailing the difficulties involved in obtaining Decatur's prize money are to be found among the "War of 1812 Manuscripts" in the Lilly Library at the University of Indiana at Bloomington. Once again, I am indebted to Dr. W. M. P. Dunne for bringing them to my attention. One question remains up in the air: Did Decatur ever get the other $100,000, or was Secretary Gallatin successful in reassigning it to the sailors' pension fund? I have left the matter moot, in the hopes that some luckier or more dedicated researcher will in time come up with the facts. In a telephone conversation, Dr. Christopher McKee of Grinell College, one of the country's leading authorities on the early navy, expressed his firm belief that Decatur eventually got the money.

NEW LONDON

The letters quoted from the Secretary of the Navy to Jacob Jones are in the National Archives. Decatur's disconsolate quote to his friend and business partner, John Bullus, is from *The Commodores*, by Leonard F. Guttridge and J. D. Smith (New York, 1969). Decatur's failed attempt to kidnap Hardy is described in detail in my own *Battle of Stonington* (Annapolis, 1990). The details of the ships' challenge, including the correspondence between

Decatur and Hardy, can be found in *Niles' Weekly Register*, January 29, February 19, and February 26, 1814.

TUNIS

The discussion between Mordecai Noah and the Bey is based on an account in *History of the Navy of the United States* by J. Fenimore Cooper (New York, 1854). Much of the credit for Decatur's diplomatic success with the Bey of Tunis clearly belongs to the American consul, Noah. Another of his diplomatic initiatives on the Barbary Coast was to have far-reaching effects on America's global posture.

During the War of 1812, a Yankee privateer sailed into the port of Tripoli with a captured British merchantman in tow. The American captain wanted the prize condemned and sold by the Barbary courts, but the British minister at Tripoli protested, pointing to a clause in the treaty between England and the Bey of Tunis, which stated that the Bey's ports "should not be used as ports of condemnation for the sale of British vessels as prizes, when captured in any war between England and any other Christian nation." In answer, Noah produced a copy of the U.S. Constitution to convince the Bey that in America, Jew and Gentile, Hindu and Chinese, all stood equal, regardless of belief. How then, he argued, could America be called "a Christian nation"? The Bey agreed. The British merchantman was condemned and the Bey pocketed 20 percent of the sale price. The story is told in *Navy Maverick* by Donovan Fitzpatrick and Paul Saphire (Garden City, NY, 1963).

The log of the *Macedonian* covering her cruise to the Mediterranean in 1815 attests to the prodigious consumption of alcoholic spirits taken on board. The following abstracts pretty much tell the story:

April 5 (New London) "Took on board 32 Gallons of Whiskey."

April 7 (New London) ". . . one cask of Whiskey—105 gallons."

April 14 (New London) "Received four pipes of whiskey (437 gallons)."

May 1 (New York) "9 puncheons of whiskey—1302 gallons, 14 barrels of ditto." [Total of 1743 gallons]

May 2 (New York) "Received eleven casks of whiskey—708 galls."

May 3 (New York) "6 puncheons of whiskey—708 galls."

August 27 (Messina) "Received on board 330 Gallons Wine for ship's use. . . . ."

August 28 (Messina) "Received on board 380 Gallons Wine for ship's use. . . ."

August 30 (Messina) "Received on board 100 Gallons Wine for ship's use. . . ."

September 13 (Naples) "Received 522 Gallons Red Wine. . . ."

September 27 (Cartagena) "One cask of whiskey 50 Gallons and one cask of Brandy 130 Gallons. . . ." [Total of 180 gallons]

October 5 (Gibraltar) "Received on board 1280 Gallons of Rum . . . 8 Hhds Whiskey. . . ." [Total of 1784 gallons]

The ship was well supplied with whiskey—the staple tipple of the American Navy—prior to her departure from New York on May 20, but by August she was running so low that she was forced to make do with local wines from Sicily and the mainland until she could resupply with the more potent distilled spirits (rum, for the most part) from the British at Gibraltar. The *Macedonian*'s consumption of spirits—which was about standard for a man-of-war—amounted to about 25 gallons a day, or a shade less than ¾ pint per man. Given that at least some of the crew were teetotalers or only light drinkers, this is an enormous rate of consumption that translates to 35 gallons a year per man. To gain some perspective on the figure, Christopher McKee, in his masterful *A Gentlemanly and Honorable Profession* (Annapolis, 1991), notes that during the 140 years from 1845 until 1985, the annual per capita consumption of alcohol for each person aged fifteen or older in the general population fluctuated between 1.5 and 2.8 gallons. The officers and crew of the *Macedonian* were knocking the stuff back at fifteen to twenty times that rate.

In Ordinary

The account of Warrington's brief summer cruise to the Caribbean in 1816 is based on the ship's log in the National Archives. Details of her subsequent repairs in Boston are from *The Captain from Connecticut: The Life and Naval Times of Isaac Hull*, by Linda M. Maloney (Boston, 1986).

Storm

The description of the hurricane that overwhelmed the *Macedonian* in 1818 is drawn largely from an eyewitness account by Alexander Slidell MacKenzie, who was a midshipman on the cruise, and who included it as an extended footnote in his *Life of Stephen Decatur* (Boston, 1846). Dr. W. M. P. Dunne brought this obscure citation to my attention. The MacKenzie description of the storm is far and away the most detailed and graphic, although I was also able to find important details in John Downes's report to the Secretary of the Navy, in "Captains' Letters" in the National Archives, as well as in the personal journals of Lieutenant Charles Gauntt and Charles J. Deblois, both of which are also in the National Archives. For details on the modern understanding of the nature of hurricanes, I am particularly indebted to Don Treworgy, resident meteorologist at the Mystic Seaport Museum in Mystic, Connecticut, and to *The Oxford Companion to Ships and the Sea*, edited by Peter Kemp (Oxford, 1990). Another important source was *Seamanship in the Age of Sail*, by John Harland (London, 1984).

NAVAL FREIGHT

The three-year cruise of the *Macedonian* to the "South Seas" is well documented. Captain Downes wrote a detailed narrative report for the Secretary of the Navy, and the private journals of Lieutenant Charles Gauntt and Charles J. Deblois, the captain's clerk (all three manuscripts in the National Archives), provide a useful and sometimes revealing perspective. While Downes admits to shipping a "considerable" amount of specie from the brig *Thomas*, Deblois reveals the fact that it was $66,000, and that the captain was taking a 6 percent cut on the total. Even when reporting on legitimate freight—that is, shipping American specie to be landed at American destinations—Downes was suspiciously vague. He writes of taking on board "about" $480,000 at one point and "about" $490,000 at another. Since it is inconceivable that he would have accepted such large consignments without bills of lading, and since common prudence would have induced him to retain copies of such records for his own protection, he must have had precise figures for the amounts taken on board and landed. The fact that he deliberately chose to remain vague strongly suggests he had something to hide. I found *In Defense of Neutral Rights: The United States Navy and the Wars of Independence in Chile and Peru*, by Edward Baxter Billingsley (Chapel Hill, 1967), particularly useful in the preparation of this part of the narrative, as well as the account in *Thence Round Cape Horn*, by Robert E. Johnson (Annapolis, 1963). I would also like to acknowledge my debt to *A Gentlemanly and Honorable Profession*, by Christopher McKee, for providing the most complete and comprehensible description of the origins and mechanics of naval freight I have been able to find anywhere.

Equating the historical value of money is always tricky. My estimate that $100,000 in 1821 equals $2,000,000 today is based on data compiled by Paul E. Greenberg and Michael J. Ahearn and used in an article written by Mr. Ahearn and published in *The Wall Street Journal* on April 7, 1994.

Lastly, I would like to acknowledge my debt to *Sharpe's Devil*, by Bernard Cornwell (New York, 1992), a well-researched and exciting novel that gave me a sense of what it must have been like to be operating on the west coast of South America in 1820 and 1821.

Two Visitors

The visit by Hardy to the *Macedonian* is in the ship's log in the National Archives, and the simultaneous presence of Owen Chase on board is described in *Stove by a Whale*, by Thomas Farel Heffernan (Middletown, CT, 1981). As it turned out, Chase did not make the return voyage to the United States in the *Macedonian*, but transferred to another vessel prior to the departure of John Downes and his crew.

Bladensburg

The duel between Decatur and Barron probably had an impact upon the country as profound as that between Alexander Hamilton and Aaron Burr. Certainly there is reason to believe that Decatur might have succeeded to the presidency had he lived, with results that almost certainly would have changed the course of history. The prevalence of dueling as a means of satisfying issues of honor in the early days of the American Republic is one of the more grisly manifestations of the overblown romanticism that characterized the era. Even sober statesmen, men whose profession called for a high degree of practicality and judicious reflection, succumbed to the practice—not only Hamilton and Burr, but John Randolph, Henry Clay, Andrew Jackson, and Thomas Hart Benton all fought duels. A particularly useful examination of this curious and deadly practice can be found in "Dueling in the Old Navy," by Charles Oscar Paullin, in the December 1909 issue of the *Proceedings* of the United States Naval Institute.

Vomito Negro

The story of the *Macedonian*'s horrific 1822 cruise in the Caribbean is drawn largely from the records of the court of inquiry called to investigate James Biddle's charges against Isaac Hull, as reported in *Niles' Weekly Register*, November 30, 1822, supported by additional data in *Sailor-Diplomat, a Biography of Commodore James Biddle 1783–1848*, by David F. Long (Boston, 1983); *The Captain from Connecticut: The Life and Naval Times of Isaac Hull*, by Linda M. Maloney; and *History of Boston Navy Yard, 1797–1874*, by George Henry Preble (National Archives). Although the ordeal of the *Macedonian* was extreme, it was hardly unique. David Long cites Charles L. Lewis, who observed in 1941 that "of all the wars it had fought up to that date, the U.S. Navy lost from yellow fever in the Caribbean during the early 1820's more officers and men, in proportion, than in any service in which they were engaged," and Long adds that the generalization was still true after including World War II, Korea, and Indochina. The particularly virulent strain of yellow fever of 1822 that cost the *Macedonian* 101 dead also killed 588 in New York that same summer.

Rio and Rot

The authority on ship's rot cited in the second paragraph is Commodore John Rodgers, president of the Board of Naval Commissioners. The quote is from a long and surprisingly interesting treatise on the subject included in the Secretary of the Navy's annual report for 1821.

As it happened, two future captains of the *Macedonian* were active in the otherwise inconsequential war between Brazil and Buenos Aires. Uriah Phillips Levy (see "Chutzpah") was at the time a lieutenant in the *Cyane* and at one point in Rio was approached by the emperor of Brazil, who personally offered him the command of a new 60-gun frigate and the rank of captain in the Brazilian Navy. Levy turned down the flattering proposal with a grandiloquence that quickly became famous throughout the navy: "I would rather serve as a cabin boy in the United States Navy, than be admiral in any other service in the world." The other future *Macedonian* skipper, George Colman De Kay (see "Mission to Ireland"), served in the Argentine Navy and made his personal fortune during the war by capturing Brazilian prizes.

Death and Resurrection

Francis Grice's extensive survey of the *Macedonian* is in the National Archives. So is the correspondence between John Rodgers and James Barron, and between Rodgers and Lewis Warrington, as well as Samuel Humphreys's plans for the *Macedonian*.

Material on John Rodgers and the Decatur party is taken largely from *The United States Navy: 200 Years*, by Edward L. Beach, and "John Rodgers: The Stalwart Conservative," by K. Jack Bauer, in *Command Under Sail: Makers of the American Naval Tradition 1775–1850*, James C. Bradford, editor (Annapolis, 1985).

As for my assertion that the rebuilt *Macedonian* looked the same as the Woolwich original, I relied primarily on personal observation. Although I cannot claim any special skill in reading ship's drafts, I was able to project a slide of the *Macedonian*'s original 1809 design from the National Maritime Museum onto a photocopy of Humphreys's draft from the National Archives, and compare the two directly. My interpretation of that comparison can be found in the text.

Any consideration of the rebuilding of the *Macedonian* in the 1830s automatically embroils one in a scholarly controversy involving the U.S. Navy, the city of Baltimore, and myriad naval historians. The controversy is known as the "*Constellation* Question," and concerns the provenance of the wooden vessel of that name currently on display in Baltimore Harbor. Is she the same vessel that was built in Baltimore in 1797, or a distinctly different ship? The 1797 *Constellation* was extensively rebuilt in 1855, and some authorities maintain that the navy played fast and loose with the use of the word "rebuilt," and that in fact the 1855 *Constellation* was an entirely new and different ship from the 1797 frigate. In its broader context, the *Constellation* Question concerns the reputation of the late Howard I. Chapelle, who for many years was an undisputed doyen of American naval historians. In his *History of the American Sailing Navy* (New York, 1949), Chapelle vigorously maintained that the present *Constellation* was a totally different vessel from the one built in 1797 (and on similar grounds he also maintained there were two *Macedonians*), and for many years his opinion was accepted by almost every specialist. In 1989, Dr. W. M. P. Dunne published "An Inquiry into H. I. Chapelle's Research" in *The American Neptune* (Winter 1989), which among other things cast doubt on Chapelle's understanding of the *Constellation*'s history. Dunne's broadside set off a glorious battle of scholars, and was soon answered by Dana M. Wegner in a large book, published at government expense, entitled *Fouled Anchors: The Constellation Question Answered* (Bethesda, MD, 1991), which maintained that Dunne was wrong and Chapelle was right.

The battle continues to this day, and despite Wegner's confident title, many parties believe the *Constellation* Question remains unanswered, or more precisely, incorrectly answered.

In telling the story of the *Macedonian*, I have tried scrupulously to deal with the facts evenhandedly. I do not agree with Chapelle's contention that there were two *Macedonians*, but since his conclusion was based on many of the same data I have used, some readers may decide, after reading my account, that I have proved Chapelle's case. I vigorously disagree. As far as I can make out, considering the understandings of that time, there was only one *Macedonian*, and my "single *Macedonian*" opinion is supported by two unbiased sailors—Samuel Leech and Matthew Calbraith Perry—both of whom recorded their opinions on the matter and passed on to their reward long before the ascendency of Howard Chapelle.

Their understanding of the *Macedonian*'s provenance can be

found in the two very short chapters here, "A Veteran Returns" and " 'Another Curious Incident.' "

My key source for this chapter was an unpublished thesis written by Brina J. Agranat for the Department of History at East Carolina University, entitled *Thorough and Efficient Repair: Rebuilding in the American Sailing Navy* (Greenville, SC, 1993). This remarkable work—I can only hope it will in time find a publisher—does what Chapelle never bothered to do, namely, to delve into the dullest and dryest of government records and to tease from them the relevance that makes the navy's antebellum building program clear and unambiguous.

The fragment of the hull of the *Macedonian* sent by Lewis Warrington to James Biddle in 1835 is cited in *Commodore Biddle and His Sketch Book*, by N. B. Wainwright (Philadelphia, 1966). The same relic surfaces again in 1841, when Biddle gave it to his friend Dr. S. Weir Mitchell, and again in 1901, when Dr. Mitchell in turn gave it to Charles E. Clark, as described by Clark in his autobiography, *My Fifty Years in the Navy* (Annapolis, 1984).

While circumstances prevented the *Macedonian* from serving as flagship of the U.S. Exploring Expedition of 1838–42, a tenuous relationship remains to connect her to HMS *Beagle*, Charles Darwin's famous vessel, which had only recently returned from a similar exploration and scientific survey of South America in 1836. By coincidence, Robert FitzRoy, captain of the *Beagle*, was the nephew of Lord William FitzRoy, first captain of the *Macedonian*.

A Veteran Returns

In *Thirty Years from Home*, Samuel Leech does not give us a specific date for his visit to the *Macedonian* in New York, but judging from the cruising record of the ship, it seems most likely that his visit occurred in the autumn of 1840.

ECHOES

The sources for Herman Melville's encounter with Captain Car-
den's old musical band are *The Melville Log*, by Jay Leda (New
York, 1951), and *White-Jacket or the World in a Man-of-War*, by
Herman Melville (Annapolis, 1988).

INCIDENT AT LITTLE BEREBEE

The principal source for the Little Berebee raid was Matthew
Perry's own account in his Letter Books of 1843–45, in the Na-
tional Archives. For an important interpretive overview, I am
indebted to the article "Matthew Perry and the African Squad-
ron," by Donald R. Wright, included in *America Spreads Her Sails*:
U.S. Seapower in the 19th Century, Clayton R. Barrow, Jr., editor
(Annapolis, 1973), and to a lesser extent to *"Old Bruin"*: *Matthew
Calbraith Perry, 1794–1858*, by Samuel Eliot Morison. I found
Admiral Morison's biography more helpful in his coverage of
Perry's Japanese expedition (see "Japan") than his African duty
in the *Macedonian*. Morison barely touches on Perry's notorious
denials of American participation in the slave trade, and limits
his account of the 1843–45 tour to a description of the commodore's successful efforts to protect the health of his crew along
the disease-ridden African coast. Morison provides the interesting detail that it was Isaac Mayo who delivered Ben Krako's
mortal wound with a pistol bayonet.

The quote concerning American slavers in Rio is from a letter
of David Tod, U. S. minister to Brazil, written in 1847. Although
the letter postdates Perry's tour of duty on the African Station,
it clearly refers to a situation that pertained at the time of Perry's
cruise.

The navy's high estimation of the *Macedonian*'s symbolic value
is shown by the fact that she was the invariable choice for opening up new foreign stations. Under John Downes she inaugu-
rated the Pacific Station in 1818; under James Biddle, the West
India Station in 1822; again under Biddle, the Brazil Station, in

1826; and finally, under Perry, the Africa Station in 1843. The only foreign stations she did not inaugurate were the Mediterranean and Far Eastern. Before her navy career was over, she would serve as flagship in both.

"ANOTHER CURIOUS INCIDENT"

The letter from Perry to the Secretary of the Navy is from Matthew Calbraith Perry's Letter Books, 1843–45, in the National Archives.

A NEW WORD ENTERS THE NAVY'S LEXICON

The quote is from Navy Department General Orders and Circulars, 1798–1862, in the National Archives.

MISSION TO IRELAND

Principal sources for this chapter were two long articles by my late aunt, Phyllis de Kay Wheelock, in *The American Neptune*, "An American Commodore in the Argentine Navy" (January 1946), and "Commodore George De Kay and the Voyage of the Macedonian to Ireland" (October 1953), and *Personal Reminiscences by Robert B. Forbes* (Boston, 1892). Of particular help was *Massachusetts Help to Ireland During the Great Irish Famine*, by H. A. Crosby Forbes and Henry Lee (Milton, MA, 1967), published in conjunction with a commemorative exhibition at Captain Robert Bennet Forbes House, Milton, Massachusetts. Also useful was the *Outline of the Life of George C. De Kay of New-York*, by "one of his contemporaries," who was probably Fitz-Greene Halleck (New York, 1847). The record of repairs and refitting performed on the *Macedonian* at the New York Navy Yard in March and April 1847 are in the National Archives, and the article on the *Macedonian*'s arrival at Cork in the *Illustrated London*

News of August 7, 1847, is from the personal collection of my brother Ormonde de Kay.

MEMORIES

Material for this chapter is taken almost exclusively from *A Curtail'd Memoir of Events and Occurrences in the Life of John Surman Carden*, Written by Himself in 1850.

JAPAN

Lieutenant Maury's testimony before Congress is from *Yankees in the Land of the Gods*, by Peter Booth Wiley with Korogi Ichiro (New York, 1990); details on the 1852 rebuilding of the *Macedonian* and her subsequent sailing improvement are from *History of the American Sailing Navy*, by Howard I. Chapelle; *Statistical History of the Navy of the United States*, by Lieutenant George F. Emmons, USN (Washington, DC, 1853); *Arming the Fleet: US Navy Ordnance in the Muzzle-Loading Era*, by Spencer Tucker (Annapolis, 1989); and an article in *the Daily Transcript*, Portsmouth, Virginia, June 6, 1853. For details of the actual cruise of the *Macedonian* to Japan, I relied primarily on *The Opening of Japan: A Diary of Discovery in the Far East, 1853–1856*, by Rear Admiral George Henry Preble, USN, Boleslaw Szczesniak, editor (Norman, OK, 1962); as well as on *"Old Bruin": Commodore Matthew Calbraith Perry 1794–1858*, by Samuel Eliot Morison; *Correspondence Relative to the Naval Expedition to Japan*, printed as 33 Cong. 2 Sess. Exec. Doc. 34, and reprinted with title on spine JAPAN/ PERRY (Washington, D.C., 1855); and *A Private Journal of John Glendy Sproston, USN*, Shio Sakanishi, editor (Tokyo, 1968). The incident of the American graffiti is from *The Black Ship Scroll*, by Oliver Statler (Rutland, VT, 1963).

IDENTITY CRISIS

This chapter is dependent in its entirety upon the research in the unpublished thesis entitled *Thorough and Efficient Repair: Rebuilding in the American Sailing Navy*, by Brina J. Agranat, described in greater detail in the notes on "Death and Resurrection."

CHUTZPAH

Any attempt to cram a character as large as Uriah Phillips Levy into a single chapter is bound to run into problems, and I can only plead that I did my best. I have relied on three biographies, primarily *Navy Maverick: Uriah Phillips Levy*, by Donavan Patrick and Paul Saphire; also, *Uriah Phillips Levy*, by Harold W. Felton (New York, 1978); and a biography for young readers, *The Commodore: The Adventurous Life of Uriah Phillips Levy*, by Robert D. Abrahams (Philadelphia, 1954).

The court-martial decision given on board the *Macedonian* is from the ship's log in the National Archives, and details of the incident on board the *Vandalia* are taken from the court-martial records, also in the National Archives.

Uriah Levy unsuccessfully sought command of the *Macedonian* some eleven years prior to 1858. In February 1847, during the long period when he was deliberately denied sea duty, he wrote from New York to Secretary of the Navy John Y. Mason: "Sir: Understanding that a vessel of war may be detailed for the conveyance of food to the distressed people of Ireland, I beg permission that should the government select a vessel for that purpose to tender my services to take command of her, having already intimated to the committee not only my willingness to render my service, but at the same time to devote all my pay during the performance of this duty in aid of the benevolent object in view." Secretary Mason never bothered to answer the letter.

I have stated as fact that Isaac Toucey made some sort of promise of sea duty to Levy after the captain's exoneration in the court of inquiry. None of Levy's biographers mention such a promise, implying that Levy's sudden return to a sea command was simply part of the normal running of the Navy Department, but it seems evident to me that Secretary Toucey would have felt constrained to do something to redress the highly publicized wrong that the navy had inflicted on Levy, and that the promise of some sort of sea duty commensurate with his rank would have been a natural response to the court's decision. Certainly Levy acted as though such a promise had been made to him. Nothing else could explain his otherwise querulous and acerbic acceptance of the command of the *Macedonian*, nor his unprecedented request a few days later to allow his wife to accompany him on board, a request that the Secretary of the Navy approved with an alacrity that was equally unprecedented.

Paris

Sources include logs of the *Macedonian* in the National Archives, as well as *My Fifty Years in the Navy*, by Charles E. Clark, Rear Admiral, USN, and *The United States Naval Academy*, by Park Benjamin. Both writers agree that Captain Luce disguised his ship in hopes of deceiving a Confederate raider, but where Clark claims he modified the *Macedonian* to look like a British vessel, Benjamin states that the disguise was to make her look Spanish. Perhaps Captain Luce tried both ruses.

City Island, the Bronx

Details on the navy's sale of the *Macedonian* are from the *New York Times*, January 1, 1876. The story of Charles McClennan's purchase of the ship and her subsequent resale to Jake Smith is from a piece entitled "Measure for Measure," by Captain Edgar K. Thompson, USN (Ret.) in *The American Neptune* (January 1968), as well as from *City Island: Tales of the Clam Diggers*, by Alice Payne (New York, 1969), and *City Island: History, Legend and Tradition*, by Allen Flood (no date or place of publication). The two last-named sources are in the New York Public Library. Additional material is from the feature article called "Fifty Years Behind the Times," in the *New York Herald* of March 30, 1902, a copy of which is reproduced in the text. The details of the burning of the Macedonian Hotel, unless otherwise stated, are from the *Herald* of June 10, 1922, and *the Bronx Home News* for June 11, 1922.

INDEX